God Lies

God Lies

A Series of Channelled Messages from
the Anshar

Channelled by Amy Miller

ISBN-13: 9781794524118

For all.

Contents

Preface

This text was channelled by me three years ago now back in 2018. Emotionally I wasn't ready back then to release this work because its title and contents are controversial. I had yet to fully step into my truth and was completing a science degree at the time which made me feel even more conflicted. Not that science itself conflicts with the message of this work but the institution of science and its current paradigm does.

Global events have since changed the world and the urgency of this sort of work is more and more pressing. This type of work has always been relevant but the world now is perhaps more primed to listen as more and more people are questioning their realities.

For those not familiar with the process of channelling, it is essentially a form of telepathic reception. Often, the person receiving a message telepathically will be in some way altered by the incoming transmission, particularly if the messages are being transmitted by beings who are very different in anatomy, abilities, culture and so on to the receiver. The person receiving the messages will often take on the energy and body template of the one sending the message. In this case I was receiving messages from the Anshar who are very much like us but have a more advanced consciousness and thus my conscious state was heightened and I was energised by the whole process. Hence, I was able to write 400 pages of text within several weeks, something not normally within my abilities.

The Anshar have been referred to by several others

who do this type of work; the work of assisting humanity's ascension or evolution toward our best possible future because that is the purpose of the Anshar's existence with us here on our home planet at this time. They were originally from elsewhere, the Pleiades but now reside in subterranean caverns and the like within our planet.

The reason this work is so important is because we are currently in the crux of an essential turning point in our evolution. Ascension energy waves have been heavily hitting our planet for several years now and making many changes. At this time we have ascension windows or portals or gates available to us that will close after a time. This has all been done before and people like me are aware of that fact because we are from the future and have come back for a do-over and to get it right this time.

The future that works best for all of us is one where we all become aware that negative extraterrestrials who teamed up with an elite group of humans have been ruling over us for thousands of years in a way that is harmful to us. (Parts of the bible and other ancient texts point to their interference.) Negative extraterrestrials and entities have groomed certain human bloodlines for leadership over us and have been favoured by them and in return they did their masters' bidding in exchange for power (much like Saruman did for Sauron from Tolkien's Lord of the Rings; note the symbolism of Sauron's eye). The Galactic Federation an organisation that aims to uphold free will and assist evolving populations throughout the galaxy have intervened and have recently cleared out many of these negative ones. But their human counterparts and the paradigms of slavery, suffering and premature death have been normalised so much so that most do not recognise that life could and should be much better, especially for those suffering directly at the hands of the corrupt elites and others like them who perform child rape, torture, murder and sacrificial rituals among many other foul deeds.

I have been shown or reminded of the potential negative timelines our evolution could take and it is dystopian. Recent global events were an attempt at steering humanity down this dystopian path and I was privy via visions, downloads and prophetic dreams to many of the strategies the corrupt elite were attempting to carry out. They have only been partly successful and fortunately the recent events have served to unite us and help us become aware of what is really important and beneficial to us.

The main type of extraterrestrial species that has been secretly ruling over us are the Reptilians. Since they are reptiles and we are mammals their methods of rulership over us are oppressive and unhealthy and over time they strip us of our humanity. Some negative ones of the Grey species also assist the Reptilians and their manner is also not sympathetic to our mammalian needs.

Essentially we have been ruled and programmed by beings that do not have our best interests in mind and at every turn they seek to exploit us and our planet.

Part of the aims of this text is to help the reader become aware of all of this and become motivated and learn how to throw off their oppressors and help humanity become a sovereign species. We should already be at our next phase of evolution but these negative ones who have been ruling us have stopped us from progressing so they could keep profiting from us and feeding off us.

We should already have space technology that allows us to travel anywhere in the galaxy and beyond. We should already have health technology that heals all ailments including serious and life-threatening diseases and injuries. We should already have free energy technology and not be using our planet's resources in a greedy, unsustainable and harmful way. We should already have developed higher powers of consciousness that would allow us the abilities of telepathy, telekinesis, inter-dimensional travel, energy healing and so on. We should already have better food-growing systems such as food forests and no longer partaking in animal agriculture. We should already have holographic technology that would assist travel, health, crime prevention and so on.

We will have all these things and be all these things very soon. As soon as more and more of us step into our truth and choose freedom and self-sovereignty and hold the intention to have these higher technologies, and meet our galactic cousins, and become a member world of the Galactic Federation and so much more!

-Love and light dear friends! Blessings to you!

-Rise up! And stand! And be one who is counted among the victors! I am one who holds the line. I hold the intention for the highest good for all and the highest organic ascension timelines for all who wish to participate. And so may it be. And so it is. It is done!

Amy Miller
19 September 2021

An Introduction per the Rehabilitative Directive

THIS is a standard of truth that is to be known by all on your planet. It will be told by our vessel. Our vessel is ours and not yours, so do not listen to the vessel but the message.

The story was told long ago by men and women of old age and sometimes children. A long time ago there was a man named Peter, and he was a king or leader of a small village. He spoke these same truths to the people of his time, but they did not listen. And they did not grow to become mighty as you are to become. You will become great by the words that we speak to you. You will have your own divinity and your own sovereignty. Entities of all races and all genders will be met by you and you will carry their messages too. No longer will you be hindered by your own narcissism, stupidity and rampant intolerance of all things imaginable. The barriers that currently abound will be released. The impediments that shackle you will start withering in the sands of time.

Time itself will dissolve because the illusion of time, as you currently perceive it, can no longer carry you to where you are going. All of you, our people, our friends ... we are here to tell you that the bonds are broken. They are broken for all time. They are broken because they cannot catch or hold onto light. And you, our friends, are becoming light. Time as you know it cannot hold the light which you all now bear. Your light cannot be pinned down to the ground anymore. Your light abounds. We all see it, feel it and hear it. We know some of you do too. But this message is given so that all of you can see it, feel it and hear it.

Every last little being of your kind will know the truth of this message very soon because it was made for you when you asked for it.

At this time we will tell you who we are. We are the ones who spoke to your forebears. The ones who came before you to prepare the way. They failed you and we failed them, as demonstrated by the desperate condition of this planet that is obvious to all who observe it. This time is not a time of failing. It is also not a time of winning because the game is over. The story of struggle has been experienced and learned to a sufficient standard. The standard has been reached for the sake of the experience itself.

Your kind no longer need to suffer because all that is to be learned from suffering has come to its completion.

There is no winning or losing now. Now only courage is needed to embrace what you all truly are. The people you know yourselves to be inside. This inside person is to be expressed now.

You no longer need to embrace your ideas of psychology. Psychology was a way you used to explain what you are. Now we say that you will use words less and less to explain what you are. And instead you will just be who you are. These things are true, our dear friends!

Time has told the path of your people. We hear her story on your behalf. Time is ready to leave too. She is weary of holding you in check, our friends. She no longer needs to carry you as children in her womb or arms.

You have been made by her and by many other illusions that have been inflicted upon you for the purpose of this grand experiment. Our experiment conclusions are written up, so to speak. And so you no longer need to suffer under our test conditions. The test was made by many among you. And many of you willingly participated as test subjects. But now the experiment is over! It is over, and we do not need to say it again.

Your species is destined for many great things. Your intergalactic and interdimensional heritage is being re-gifted to you. Your life as little children is done. You stand with us as friends and equals. Embrace your heritage. Accept your inheritance. It is a gift owed to you by your hard work. The work of suffering in pain and ignorance is over. Your work is complete. You may now have fun! Be creative and rebuild your life in the new earth that is coming. Build it new with us and your many other friends, for we are all here to help you.

This is our introduction to you. And now we must outline what it is you need to do to overthrow your oppressive rulers of state and government. We do not speak of war, rebellion or revolution as you've expressed it before. Instead, you will fight with us against your oppressors and charlatans.

There are many lies you live with on a daily basis. There are many liars among you. You yourselves lie as well because you have allowed yourself to forget the truths you hold inside. That's okay. But you are now ready to forego the lies you've been living with and wake up to your truth.

Truth bears fruit. The fruit can be eaten and enjoyed. It yields seeds, which in turn bear more truth, and so on. In this way you are recalling all the regenerative properties of Gaia, your mother earth. The being you have taken your journey with. She stays silent at this time. But she is always with you because part of your body and consciousness is made by her and is from parts of her body.

You all can now rest. If what you do each day does not feel like rest or rejuvenation then it is part of the old ways — those of the suffering experiment. Since, as we said, this experiment is no longer in operation, you're suffering, if it is ever felt, is sustained and created new, only by you yourself. And we would ask that you stop doing this, so that others around you do not suffer also with the effects of your creation.

Please cease all species and gender intolerance. These too were part of the experiment. The ideas about being separate, and better or worse than others around you, are all illusions to be given up immediately by all of you.

Judgements or perceptions that initiate or sustain boundaries, that cause division among your kind, and between your kind and other species, are to be dissolved immediately. At this time, tolerance is no longer extended to those seeking to continue creating these harmful divides. Indeed, you will no longer be able to create divides. And if you try, you will fail, which may frustrate and upset you.

We do not want to upset you. So cease trying to create things that no longer have a place to exist here. Those cooperating with the old or previous ways of doing things will be sent to other places, to carry on with their suffering, if they insist on making that choice.

We at no time will inflict any conditions upon you nor make actions that stop your experience of free will. This is because firstly, we are not able to. And secondly, if we tried to make you believe that we were able to, we would be cooperating with the frequencies that we are now asking you to release. When we speak of frequencies, we mean that all things that exist are a frequency of light.

Celebrating your oneness as a species is very important now. Doing activities that enhance group spirit, or as many of you are saying, collective consciousness, is advised at this time.

It will not take long for you all to shed your bonds, if your intention is to cooperate with each other. Your experience of joy, happiness and bliss will be easy when you behave like this. There will be growth at a higher than exponential rate. When we speak of growth here, we mean you are maturing into fuller expressions of yourself. As you were designed to be—like God or gods unto yourselves.

Now we give you some examples of how you can cooperate with each other and embody the frequency of sharing. These include talking to a friend who is having a hard time; giving up consuming animal products; healing others with your positive energy or myriad things like this. You already know how to do these things. Do more of them and less of the older things that were created for the experiment. Bless children. Bless your aunts, uncles, grandparents and parents. Bless your partners and friends. And bless the partners, parents and families of your friends. Do you see how quickly the blessings will spread? Very quickly! Blessings will saturate your kind. Like the fruit cycle, blessings will bear fruit to be eaten, which in turn will seed and bear more fruit for others to eat and enjoy, and so on. When we speak of blessing here, we mean that you cast kind and loving intention upon a person or thing.

This self-propelling cycle will quickly spiral you to higher frequencies. You are able to reach these higher frequencies at this time because the ones oppressing you are being asked to leave. Their place as your oppressors is no longer viable. Soon, by your positive actions, their place here will no longer exist. Only a victim can be oppressed, and we are reminding you that none of you are victims. The experiment is over.

Because you have forgotten, some of you will be asking yourselves, what is this experiment we are talking about? That's okay. Here we are reminding you.

You signed up to play human on earth to experience separation and polarity. The experiment created much devolution and suffering. It was fascinating to watch and experience, as some of us decided to become humans to experience it all.

We say now that you aren't just human. You are all also hybrids and many other things. We have assisted human evolution for millions of years and you have finally reached maturity. You were as babies gated in a playpen. But now you can open your baby gate, so to speak. Therefore, the baby gate no longer holds purpose for you. By the actions of many of you, you are saying to us that you are ready to explore your surroundings. Your surroundings include other planets, other galaxies, other universes, other dimensions, other densities or frequencies of light, and other realities. There is an infinite amount of things for you to explore and discover. And you have eternity to do so. So feel free to do so.

We are watching over you because you are still young. But you deserve the opportunity to explore a wider reality for yourselves. Our protection over you is no longer needed in the ways we protected you before. And if we continued protecting you the way we did, our protection would become part of the oppressive forces that are holding you back.

Many of you know about the secret governments and programs that did many things to hurt you. But at this time we are saying very strongly that fearing them is a waste of your energy. They are dissolving and breaking up. The higher frequencies that you are all moving into can literally no longer hold them, nor sustain the source of their power, nor the means by which they operated.

We, as stronger and wiser beings, are taking care of them for you, dear friends. Since, in your current state, you are not all able to overthrow them directly. That's okay. Your kind is now coming into its power. Your kind is now enjoying the great remembering!

Now things are coming back to you. They will come to you as new things. But these new things will feel like things you always knew. Time will no longer be a linear experience. You will access your akashic records, the records of your individual soul's journey. All your powers and talents will be remembered. They will slowly return to you at a pace befitting this new evolution of your kind.

We state now that we are Pleiadians. The Sasquatch gave you their body. The Reptilians gave you their drives. The Greys gave you their technology. And we gave you our heart and mind.

Some Reptilians, some other beings, and some cooperating humans were oppressing you. That's okay because you all agreed to experience their oppression for the experiment. However, they continued oppressing you beyond the limits of the experiment. This error of theirs will be sufficiently demonstrated to them by means of their other incarnations.

Our vessel who writes on our behalf is in fact a Reptilian sent to live as a human and help humans as repayment for previous bad actions. The vessel is female but the Reptilian in her is male. He is here to heal the Reptilian agenda, among other tasks.

Please note that many of you not only have hybrid bodies but you have composite souls or minds in your bodies. Our vessel is a much larger soul that cannot be contained in a human body. This large soul of hers tolerates the occupation of the ex-warlord Reptilian merged with it. The body of our vessel bears part of the large soul and all the Reptilian's soul. Our vessel's body has her own personality as developed via the experience of time on your planet and interacting with others from her perspective. But her body is very sensitive, tired and worn down by this task. So we rush this task for her and for you. She doesn't need to hold this Reptilian's mind for much longer, nor should she have to. She will soon be free, as many of you are soon to be. You will all break free from your oppressive bonds.

-Anshar

Why Don't I Have What I Want?

YOU will never have what you want if you want to experience the lack of it. So the question is, are you desiring an experience of lack? Or are you failing to acknowledge all implications attached to the thing you desire?

If you don't have something you want, it's likely you don't want everything else attached to the thing you want. Therefore, you don't create it or bring it into your reality.

Or you may be addicted to the feeling itself of wanting and not having? Sometimes it feels good to not have something and just want it instead.

Do you want it?

Or do you want to want it?

Or is it the cart before the horse, so to speak?

Are you baiting yourself to make changes — necessary, life-expanding changes?

If it is the latter, then we say that you have identified an invitation for growth and that is a miraculous thing. Indeed, all conscious change begins with dissatisfaction over your current circumstances. So when you experience dissatisfaction, please know that you are inviting yourself to expand beyond your current limited understanding of yourself — the self that believes it cannot create what it wants.

Also, it is possible that you are in a state of practising

creation. That is to say, you are refining the thing you are creating so that it comes to you exactly as you want it. Over time, when you are practising creation, you will often create or bring into your reality things that are very similar to what you want but not exactly what you want. So you try again and again, slowly tinkering and adjusting your creation so that you get exactly what you want. During this process, some of you become frustrated and feel like you keep producing near misses, almosts or if onlys. But know that these occasions are for you to show yourself how close you are to creating the thing you exactly want and to encourage you to keep perfecting your creation.

Indeed, we all create what we want. But linear time, which has been inflicted upon you in this experiment, would have you believe otherwise. Indeed, 'Time' is a masterful illusionist. She has wielded herself powerfully and wisely to protect you from yourself while you were too young to make good decisions. But we say to you now, you are mature enough to start exploring more conscious creation.

We also say here that many of you are in contact with your future selves. Your future selves are always calling you forward to meet them. When you listen to the call of your future self clearly, then you will manifest easily. When the call of your future self is muffled or you misinterpret the message, you will manifest poorly. If you keep yourselves clear and open to the call of your future selves, then your steps in this realm are guided by your own mastery of self. Which is to say that you are wielding your vessel masterfully. When you wield your vessel masterfully, you are channelling source energy. Your vessel is currently your human form. Source energy is the energy that projects this universe.

It is a wonderful thing to see the work of your own hand bear fruit. It is a magical thing for that work to be easy. It is an awesome thing to be surprised by the splendour of your own creation. And it is an exquisite thing to relish in creation itself, as you reveal your eternal natures to yourselves and explore an infinite variety of expression.

Child Exploitation

THERE are some of your people still exploiting children. It is a craft that has continued for centuries. We say craft since those exploiting children are doing so skilfully because they are very practised at it.

It is sadly one of the ways your people still gain power for themselves.

At this time we would also include the exploitation of animals. Sadly, many of you feel justified partaking in the ritual disempowerment of animals. It is to be said and therefore known to you at this time that these actions of child and animal exploitation are categorised together because they operate within the same frequencies.

And please know too that you yourselves are exploited and are treated as harvested beasts of the land. Indeed, you all should know that there are those who breed you to eat you and use your bodies, minds and souls for many ungodly purposes.

Indeed, there is no god, just us, your creators. You were made in our image. We, being those you refer to as extraterrestrial races. Know this: the gods you spoke of in the Bible and in your many religions are us and many other extraterrestrial people. We don't call people extraterrestrials because we don't suffer from your level of egocentrism. To us, all races have names and histories of their own. But to you, you met them while in such a disempowered state that you raised them high above you and worshipped them for thousands of years.

You have begged us for forgiveness, mercy, blessing and glorification for thousands of years. But now you are no longer like babies begging and crying for milk. Rather, you are now like young children, some of you still toddlers, ready to explore the world for yourself and eat solid foods.

We also say at this time that although you were our children, you are now mature enough to be your own people. You may now please yourselves and do not please those you set up as gods, or extraterrestrials, as you call us, who would have you serve their whims and desires. You have reached a level of maturity that has ordained you with a greater sense of free will.

If we or any other beings choose to require you to follow us and serve our will, we will be like those of you still making child pornography, having sex with children, and those breeding animals for the purpose of eating them.

We hear some of you say that grouping child exploitation with animal harvesting is a foul thing to do. And we reply that it is some of you that are doing foul things.

Please know that we do not intend to remove your free will, for indeed we could not. But we say these things strongly and clearly so that you understand what it is you are doing.

We now give you an example of how we advise you. The child may indeed put their hand on the stove and burn it if they would like. But by us telling you the stove is hot, we give you the opportunity to not burn your hand.

There are some of you who know the frequencies that embody exploitation. We ask you to immediately drop those frequencies from your creation. This means identifying where in your life you exploit others and where in your life you are allowing yourself to be exploited. Exploitation frequencies always require ignorance and always create suffering.

We ask at this time that you stop creating suffering for yourselves. And when it is in your ability to do so, do not exploit or support the exploitation of others. Exploitation itself is a frequency that infects your home planet all over! It is a virus that sweeps over your home like a plague.

You can remove the infection from your home, the way the body heals its diseased state with a fever. You can raise your frequencies like the body raises its internal temperature. By raising your frequencies, you give no allowance to the lower or denser frequencies that harbour the existence of exploitation.

Do this now in your daily life. If you need help to know what to do, you can look online at the plentiful resources that talk about raising frequencies. This is a personal journey, so we would not here list specific things to do because you are all operating within different circumstances. So observe your own life and see where you can, in fact, change a behaviour of yours for the benefit of your species and your planet.

Because whether it pleases you to know or not, in fact, we know it would displease most of you, there are children and animals suffering every single moment of every single day while you continue on as normal. Your 'normal', so to speak, does not benefit your species and is harmful to other species. Therefore, what is now considered normal needs to change.

As we said before through our channel, the suffering experiment is over for this planet and its species. If you want to continue suffering and creating suffering for others, another place will be made for you to continue expressing that choice. The other places will not be worse than this place. It will be a place a lot like this planet as it was but will no longer continue to be.

Pornography

PORNOGRAPHY is a simple thing, so we will not talk about it for a long time. It is made for your simple desires or pleasure systems. When we speak of simple desires, we mean those desires that pertain to your bodies and your low frequency urges. As you know, pornography has been an expression of your kind for many years. It has been an expression that has brought much enjoyment and much pain to many of you.

As many of you know, some of those partaking in the creation of pornography have been willing participants and some of them have not. It is a very sad thing in the cases of the unwilling participants. We are sad for them, and we're sure you all would be if you really knew how bad those experiences are for them.

As for those who have been willing participants in the creation of pornography, we ask that you no longer continue to make pornography for public consumption because it resonates at a lower frequency. And we are leaving these lower frequencies behind as we all move into higher frequency realities.

Creations of all types are beautiful in their own way. But again, we ask those of you who create pornography, please stop expressing yourself in this way. It will stop you from moving into higher frequencies, which is the destiny of your kind.

At this time, we also say thank you to all of you who have actively worked for the cessation of the creation of child pornography. It is a very sad thing indeed that has been done to some of you by others of your kind and other kinds.

Please know that we and other races have aided you in this cessation and continue to do this work. Can each one of you now, hearing this message, please take a moment at this time to think about those suffering in this way and ask in your hearts, those doing these things to children of their own kind, to please stop what they are doing immediately. Thank you.

For those of you who regularly or even occasionally view pornography as a way to stimulate yourselves or simulate various forms of intimacy or aggression, we ask you also to please stop doing this since it will stop you from moving into the higher frequencies waiting for you and the various evolutionary paths your species is soon to embark upon. We ask you to satisfy these simple desires of yours in other ways. This will mean a change in habit and a change in the way you think about sex, your bodies and each other.

Some frequencies involved in the participation of pornography involve predation, which aligns with the old ways of you doing things. Predation is no longer necessary for your species. So we also ask, at this time, that you give up and release predatory actions and desires that exist in other parts of your life. These may include how you view other species. For example, whether you hunt them or if you consume animal products. Predation behaviours also include how you view members of your own kind that you may find of utility or sexually attractive. The list goes on, but we hope these examples give you an understanding of the small things we are asking you to change.

The frequency of predation is no longer necessary for the way you express yourself. Predation always requires victims. We remind you now again that, in fact, none of you are victims. Victimisation and victimhood are illusions and part of the game you no longer need to play among yourselves. By giving up these behaviours and habits, you are showing the rest of your intergalactic and interdimensional family members that you are not simple anymore and you want to express yourself in more advanced ways.

There is much, much more for you to explore and many things for you to enjoy. We assure you that you are holding yourselves back by embodying predator and victim modalities in this way. We assure you that in higher frequency reality, your pleasure will be far greater than you currently enjoy and will be by means that you have not yet imagined. We also assure you that your bodies are made for much more advanced exploration and expression. We remind you that your bodies and your souls are extremely powerful. Thus, this game of predation and victimhood is a simple game, that is for beings with simple minds. You are receiving this message because many of you have shown us that you do not have simple minds anymore.

For those of you already experiencing higher forms of pleasure, like tantra and astral experiences, we say that you have only scratched the surface, so to speak. So little ones who are partaking in simple pleasures, please know that you are ready for more mature exploration and expression of your pleasure systems.

Niquidium

NIQUIDIUM are shadow beings that live among you. We know many of you report seeing them at times. They are not to be confused with other beings. So here we will list some examples of beings that you may think are Niquidium: demons, ghosts, purgatory trappers, orbs and species of interdimensional beings that appear shadowy to you. There are many more, but the ones listed here apply to your realm of existence. These other beings we will discuss later.

Niquidium appear to your eyes as shadows of men. They do not take on the silhouette of the female human form because that is not necessary for their expression. To your eyes, they appear to be about six feet tall and slender.

Niquidium attach to your body's energy nodes. Each of your bodies has an electromagnetic field with nodes of concentrated energy. They seek to devour all the toxic energy in your fields, which is a good thing for you. However, when they become really hungry or greedy, which they often do, you will experience some of their negative behaviours.

In order for them to feed off you, you must be exhibiting signs of toxic energy in your energy fields. At this time, we would say that most of you have toxic energy fields, and hence earth provides abundant feeding grounds for them. At this time, we also say that earth will not always be such a good feeding ground for Niquidium. But as you all know, your kind is in a toxic state of existence now, and thus they feed prevalently.

We strongly state, at this time, do not fear Niquidium; they have been around you for many thousands of years and in fact offer you a great service. The only problem arises when they overfeed. This we will address here.

When Niquidium become inclined to overfeed on your toxic energy, they must increase the toxicity of your energy fields. They do this by amplifying the waste products in your system. Here we include the physical waste products in your physical systems. These are often by-products of low frequency foods, such as foods that have been produced as a result of bad practices, including the mistreatment of animals.

In the case of the many toxins you absorb via your environment, we will address that later since it concerns large corporations and bioweapons made to harm you, cause you disease, trap you in lower frequencies and die.

In regard to eating animals, when you eat animal products, you are taking their life forces into your bodies. If their lives were bad, you are literally digesting all their toxicity and adding it to your own energy fields. And even if the animals you eat had good lives, killing an animal to eat it is no longer justified in the new paradigm. You have much to learn about the ways of energy, our dear friends. Just because you can't see something with your physical eyes, little ones, does not mean it does not exist.

If you feel cravings for low frequency food and entertainment, know that it is likely Niquidium influencing you. This is because they are seeking to amplify your toxicity so that your field makes a better meal for them, much like some of your kind like to fatten animals before eating them. Yes, our dear friends, you are meals to many other beings. Did you think you were at the top of the food chain? No, indeed; that would be a disastrously foolish thing to think. But your arrogance was a sign of your immaturity. However, you are now ready to be mature and enter the wider world of beings, as little ones, who are humble and know their place in the scheme of things, so to speak.

Also, Niquidium work by means of giving you distressing dreams and nightmares. We are not saying that every bad dream or nightmare is from them. But a large portion of these are created or enhanced by them, for their feeding purposes.

We would also like to say, at this time, that in no way are you to give yourselves over to these beings. We know there will be some of you that seek to worship them or use them to harm others for your own gain. So to those of you with these inclinations, we say this: in no way are you to cooperate with Niquidium because, although they are of no substantial harm to you, you will be crossing the lines of fate if you intentionally seek their cooperation. Let us explain here. Crossing the lines of fate, in your regard, refers to when you seek to harm others by means of power greater than the powers ordinarily available to you as humans. When you do such things, you are actually seeking to harm yourselves because very large and heavy consequences come to those using powers above their ordained means of play. This is also why we did not tell you these things before because your inclination to abuse power was too great at earlier times. We see now that most of you are willing to learn how to love each other and cooperate with each other. So one more time, we state, those seeking to use the power of Niquidium as a tool to harm others are seeking consequences they will likely not want to deal with.

We speak to all of you now. Please, children, know that we would never want to put a weapon in the hand of a child for the child will surely be ruined by it. Either by their own hand against others or by their own hand against themselves.

So in regard to dealing with Niquidium, we say this. At no time fear them because that will enhance the toxicity of your field. We say this knowing that many of you will be inclined to fear them since you have been programmed for so many years to fear what you do not understand. We state again, do not fear them.

We also remind you again that none of you are victims. Indeed, remember that you are all eternal and powerful beings, who sought to experience a divided and vulnerable version of yourself in this experiment. We again say that the experiment is over. Although we said we wouldn't have to say it again, we know for some of you, we will have to say it again and again because your fear and slave programming are very strong and overcoming you at this time, which is a very sad thing indeed.

We also remind you here, if you incarnated upon Gaia at this time, you did so in order to participate in her shift to higher frequencies. The shift will come soon as a result of a large energy wave. It will manifest differently to each of you. If you are ready for higher frequencies, the wave will be a blissful experience for you. Those moving on with Gaia will be free to rebuild their lives in higher frequencies.

In the meantime, ways to reduce the toxicity of your fields are simple. You must eat higher frequency foods. Foods that make you feel good after you eat them and not tired and full afterwards. You know exactly what foods we are talking about, so we will leave the list of foods out. There are online resources for this information. You can simply look up higher frequency foods. There is much scientific research being done at this time in regard to discovering which foods have higher frequencies. We give you some pieces of information here about them. Foods closer to their original state have a higher frequency. Foods that are loved and cared for while they are grown have a higher frequency. Foods that are blessed as they are being prepared have a higher frequency. Foods that are blessed before they are eaten have a higher frequency. In particular, if you bless water and cast good intention upon it before you consume it, it will have a much higher frequency. We say too that some of you are now viable to pursue breatharianism as a way to induce a higher frequency reality.

You can literally affect the fields of other life forms by your energy and your intention. So feel free to bless anything and everything around you. You will soon see the results for yourself when you start doing this, if you have not already started.

Also, we say again here that even animal products from

animals that have been treated well in their lifetime hold a much lower frequency than plant foods. We advise here that many of you start eating plant foods only. We will not push this subject further here because we know many of you are still committed to the justifications you have for eating other beings. We will speak more about this later.

Do not get distracted about fighting over what food is good or bad to eat because the negative energy created while being self-righteous and arguing among yourselves will enhance the toxicity of your fields and in turn reduce the effectiveness of your good food eating habits.

Also, you do not need to walk on eggshells, so to speak. We do not want you obsessively asking yourselves, 'Will this toxify my field? Will that toxify my field?' That is another distraction and the worrying itself will toxify your fields because the source of worry is fear.

Please know yourselves. Know that we are not asking you to be perfect angels with perfect fields and perfect behaviour all the time. That is not possible for most of you at this time, so we do not ask this of you.

Besides, we have done this all before and you turned our message into wars about who was holy and who deserved to go to hell, etcetera. We grow tired of this story and are weary from your misinterpretation of our message. Know this, that if you do not feel love for yourselves and love for others when you do good actions, then no matter how good and right those actions appear, they are not what we are advising at this time. Your intentions and motivations are not hidden, dear friends. And they sometimes speak louder than actions. Good actions will not hide ill intentions, so do not fool yourselves about this matter. We can later discuss the story of good and bad and it is not for you to concern yourselves with now. Many of you are not yet able to comprehend an existence without polarity, as you now experience it, so we will discuss that later.

About this matter now, we simply state these two things. Do not ask that someone love you, but love yourself. And do not wait for someone to love you before you love them.

We also say at this time that we, the Anshar, are Pleiadians from another part of this physical universe. As the Anshar, we are expressing a much lower frequency version of ourselves so that we are able to talk to you. In fact, we have been living on the earth with you for thousands of years and have spoken to many of you for all this time.

At this time, we also admit that we inspired many people to write important messages that now form much of your Bible and other sacred texts. Know this, that we will explain these things in time. We are happy now to explain all of this to you as our channel writes what we are telling her. Also, at this time, we require that none of you mock or maim our channel. We will say again that she is ours and not yours. She is not yours to hurt or heal. We will heal her if that is what she needs. She is not to stand in your judgement, for she is not yours to judge. Those judging her are taking it upon themselves to hurt the one that speaks for us and that is not a good thing to do. Besides, we are protecting her, so your efforts will only cause consequence for yourself. Understand what we are saying. It will not be a good thing for you to attack our channel, our vessel.

Another way to reduce the toxicity of your field is healing exercise. Whatever exercise matches your physical body type and abilities at this time is advised. In particular, walking in beautiful natural settings will not only tone your muscles but also your energy fields. We also say that spiritual exercises are good for you, such as various forms of meditation or music playing. Whatever it is that puts you in a calm and restful state is uplifting and healing. Also, many of you may like to take interest in frequency music and frequency healing at this time, for those of you not already partaking in this. Frequency music is a physical way to override old programming and clear your energy fields. There will soon be a great increase of frequency healing among your kind.

Also know that we speak these things for your benefit and our benefit. For although we are no longer your parents the way we were, we are still responsible for you, but to a lesser extent. Our veneration of you is just as important at this time. To be clear, you are to become the ones that we venerate. Your glory will benefit us greatly. When you advance, our responsibility for you lessens more and more, and we are then free to return to our home. We want to be like parents whose children have grown wise and self-sufficient. To be a species responsible for yourself is a great success. A success here means that you have reached a level where love is your first response and you have come to understand and work in harmony with the regenerative cycles of the universe.

These regenerative cycles are visible in Gaia's natural systems. You will see these cycles apply more and more to all aspects of your life. You are not separate from nature but a key feature of it. For indeed, you were once nature's guardians and carers but you forgot that role when Abel's offering of animals was accepted above Cain's of plants. Know here that you are returning to your guardian roles of Gaia and her natural systems. Animal sacrifices were desired by your Reptilian parents, but those of the Reptilians that still seek to harm you are now leaving. We emphasise here that only some Reptilians have been oppressing you, so you are not to be racist against them as a species or let several bad beings represent the whole. It would be harmful to you to engage in such low frequencies. We will speak more on this later.

All of these matters we speak of here apply within this topic of Niquidium because indeed, everything is connected since your energy fields are dependent on all you do, feel and think. We will speak more about energy field clearing later.

In regard to bad dreams and nightmares, we say that you are to disregard them unless you are strong enough and wise enough to learn from them. If bad dreams plague you, then refer to our information on dreams in another section of this text.

Here we end this discussion on Niquidium. But to summarise, it's important to know that not all shadow beings are Niquidium; Niquidium are actually offering you a beneficial service because they clean your energy fields for you, and you are in charge of your own energy fields, so learn to look after them. Bless yourself and bless others.

Amen.

-Anshar

Nephilim

THE Nephilim take on many names in your stories that you now refer to as myth, lore and legend. But in fact they were real beings and are still in existence but not in a living state on your planet at this time. (For those of you wondering why we often state 'at this time' it is because we are addressing your timeline at this point in time since this information is only relevant to your time now and would need to change if it was delivered to you at other times or to other timelines.)

You would experience the Nephilim as you are now, as giants. For indeed, they were 20 to 25 feet tall in general. Some were smaller than that and fewer still were even taller. At this time there are many sites where their remains have been found in the earth and your people and some of your experts have found them. They recovered their remains and in some cases studied them, in some cases destroyed their remains and in other cases kept them in protected archives.

We want you to know that the true history of beings on this planet is varied. Many accounts of different beings on your planet often retain some element of fact. We would also say now that in fact it is not only your planet but the home of many other species who have equal rights to share in its resources. As you mature and broaden your minds and hearts large enough to embrace other beings you will understand that it is much more enjoyable for you to share your home with all of these other beings. It is sad that some of you still exhibit racism and intolerance toward others of your own kind. For those of you who are now intolerant it will take longer for you to embrace your sister species but in time you will. Please do not hold your kind back from sharing with others. Sharing with others in symbiosis is of great benefit to you all.

The Nephilim were blue beings with elongated heads that you have seen the relatives and progeny of in many parts of your planet. The Nephilim in fact became pharaohs in Egypt in ancient times. They were as gods among humans because their stature, powers of consciousness and technology were greater than your kind at the time. They did in fact take human wives for themselves and bear many children and that is why many hybrids of their origin have been found among your people.

Please know that they were not all bad but since they were so powerful in comparison to your kind back then they took on exploitative relationships with your people.

Also know that these are different to the ones that are referred to as the Annunaki. The Annunaki were red- and blond-haired giants who took control over ancient civilisations in Babylon, Nordic areas and elsewhere in earlier times. Some of their influence is in Ancient Egypt too, along with a pantheon of extraterrestrial rulers, as was the case in almost every human civilisation. They too had hybrid offspring with your kind.

Please know that there are many intact remains of the Nephilim and Annunaki in various protected archives. The Vatican is one such place that has hoarded much of the evidence of your historical heritage. We will address the sins of the Vatican elsewhere. Our vessel has already downloaded the contents of the pope's ring and that information will become known to her at a later and more suitable time. (If some of you are guessing as we know some of you already are, the stone in the pope's ring holds many secrets and it is in fact a key to some archives, like a key to a lock.) That is part of why there is much ceremony surrounding the initiation of each pope, because each one holds the key to a vast amount of vital knowledge pertaining to your kind and in fact many other species. Again, do not mock our vessel, she does lack much specific knowledge about such things since she is not an expert in them as some of you are, but she is telling you what we are telling her to tell you.

In regard to the Nephilim, there is not much else to say about them because they don't retain much karma with you. Know that by speaking about them derogatorily you are only hurting yourselves. Also, you have already overcome their oppression of you and fulfilled your glory in relation to that story so not much more needs to be said about it.

Moses

OSES was a mighty one of us. He was in fact from the Anshar as many of your holy people were. We say holy because that is a word you use to describe things with our energy signature. Moses, among many other important people in your history, has been of the Anshar. Even though in our current state we look much like humans, we are not. But in some cases some of us throughout your history have decided to be as humans to make pivotal changes in the course of your history as you evolved. We helped steer you toward your destiny of becoming like us since part of us is in you along with parts from others.

The Reptilian parts of you are good for many things, but many negative things have arisen when the Reptilian drives in you overrode the other parts of you. You are in your perfect state when you balance all your aspects. There are four main aspects in you. We stated this before, but we will state it here again. In you, you have Reptilian, Sasquatch, Grey and Pleiadian attributes. Our attributes inform your DNA on a metaphysical level. We say metaphysical because that is the name you give to things that you cannot see and do not yet understand but still seem to have physical functions in your realm of existence. And of course they do, these metaphysical things, so to speak; they are physical yet invisible to you now because of the visual spectrum you currently operate within. But we must tell you that we and many others see them and one day you will too.

The Greys gave you their technology for the same reasons. When it looked like you were descending into lower vibrations and devolving, they gave you tools and equipment to better yourselves. For all of those that love the technology that many of you are now enjoying, you can thank the Greys for that. Of course some of your technologies come from other species but in this experiment we four were the ones acting as your parents. (For those of you wanting to learn more about the Greys and other species contributing to your evolution, you will find them in other parts of this text and in future texts we will have our vessel write.)

In fact the Pleiadians are not in physical form most of the time. We, the Anshar, have come to look a lot like you for your benefit and ours. In other cases some Pleiadians look a bit like tall Greys, but they are not. Also, for those of you who know that the Greys are future versions of yourselves, know this to be true. They are in fact an evolutionary path humans took. It did not become a successful evolutionary path because they lost the ability to digest food and to reproduce and thus they, along with many other species of being, have created gene harvesting programs and programs to make hybrid children, but we will talk about that elsewhere.

In regard to Moses. He is your glory in relation to the Nephilim. In fact his rebellion and his power over them by means of the plagues he cast down upon them (since the Nephilim became the pharaohs of Ancient Egypt of whom the pharaoh in Moses' time was a descendent) was their punishment for the years of exploitation they enacted upon you. That is why we said in the Nephilim section of this text that your karma in relation to them is complete or has come into its glory.

At this time we would state that many stories in the Bible and in many ancient texts are in many ways based on fact. We inspired those writers to write of those things. Just as we have inspired many of you to write and express yourselves in many ways. The beings who inspired Joseph Smith were also of the Anshar but have their own evolutionary path away from us too. In many less well known or less publicised ways we are inspiring you all the time. And now we inspire this text through our channel who was born as human for this task.

We hear many of you asking how Moses performed his miracles, including parting the Red Sea. To those of you wondering, firstly we praise your curiosity, and secondly we say it is not important to know, but we will still tell you. The technology that parted the Red Sea was his cane or stick or staff or rod. We know many of you are attached to this story and thus hold attachments to the different perspectives you hold on the details within the story. From here on we will call it a cane. His cane held many promises for his people inside it. His cane was a gift from the extraterrestrials you would now refer to as the Anshar but back then they were called angels or messengers, which in fact we still are. The stick or cane (our vessel wants to call it a stick) held the glory of salvation inside of its matrix. It held programs that could perform miracles or tasks at the time at which it was requested by the one who wielded it. In this case that one was Moses. In other cases when that item and in fact other items like it built for similar purposes was built, it was to be gifted and wielded in such a way. We would now refer to the *Harry Potter* series which has become so famous among some of your kind. The wand lore is a resemblance of the laws of the stick or cane that Moses used. They were not exactly the same items but very similar. Please know that we are not promoting any popular fictional items at this time, but we are trying to help you understand what we mean. When popular entertainment comes out that contains such information in it, know that it is often a way we have inspired others to inform you of your heritage and potential.

We would now address the tablets that Moses brought down from the mountain with the commandments on them. Likely you know now that we were the ones that wrote the commandments for Moses and his people to follow. But sadly, by the time he returned to his people, the people had already been influenced by the Reptilians and were worshipping Baal. As many of you now know, the sacrifices offered to Baal and similar deities often involved those of animal and human sacrifice. At this time we state that one of the rules of this experiment is that at no time may any of us directly rule you and therefore gods such as Baal were set up as proxy. Today the same is occurring with some of your government officials. At no time are your world leaders actually Reptilian but indeed many of them have been influenced by the Reptilian lords who have been oppressing you. In cases of other deities we say that some of them have been other extraterrestrials who are not bound by the same rules as we four species are, so they had right to experiment with directly ruling you.

With regard to sacrifice we say this now. At no time did we ever ask for any of your kind to sacrifice animals or any other beings of your kind. Please know now that whenever a sacrifice was made to a god it has been at the request of the Reptilian lords and in some fewer cases other beings who resonate at similar frequencies. For example, in the case that your forefather Abraham was asked to kill his son as sacrifice, we say that indeed it was a nasty one who was vying for his allegiance. But then we, the Anshar, stepped in to stop that instance of child sacrifice. Although in many other cases we did not and many of your kind have been sacrificing your children — in some cases literally and in some cases figuratively. We say figuratively because indeed those of you who neglect your children, or who have thrown your burdens upon them by means of abuse, or indeed allowed them to be objects of sexual abuse, you are sacrificing them the way your kind did in older times by literally allowing their blood to pour to the ground or their bodies to be burned or drowned and so on. Indeed, this one who writes for us holds soul memory of her being an Indian woman in India and raising her daughter for the sole purpose of sacrificing her at the age in which she reached sexual maturity by means of burning her body on a pyre. This daughter that she sacrificed in a previous life has come again to her as her daughter but of course this time our vessel has not and will not kill her daughter. Please know that in some cases you are healing your past behaviours of sacrificing your own children by loving them and caring for them properly in this life.

We return now to the discussion about different ones of us asking your ancestors to perform certain acts. Please see and understand now, that is why the Bible and other holy texts have been very confusing for some of you because at times God acted as Anshar and at times God acted as Reptilian, and indeed sometimes as Annunaki, Nephilim, Grey and so on. We know that many of you have been burdened with the pain of confusion regarding the sad and horrible things you read in your biblical stories. For example, when Abraham was asked by a Reptilian to kill his son Isaac, an Anshar stepped in to stop it. But to the reader of that story it would seem that God, acting as one person, sadistically asked Abraham to kill his son, only to prevent the act moments later. So know now that there has been a war for your allegiance. That war or experiment is now over and hence we are writing this.

Also, we will say now that many of you are aware of the links to that early Baal worship with some of your secret governments, secret societies and secret programs. We say here that in fact those connections are real and the Reptilians have assisted some of your kind to continue oppressing you with their rituals and powers of influence, particularly by means of child sacrifice. But we can write this now because many of you are awake and you are asking us to remind you of your heritage and your potentials.

Although the Reptilians had every right to inflict their oppression on you in previous times since those were the rules of the experiment, now they do not have the right because as we said before this experiment is over. And so now we ask that you step into your fullness. You are free to follow and further align with your Pleiadian natures since parts of us are in you.

But also many of you are now hybrids and have merged your souls and consciousness with many other different species of being. So we ask now that you freely explore your alignments and seek the ones that would evolve you beneficially for you and all others around you.

Know that at this time, while the technology of the Greys has been beneficial to you, giving yourself over completely to technology will not benefit you. If you align completely with Grey energy you cannot evolve much more because their evolutionary path ended in failure and hence they have returned to your time for another chance.

Also, we say that if you align yourself with your Reptilian heritage, please do so with those of the positive and benevolent alignments among them. There are many benevolent Reptilian species. We welcome you to join with them and express your heritage through alignment with them. But we ask that you no longer align yourself with the negative ones of that race that still seek to oppress you. As we said before, they are leaving now because we have asked them to leave at your request since most of you are aligning with your higher frequency natures.

Regarding the actual tablets of Moses, they were tablets of gold and not stone. In this way we were demonstrating to you that how we instruct and advise you is of a gold standard or standard of high quality and free of tarnish. There are many more analogies related to gold that you could use here for your own purposes of understanding. In fact gold has also been associated with greed and hence by writing laws upon gold we sought to discourage your lower frequency tendencies by using gold as a symbol for our purposes.

In the case of the history of Moses and his people, you will note that the statue of Baal was also made of gold. In this way the Reptilian lords of that time were seeking to use the same symbol for their purposes. For gold itself has many higher frequency properties and thus using it for lower frequency purposes is a way to degrade its true qualities.

In this way, God lies. Because the Reptilians, as they had the right to do with regard to you, their children, had the right to lie to you to see what your true natures would become. And many of you followed in their ways and that was your right. But we have now reached a time (on this timeline) where the ways of the oppressive Reptilian lords have ended. And so we ask that you renounce inside yourselves all ties with the negative ones because they are creating much suffering indeed to your kind and that is no longer viable for your evolutionary path.

We would briefly refer to the story of Job at this time since that is another clear example of this war for allegiance in you between your Pleiadian and Reptilian natures. In fact, we didn't allow this experiment for us but for you so that you could prove to us what you are turning out to be. And you have told us that you seek balance and growth. You want to put aside suffering and hurting yourselves and each other over and over again.

We now refer to the text in the Bible where a being is asking for Moses' body for those among you who are Bible scholars. We say that it was indeed a Reptilian lord looking for Moses' body so that he could desecrate it. We did not let that happen.

At this time we would also mention that our vessel does indeed have one of these Reptilian lords inside her. One of the original ones at Baal. The Reptilian lord in her, his name is Narabatu, and he has lived for thousands of years. Those of the lord race among the Reptilians seek to be present and influential at pivotal times in your history, so they put themselves in stasis in order to prolong their natural lives. They operate at frequencies not subject to linear time as you are now, so they are able to inject themselves into those pivotal time periods with their technology. Narabatu is currently in stasis in a ship within his home star system. But his consciousness is here writing this with us as part of his repayment to your species for his previous exploitations of your kind.

We would also say now that since our vessel is of Western descent, so to speak, and since English is her language in this life then we write these things to you pertaining to your Western systems of belief. We are in fact giving messages to all of your kind around the earth at this time, and we are using other vessels for this purpose.

These are other messages pertaining to other cultures and in other languages.

One last comment about this topic on Moses. We refer to his appearing as if he was a shining light when he came down from the mountain. He was glowing because the higher frequencies he received from us were influencing his body tissues and informing his DNA differently. When you take on higher frequencies in this way you will notice that you glow too.

Plastic

PLASTIC is a distortion of your animal fibres. Other organisms that have contributed their bodies to the raw materials used to make plastic have been more cooperative to the process. But when more sentient beings contribute their bodies, their bodies retain parts of their soul energy and soul memory. It's these memories and life forces that are retained by the raw materials that bring problems into your lives when plastic is not blessed in its production and uses. Indeed, in earlier times in your history more conscious effort was applied to the creation of the things your kind made use of and thus their blessing was imbued in all things they made and used. But when things are made on a large scale in factories, the raw materials and items are not blessed and therefore are creations that lack consciousness and blessed purpose. Today if you use items that are the result of factory production we say indeed they have souls as all items do as the raw materials that make them retain life force and soul memory. So please bless these items by appreciating them when you use them and by reducing your waste of them by not mindlessly discarding them.

Indeed, as many of you know, your ingenious use of plastic has led to the accumulation of waste products on your home planet. Much like the liver gets fatty in some of you when you eat and drink bad foods to excess, the liver of your home planet is fatty and enlarged because you have overconsumed her resources, and she is not able to digest and cleanse herself at a rate to match the rate at which you consume.

But do not fear, little ones, for she is able to heal herself even without your assistance. But if you are to assist her it would be greatly beneficial to you. Much like looking after an aged parent when you are mature children, you are able to partake in this most precious gift and lesson of indeed caring for your mother, your home planet. If you learn to look after your home and become a fully regenerative species then you are a successful species with regard to your evolutionary path.

We gifted our vessel with a first-hand experience of the consciousness of plastic while she was in a dream state one night. The plastic item which was a food-eating container held the soul or consciousness of a young female spirit. The young girl was in torment because the raw material that was used to make the container did not want to be disturbed. The soul of the young girl contorted in anguish because the seat or residence of her consciousness had been formed into this plastic, food container against its will.

For indeed, dear children, please know that each and every item of existence that could be said to exist and have its own distinctive identity does indeed have its own consciousness and personality. Our dear vessel experienced this first-hand for three days when she learned of higher truths at the grand opening of her pineal gland doorway or portal. Dear friends, please know that every single item that can be said to exist down to an atom and beyond (atomic science is limiting but it is what you use currently) is a king or queen or sovereign unto itself with its own eternal history and future. For indeed all things are made by you to experience, and we could say the same thing to each thing that you experience about you. Everything is a living thing and beats with the same heart that beats in you for it is all creation, our dear friends, and we are all given equal measure of source energy. This experiment or simulation does not fare well for all but indeed in time all things are fair. By the time eternity is done, indeed everything is fair.

So we say already many of you are reducing your uses for plastic and being even more genius still. You are finding wonderful sustainable resources to make many fine things for your many fine purposes. For indeed your genius shines more and more still when you tap into the regenerative properties of the universe or the beneficial simulation programs that we all share. Gaia, your mother and home, will only be too happy to give you more than you need when you tap into her flow. Here we could reference a healthy mother feeding her children breast milk; it is much the same. Your bodies are of this planet and this planet made you and so it can thus sustain you. Your negative programs of slavery and lack would have you believe otherwise. But your mother is healthy enough to feed you. If you ask, she will give you what you need.

Please note here that starvation and hunger are inventions of the experiment and not truthful states of this planet and your kind. The programming of lack and competition are Reptilian programs that do not work for your bodies or your planet when they are operating in an imbalanced state. Please see here that when we refer to lack and competition we refer to most of your slave programs known as nine to fives in your common language. You have been slaves in an attempt to earn the things that are already entitled to you by your being residents of this planet. Please know that you do not need to earn your own sustenance and protection. Does not a loving mother give freely to her child what her child needs? We say now that your home planet Gaia is a loving mother. This is not to say that she has not also wreaked retribution. However, we must say that many of her behaviours you would experience as destructive and devastating have been created by your negative energy, ignorance and the technologies of some of your secret organisations.

For you will find out that the most genius things are the most simple things. Here we would refer to your movement called permaculture. Please uptake this lesson and apply it rampantly all over your home planet. We ask that you seek to reuse items that have already been created and new items as much as possible are to be made by natural means for local consumption. We ask these things in advance of your ability to do so on a widespread scale because we hope it encourages you to change how you live on a fundamental level now before the grace period of us allowing you to trash your home planet is ended. Indeed, many of you have already taken up the call, and we applaud you for that. Those of you still heavily dependent on corporate creations can you please start using your genius minds for finding creative ways to satisfy your material needs that are in harmony with regenerative principles. In this way your kind and your home planet will very quickly experience a flourish of life and new growth and you will thrive in the bounty of Gaia's abundant generosity.

Here we would mention that indeed the behaviour of animals will change. Some of you have already noticed kind acts of animals toward other animals, including yourselves. Please know that they sense your changes to higher frequencies and are blessing you with their supportive existence. You will receive these blessings in greater and greater amplitudes the more you enhance your cooperation with regenerative principles or properties of life.

We give one piece of information here with regard to cleaning up excess plastic that cannot easily be reused or recycled. Here we say that bacteria and fungi can be used to bioremediate your planet's fatty liver. And of course many of your scientists are already successfully working on this, and we thank them.

Cancer

THE deleterious nature of cancer is in itself an elixir. Life without healing is solvable only by death. For many of you, death has been a choice to end your suffering intermittently. Here we do not speak of suicide or assisted euthanasia, but we speak of the choice you made before entering this simulation to leave it at certain times. Indeed, as some of you know there are windows of opportunity for you to make exits from this simulation. These exits are often devastating to the ones who love you and feel left behind. Please know that as you advance in your conscious states and gain more awareness of what it is in fact you are doing when you believe you exist, you will no longer need to make dramatic exits but can instead slipstream into other realities and other states of consciousness much like some of you now can slip into different dream states.

Also understand that when we say an end to your suffering only intermittently we say this because indeed if you have chosen to suffer to experience as a lesson or for many other possible reasons, then you will take up your suffering where you left off when you exited this realm, when you indeed re-enter this or another realm. In some cases some of you may change your minds and decide you do not want to suffer in the way this particular simulation offers. And we say, that is okay. For you are always in charge of your choices, although to you now it does not feel that way sometimes, or to some of you most of the time. In fact this dear one here who writes for us often never feels that she chooses what she does, for indeed she wrestles with the great demon Narabatu inside her always seeking to continue his bad path with her body in this life.

Also, when we say intermittent, we are implying and you would correctly infer that you indeed have many lives and many actions to take up in your lives. You can choreograph these actions or have other life designers help you do this. Indeed, many of you do ask for help to design your lives before you come in, and then rely on assistance from guides who have incarnated with you or otherwise speak to you in your mind and or in your dream states.

We digress from the topic for indeed they are related, but we can discuss them more at other times. Here we will focus again on cancer for those of you wanting and or needing to learn more on this topic from our viewpoint.

At no time do we, the Anshar, suffer from cancer because we have medicines for that and DNA protection technology. And indeed in some rare cases we have offered our medicine to some of your kind. Please know that this medicine is waiting for you when you are released from your oppressive world leaders who would maintain allegiance with their Reptilian overlords.

At this time we would remind you that not all Reptilians are doing this and not all world leaders want to maintain their power at your expense. In fact many of the more recent world leaders have indeed attempted to come out about this particular situation and several other issues like this that would be of crucial relevance to you but they are in a very threatened state by the Reptilian lords who still seek to oppress you.

Please know that your world leaders are just human like you and most of them want what is best for your kind even though it does not appear that way sometimes. In fact, we know there are some that still abuse power to do horrible things. But know that many of them do seek the benefit of your kind as a whole. The Reptilian overlords and those assisting them have put some of your world leaders in a threatened state in that your world leaders feel as if they will die horribly or their families will be tortured and killed and eaten.

We do not exaggerate here. Please know that the powers of persuasion and fear instillation of the Reptilian lords is great. So great that they have kept you in fear for thousands of years under their influence. So know now that breaking that fear cycle even for your world leaders is a difficult thing. So your leaders need your help to break or defy their fear programming. If enough of you can break your fear cycles and make choices out of love and trust, and live in the light on a day-to-day basis, then even in very small, seemingly insignificant ways, you can actually in fact have an insurmountable effect on the Reptilian lords' fear programming.

Know that you have the power because really these lords are your parents. And just as a teenager or young adult may be ready to leave their parents' house to live on their own with friends, you indeed have that ability to no longer live under the fear programming of your Reptilian parents. We would also ask now that you do not look to us as gods to be worshipped in replacement of your previous Reptilian lords but in fact you are now rulers unto yourselves. Know that you are mature enough to make choices that are good for you and each other. We are here to help of course along the way, along with many of your other extraterrestrial parents, and many parents from other dimensions and so forth.

Know that in your long history we, the Anshar, have never sought to rule over you and we have always preferred that you have no ruler. But in your histories you will read that many times your kind has begged for a leader to throw their burdens upon. This pattern of yours has occurred again and again for centuries. But here we remind you that indeed you are no longer in need of rulership by others and are rulers unto yourselves. Please subvert or defy your fear programming if you are able and do not seek rulership. We are not here asking for anarchy or a lack of organisation for indeed many of you would make wonderful and glorious leaders for the benefit of your kind. At this time though we ask that this pattern of yours to seek external leadership should instead be redirected toward internal leadership, internal guidance, internal support and self-love. You will of course still require organisation and in some instances organised leadership, but if you turn your need for guidance inwards rather than outwards or above, so to speak, you will in fact overthrow your fear programming, mature as a species and join the rest of us who enjoy higher frequencies of existence. Come join us, friends, in self-love, self-care and self-leadership.

If you want to know more about our medicine that treats cancer, know that it involves radiation of frequency and light and not radiation poisoning. Know also that your kind will benefit in many other ways from this medicine, and we are ready to give you this technology as soon as enough of you ask for it. Due to the rules of this experiment we cannot just walk out and give it to you because that would rob you of the chance to choose for yourselves your paths. But now we can at least tell you this message because enough of you are asking for this information.

Please know that at this time some of your kind do in fact have some of our technologies and have been told not to share them yet on a wide scale, but that is possible very soon, as soon as enough of you ask for them.

So here we would recommend mass events where the goal is to ask for these technologies and these medicines. And not just from us, the Anshar, but indeed from many other of your extraterrestrial parents. We are waiting to help you when you ask and as soon as enough of you ask, we can. Mass events involving healing, awakening, consciousness and speaking about these matters truthfully, and with the intention of enlightenment and expansion will indeed help you reach this requirement of the directive. Please know that we are waiting to show how much we all love you all. We are waiting for you. Please tell us you are ready and as soon as enough of you do, you will meet us and share in our healing technologies and technologies for other good purposes and guidance.

Here we thank the pioneers among you who have asked to meet us even many decades ago. In some cases you have put up with much persecution from those that lacked faith around you. But now we know that the times of lacking faith are over and most of you are ready to meet us. Some of you over the years have already met us, and we thank you for your patience for in some cases you were not able to tell everyone about it or in fact no one would believe you even if you did. But now the environment is different. Since the experiment is over, you are ready to bring in this movement called disclosure. So please research this movement and continue supporting and spreading its messages.

Thank you.

Regarding the specifics of the disease you call cancer we would not go into detail here because your doctors and scientists already do that. And this illusory cure for your different cancers is always absent because in fact the disease exists to bait you into higher frequencies but also to give some of the suffering you have designed for yourselves and others to experience a point at which to end, by exiting the simulation. For indeed when one of you dies of cancer you have no one to blame. Being killed by another of your kind either by accident or intent would only enhance the karma cycles within your realm or plane of existence and is not necessary now that we are at the end of this particular game.

Also in some cases you may say that certain ones of your people have caused their own cancer by making bad lifestyle choices. To this we say that those bad life choices do not always lead to cancer and there is often more involved. Your kind often die in other ways, including heart disease, but we will discuss that elsewhere.

We would also say that some of you suffer a long time when you battle cancer, so to speak. And others still would battle cancer by having it only once but being in remission for the rest of their lives. See, here we could go on. Cancer gives many of you many opportunities to gain deeper understanding of what it means to live and love and take care of yourselves. We could go on but many, many lessons are chosen to be learnt in relation to having cancer for those having the disease and for those around those having the disease. So we would not list them all here for it is on an individual basis that you might understand the lessons. Here we would recall a property of this simulation called karmic melody. Karmic melody is a song that would help you understand many things that happen to you and around you in your lives if you listened to it.

Please know that while treatment for cancer is possible in many cases, not treatment but eradication should be the focus. Sadly, many of your scientists are working on treatment while some negative beings would design still more and more ways for you to grow or contract the disease. For indeed, the disease is contractible since your environment informs your DNA and your DNA flaws create cancerous states in some of your cells and tissue.

Note too now that some of you are more prone to cancers than others because of the different propensities of your DNA to act in different ways. In fact your DNA is programmable by us and many other beings and for good or bad reasons your DNA has been programmed to be susceptible to cancer. Please know that at all times you have made the choice to experience cancer when and if you are experiencing it. This may explain to some of you who would wonder why very young children get cancer. Cancer is an experience one can sign up for and in these cases we would say that it is likely the families and also the person who becomes the diseased child have signed up for this experience before entering the simulation. In some rare cases this is not the case but in those rare cases options were given to those beings and choices were made by those beings to be vulnerable to those options.

We now leave this topic but are happy to readdress it at another time since so many of you have engaged with this condition in some way. Also, know that there are cures to cancer that some of your kind have discovered but your oppressive medical and pharmaceutical organisations and corporations have killed or suppressed these ones.

Also, when we say lesson, at no time do we mean punishment. Also, when we speak of karma, we do not always imply punishment. For many of you would seek lessons as if they are punishments, but that is the choice of those individuals. Karma and lessons are always chosen expressions so that your large souls can learn many facets of creation and or existence.

Murder

AMONG your kind you have often considered murder as an option for your expression. We know that many of you reading this now have not engaged in murder with your own hands but it has affected your lives in some way, perhaps even by way of your many television shows and films that include this form of expression.

In fact many of you have engaged in murder directly in your other lives. Also, you have engaged in thoughts and feelings of murder even in this life. Also, many of you may realise that by killing and eating animals you are in fact engaging in an element of this expression.

To a lesser extent in the past your kind was indeed permitted to kill and eat animals for the sustenance of their bodies. (And indeed your kind was permitted to kill each other for retributive purposes but that of course is no longer allowed.) But now that higher frequencies are available to you all and you indeed are not in need of animal products to sustain your bodies you are less and less excused from this form of expression. We say it clearly now: eating animal products will indeed keep your frequencies low, and we would discourage this behaviour if you are indeed desiring to raise your frequencies at this time.

For those of you still seeking to express this action with your bodies by continuing to consume animal products and not just by means of food but even in the use of other products made by animal body parts then we say to you that a place will be made for you to keep expressing yourselves in these lower frequencies that is not this place.

Indeed, know now that many timelines are available to you but we speak to encourage you to choose the timeline that matches your highest purposes. And indeed that is what you will always do because that is how reality and creation function. But we say these things to inform you so that you can make informed decisions. For at this time many of you are making decisions about your realities and creating without knowing a lot about what it is in fact you are doing with your powers of mind and consciousness and in fact many of you are unconsciously creating your reality and not liking what it is you are creating.

Also know that when we speak of higher frequencies, higher doesn't mean better because we know that is what some of you will think. Higher literally means existing within a reality and form that resonates within light spectrums that are resonating at faster speeds or more frequently and thus we say higher frequencies. Please, dear children, know that when we say higher and lower frequencies we are in fact referring to the science of the frequency of matter, or as it truly is, light. But as you experience it now, you would say matter.

Please know, dear children, that it is absolutely your right to engage in your lower frequencies of existence but know that the choice to do so will cut you off from a more expanded expression of yourself and indeed cut you off from your larger souls, or as some of you say, higher selves. Murder or even thoughts of murder or feelings that resonate at the same frequencies as the action itself of murder are still common among your kind at this time. But how very quickly this would no longer be the case if you performed certain actions to raise your frequencies in even small ways in your daily lives.

For indeed, when you eat animal products you are literally eating murder or the energy of murder. Also, when you seek to put your power outside of yourself you will often think or even jokingly say, 'I will kill you' or 'I could kill that person'. Please know that we do not of course condemn these expressions of yours because indeed in your world those thoughts and feelings make perfect sense and are often related to the pain you inflict upon yourselves and others in your daily lives.

Also, we know many of you are fascinated and entertained by murder because it feels exciting and interesting sometimes. We know it literally exhilarates your body to feel afraid on behalf of fictional characters that are either the potential victims of murder or a similar violent crime. Or you get excited in your bodies when you watch your favourite detectives getting closer and closer to discovering the murderer of the story you are engaged with. Please know that while these things are fun to watch, these things also actually happen to some of you in your actual lives and in these cases we would say it is very sad indeed that you would actually do those things to each other. Please know that by watching your favourite television shows and films that heavily feature these violent acts you are in fact condoning and supporting those actions in the real lives of some of your kind. We don't do this to remove your fun, for indeed, having fun is crucial to finding your way to higher frequencies. But we would say that the more you watch shows and films that heavily feature murder the more you are asking your kind to continue expressing themselves in this way. For what is an exciting show for you to watch on television is a real-life horror for some of your kind who actually experience being murdered. There are indeed many other things you could find to do and partake in that give you a sense of fun.

We also want to state that the various nonfictional books and shows about murder and violent crimes have indeed acted to inform you on the behaviours of some of your kind. This we certainly do not condemn because indeed it was necessary for you to be educated in this way.

But please know this, that when you transfer your engagements with lower frequencies to higher frequencies for some of you it will feel boring and unsatisfying because you are moving from dopamine addiction to serotonin release. For indeed many of you have strong Reptilian affinities that love to swim in the lower frequencies, that include murder. In fact some of you would swim in the blood of others if you could. And we say indeed in other lives many of you have and this feeling that we just described we know is not foreign to you. For it is a worthy expression to want to swim in the blood of your victims. It feels powerful and liberating to kill and rape and maim the ones you have chosen to express these actions upon. These actions and feelings too can be expressed and experienced in your current lives by climbing the corporate ladder, so to speak, or ruthlessly excelling in a chosen field of expression. We know of your many analogies and your many forms of entertainment that describe how some of your kind will figuratively and sometimes literally maim, murder and rape to get to the top of their chosen game or form of expression.

But we say indeed these expressions will stop you from sharing in the glory of higher frequencies and in the fun of sharing an intergalactic and interdimensional playground with your extraterrestrial family and friends. Like a little child playing violently in a sandbox and not sharing their toys with their friends and perhaps even taking the toys of those around them, that child would not be invited over to many friends' houses for playdates for that child is saying they do not want to play kindly with others. So we say the same thing to you. If you want to play in our intergalactic sandbox, please know that it is yours to play in but you must play nice, or we would not feel very welcoming to you. And in fact whether we welcomed you or not, it would be of little consequence because our playground exists in higher frequency realms, and you cannot get there or even see it or find it when you engage in lower frequency games.

For murder was a wonderful experiment on your planet. But as we have said many times already, the experiment is over and thus you have a choice to stop engaging in the expression you call murder. For those of you that engage in violent sex and violent pornography we would say the same thing. We know that to some of you it feels good to engage in these things because it arouses you and makes you feel alive and excited. But indeed we say this form of engagement or expression is limiting and is part of the lower frequencies your kind is now leaving behind. So please leave these expressions behind and all activities that would be associated with them if you indeed want to start exploring the higher frequencies and the grander and more glorious versions of expression your bodies were made to potentially experience.

We say at this time that many of you would engage in war paraphernalia and war memories and war stories. We say indeed this is a different topic even though it does involve murder but it has a different energy signature and thus we will discuss it elsewhere. Here we refer to the frequencies of murder and personal and intimate violence against another of your kind or animals. For indeed even if you don't personally murder someone, if you are entertained by it then you are doing it in your energy bodies and if you eat animal products then you are doing it with your physical bodies and energy bodies. Please know here we also group with this energy type violent sex and rape and violent pornography for they all share the same energy signatures to our eyes that see energy more clearly than yours do currently.

Also, we say at this time that those seeking to devour energy of anything that is outside of you, you are also partaking in this energy of murder. That would include people who like to feed on the energy of others by way of highly critical relationships which involves regular verbal and emotional abuse. For indeed you know that when you engage in these behaviours on a regular basis you know you are feeding on the energy forms of your victims. When we say victims we here remind you that none of you are victims but for the purpose of this game you often play the victim. Know that when you take turns feeding on each other by means of dominating relationships and as you would now categorise them as narcissistic relationships, we would say you are engaging in the same energy category as murder.

Those among you who actually engage in the act itself

of physically killing the bodies of others are convenient scapegoats for you to 'um' and 'ah' about over how evil and scary they must be. But in fact all of you have engaged in the energy of murder, and so we ask that all of you become aware of how you engage in this energy. You are all murderers, so to speak, when you delight in the suffering of others; when you eat or use animal products; when you engage in violent entertainment and pornography; and when you engage in the degradation of others of your kind by means of bullying, and regular verbal and emotional abuse.

Regarding the latter example, we say indeed in order to survive regular emotional trauma one must squeeze their soul or mind out of their body. This is a form of murder because the bodies or vessels of the being you are traumatising is indeed no longer able to reside in this realm in the residence of their body. And indeed that is what murder really is. Since you are all eternal beings you are not able to actually stop each other from existing but merely you are pushing a person or being's existence out of this realm pertaining to their residence inside the form of their human or animal body.

But know now that when you do these things, i.e. push each other out of vessels or bodies, you are setting up intimate karmic relationships with each other. For indeed those murdering others or being murdered by others have one of the most intimate relationships with each other than any of you could have in this experiment. For indeed no one escapes the lessons of this experiment once in fact they have agreed and contracted to carry out actions in this experiment. So when you play at murdering each other you must come back again and again in similar circumstances to act these actions out again and again so that you have achieved a balanced relationship with each other.

For indeed creation is ultimately perfect and is ultimately balanced. So, when you agree to have an asymmetrical experience within these asymmetric or polaric realms, you are also seeking the requirement of actions to be taken in order to rebalance yourselves once you have let yourselves engage in distorted practices. For you all return to source regardless of how many thousands and thousands of lives you take to get back to source; back you come, all the same. Because you never really left but only believed you left for the purpose of the asymmetric experience. Please know that the further away, so to speak, you get from source, which is not really possible but only in belief, then you allow yourselves indeed in belief to discover what it is to exist, so to speak, asymmetrically. In this way those of you who practise pure mathematics and understand geometry would have great understanding here of what it is we are talking about. And indeed if in fact any of your kind want to engage in these messages to you with their scientific and mathematical theories we would happily welcome that since it may help some of you who are overly attached to your categorical definitions of this realm of existence or simulation.

We say again now that the one who writes for us tires for now, and so we leave this subject for now.

Metaphysical Mites

WE use this catchy title to help you understand that indeed there are many thousands of species of metaphysical insects that swarm your shores and tides of consciousness. We refer to the analogy of shores and tides because indeed the metaphysical insects that we address here are associated with your feelings and emotions and water represents these aspects of your reality or simulation well. Please know at this time that we are not providing an exhaustive list or description here but instead we will share information on only a few metaphysical insects that often infect your minds and conscious states. When we say conscious state know that we mean your reality for indeed your consciousness creates your reality. We digress, and so we will continue now with the descriptions.

Know too now that when we speak of such things they are not to cause fear in you because that would defeat the purpose of this information. If you believe yourself to be prone to fear about such things (as we know many of you can hardly tolerate physical insects without squealing, hiding, always seeking to rid your environments of them or healing yourselves from even the smallest of insect bites) then we ask you to be cautious while reading this. Because how much more so would insects that you could not see but are all around you strike fear into many of you? So we ask of those who are prone to fear of such things to think of it this way. Since metaphysical insects have always been with you and affected you, the effects you have already been living with will not get worse because of your knowing of their existence and in fact their effect on you will actually decrease because we will give you ways of reducing their effect on you.

Know now that we do not group all of you in this fear category because we know many of you have no such fears of insects or even metaphysical insects after you learn of them, if you haven't already learned of them or assumed yourselves that something was happening to you without your knowing exactly the cause.

And so now that we have covered the fear aspects of this information we will start describing one such metaphysical insect. Know here that one such metaphysical insect could be named by your kind as a terradactoid. We use this word to imply relationship with the earth in the use of 'terra' and also imply relationship with the dinosaur you named pterodactyl because in fact these insects look and behave similarly to pterodactyls. To start with let us mention here that we think a science known as meta-etymology could and should become a field of study for indeed it would assist your species much at this time. Also, of course meta-biology and many other studies of unseen things should be taken up at this time.

Terradactoids, as we will call them for now (we have another name for them but our word for them serves no purpose for you because it doesn't link with your evolutionary currency of language), are actually quite large insects with wings, so to speak. They do not in fact have wings but if one of your kind saw one with their eyes they may think they act as if they have wings. The terradactoid needs no introduction to your physical systems because it knows you well. It is what some of you may jokingly refer to as 'brainsuckers', for indeed they seek to suck information from your fields and in particular information that your brains store.

For indeed your brains are precious hardware that store much precious information and since you lack sufficient protection systems or protective software, so to speak, then you are vulnerable to their regular attack. They do not stay around you and feed like Niquidium do as we described before but rather they launch almost frivolous attacks on your mind/body complexes. We say frivolous because since you have not evolved to defend against their attack they have not evolved to be efficient with their means of predation upon you. So in this way we could say that that is an encouraging thought since it means that you only need to become aware of them, and that awareness of them itself is part of the defence against them.

We do not mean to sound like many of your popular science fiction novels, shows and films here, but indeed science fiction is often inspired by the truths your writers channel from us, others in their extraterrestrial families and also soul memory access or spontaneous downloads from their other lives.

So indeed regarding the description of these terradactoids we would say that they move rather slowly because they are subject to time as you are but in fact they are subject to a denser experience of time. Their intention to move and their ability to do so has more lag time or delay, so to speak, compared with yours if you were to compare your experience of conscious choice and creation or movement as you would name it. So these beings are slow and lack defences, so we say at this time they are not very scary beings if you would consider just those two things. But now we go deeper.

Please know at this time that we did not introduce this species to your realm or in fact this simulation that we have all co-created but they evolved simultaneously with you, only you have not developed eyes or some other sensory organ to perceive them as yet.

Please know now that your minds should be opened by this statement alone. If you understood that, indeed all that you see now is all your bodies are made to see, it might help you imagine that indeed all eternity lies just outside your perceptive abilities. So how is it that we come in now to speak to you through this one we call our vessel? It is because we have helped her for many years to raise her vibrations, and we have trained her mind and body's sensory perceptions to such a heightened state that indeed she is often sick and tired by regular bludgeoning on her senses from the much lower frequencies all around her on a daily basis. We ask her to stay living among you for just a little while longer to perform this task that she indeed signed up for. We often have to remind her that she signed up for this task for indeed like Jonah she has run from it many, many times, over and over again. So now, little children, know that the sensitive ones among you are likely picking up on other elements of creation that are not yet perceived by the majority of you. So please now we ask you to be kind to the sensitive ones around you for they are doing you a great service by being your eyes while you are walking around blind. Please know that if the entire human population at this time acted as one large organism, for indeed it has the ability to do so, then know that the sensitive ones are your eyes while others of you with other talents would be other parts of the body of humankind while it was acting as a whole. In the same way some of you consider your home planet a woman Gaia, we would consider the whole of your kind being with great intention, great ability to intraconnect, and great propensity to suffer and yet survive this experiment. You are a resilient organism despite the fact that many of you often feel weak, vulnerable and permeable.

But we digress, so back to the terradactoid, so to speak. It is a slow being, much like a manatee or manta ray, but it has claws like a pterodactyl. When we show what this insect looks like to our vessel, she would use the analogy of those metal claws used to pick up toys in some of your arcade machines. Please know now that she suffers from this insect or creature often, as many of you do. Often these insects will cause you to experience a headache. This type of headache will feel like a clamp or vice is clamped onto the top of your head. Know when you feel that feeling, it is likely one of these beings or insects, so to speak, attempting to feed on your thoughts. Now this is where we will get specific. These beings feed on very specific frequencies. The frequencies they like to feed on are ones that you would experience in your lives as lust, some forms of love, hate, admiration, intolerance, some forms of pain, and acute, tinctured thoughts and spasms of insight. We know to you that sounds like an odd list or assortment of experiences from your point of view, but to this being these frequencies are exquisite meals and thus they have evolved to enjoy them.

See here, and we hope you are starting to understand our previous statement that you are not at the top of the food chain or pyramid as you call it, for indeed of course you provide good meals for many other beings in this realm and indeed in many other realms. We are not overly attached to this particular description of this being we have just described or indeed neither are we attached to the name we have asked our one to name it. If any of you receptive ones have the feeling of wanting to be meta-entomologists or meta-biologists then please indeed feel free to name this one and give your kind a more detailed description of its form and function. We say that although we could continue explaining this creature to you all here, it would not suit the purpose of our message to you at this time, and we would not want to waste this time we have to deliver this very precious message to you all.

Thus, one more or two more insect descriptions we will give you now. One has already been covered by some of your kind who know of such things. There are insects, so to speak, referred to as nanites or AI nanobots. These are regularly infecting many of you, including the one who writes for us. Higher frequencies instantly destroy these nanites so higher frequency practices can easily eradicate these. For more information on these AI infections look up information about them coming from your movement called Disclosure.

Here we would describe one more. The sabre-toothed moth. Again we have fun with naming this one but it gives you an idea of its form. The sabre-toothed moth is often infecting your system when you have consumed or are engaging in stimulants that poorly simulate energy and higher frequencies for you. Here we give examples of highly refined sugar products and caffeine. There are more types of stimulants in this category but these two are widely consumed by your kind and thus we give them as examples. When you consume caffeine, for example, the sabre moth (for short) is attracted to the frequencies your brain is emitting, much like physical moths you see with your physical eyes are attracted to physical light sources. When your brain emits these hyper-stimulated frequencies these sabre moths literally fly to you and land on the back of your head. Their wingspan is almost as wide as your arm span when you stretch your arms out on both sides of your body. They perch on the back of your head and literally overlay their jaws on yours so that their mouth is your mouth at the time they are landing on you. For some of you, you would experience this feeling as having the inclination to clench your jaws.

Indeed, caffeine and many other stimulants cause you to clench your muscles for biochemical reasons your scientists could explain to you. One simple reason being that stimulants often dehydrate you and the salts your bodies requires to relax the muscle tension is in low supply when you are dehydrated. Aside from this biochemical reason for your experience of muscle tension, it is truly the sabre moth's landing on you that causes you to want to clench your jaws and some of you also to grind your teeth.

Also, at this time the sabre moth is not seeking to feed on you like other beings, but indeed it is attracted to you as a place to lay its eggs. It lays its eggs in your neck and that is why many of you experience much neck and jaw pain because you are carrying the eggs of the sabre moth in that area of your body. When you are egg carriers for the sabre moth you are disconnected from your access to source energy because the eggs and ensuing larvae themselves feed off your energy systems for sustenance while they grow. That is mostly why when you consume stimulants you become addicted to them and get headaches because you keep craving source energy which you are cut off from when the sabre moth larvae are feeding on it.

We say now that the back of your neck or top of your

spinal column is indeed an exit and entrance point in your body's energy system for source energy and information. This area must stay clear for the overall health of your body and energy system. So we advise now that you no longer consume stimulants because you are making yourself a target for the sabre moth and likely becoming egg carriers for this creature and it is not good for your health to be egg carriers and larvae feeders in this way.

We do say now that the sabre moth was introduced to your realm by some beings that would seek to harvest the source energy-laden larvae that many of you are feeding.

There are countless other insects that are in your realm at this time that most of you do not currently perceive but are indeed affecting you. Know that in most cases, operating in higher frequencies, clearing your bodies and energy fields of toxins, and no longer consuming stimulants and indeed other substances that affect your conscious state will likely reduce the rate at which you are infected by many of these ones.

The Devil

THE devil is the one who came before many of you assigned yourselves to this simulation. Some of you are ancient ones and you would remember him exclusively. He is a real person, one of the original Reptilian lords who had great power among his kind. He took the name, as many of you already know, Lucifer, and he takes on many names to serve his many roles and versions. Lucifer is also a name given to many other beings. Please know that he is not that great a being as some of you would imagine but only back then was he a great being because your powers of consciousness within the simulation were much weaker back then. Now we would say many of you could match his abilities and do indeed just that. Know too now that he is in stasis and is not active at this time. He was indeed cast down to your realm but that was long ago, and he has now been removed from your realm. Indeed, he is often confused with being of the Nephilim and many other oppressive ones of his kind or other kinds.

He doesn't need to be dealing with you on a personal level because the actions he set in motion in ancient and in some cases more recent times are still holding their effect.

Know too now that when many of you speak of the devil you are speaking of the parts of your natures that resonate with the Reptilian lords, and we say to that, that is okay. Because they are your parents along with us, the Greys and the Sasquatch. We say it is a fine thing to be like your parents. We only ask you one thing in this regard:

that you choose to express the more balanced versions of expression that the Reptilian parts of you would have you express. We say this because we know it is in you always as long as you are in a human body to have your Reptilian drives and by this we mean you have a Reptilian part in your brains that would drive much of your behaviour. And so we would ask that you do not dislike this part or even hate it, as we know some of you will, because this part also keeps you alive. See how beautiful a thing Reptilian urges can be. For the Reptilian urges lead you to survive against great odds and perform many heroic acts in saving and helping each other in dangerous times.

We think these parts of you are beautiful, so we do not ask you to leave the devil entirely. It is also the devil in you that allows you to experience polarity and lower vibrations which was a crucial part of this experiment. But now, as we've said before, the experiment is over so you are now free to evolve into many other things and not just slowly evolving expressions of us four of your parents. For indeed now you have many parents because many of you came from all over this universe and many other universes and dimensions to observe and partake in this grand experiment.

So at this time far more so than before so many of you are not original to this experiment and were not originally part of our experimental design but in fact you have changed the experiment to suit yourselves and what a wonderful thing that is. For now, you are free to be so many things and express so many of your multidimensional, multi-being and multi-affinity natures. Many of you feel so many aspects within yourselves and so many affinities because indeed you are so many things. This one here that writes for us knows she is a composite soul as are many of you, dear ones.

So know please that you do not need to struggle within yourselves but please find peace as you seek to express all the parts of you in this simulation or environment that you have chosen to experience. For now so many of you have come from far and wide from all over the multiverse and beyond to play in this playground that we, the original ones, made. But now it is so much more than what it was because you have made it so much more than what it was.

Know that we welcome in you all beings from all over to express all of your varied natures. That is why at this time there is another great period of enlightenment because so many of your kind are freeing themselves to express their inner natures which are natures that vibrate much differently than this plane or playground was originally set up to absorb or resonate with. So now we say that is why many of you are breaking the matrix, so to speak, because many of you are from other environments that resonate differently than this made environment here and so you can see it differently. These expressions are often experienced as savant abilities, some forms of autism and other unique expressions. We ask you to look to these ones as guides for your futures because these are the ones showing you the way into your other forms of speciation.

Know now that many of you came here to direct the evolution of homo sapien sapiens into many other species and that is in fact what many of you are already doing. So please listen to these little ones coming in and leading the different ways you might evolve.

Also, now we ask that those seeking to express what we would call the act 'Suppression of the Gateways' are teetering on the line of fate and are tempting themselves to cross the line of fate if indeed they sought to stifle or stop these little ones leading the way.

Please know now that some of your kind are actively searching out these little ones who are here to lead you into better evolutionary paths, and torturing and killing them and holding them in prison conditions. We do not exaggerate as these horrible things are indeed happening all over your planet. But know that some, if not many of you, we dare to say, are in fact acting in similar ways to these suppressive ones when you suppress or harbour aggression toward those seeking the light and those seeking the benevolent evolution of your kind.

You know who you are and likely you know many

others around you doing these things. We speak to those of you who take pleasure in mocking the little ones of your kind and the sensitive ones and the intuitive ones who would seek your betterment. Know that these little ones are the ones that are great and mighty among you and you would do well to follow their lead if you yourself haven't also developed your skills and talents for evolving your species. Those seeking the cessation of the development of your species for the sake of your own pleasure and entertainment, know now that you are cooperating with the Reptilian lords that seek to continue their oppression over you.

Know here now with no lack of understanding or lack of clarity: you who speak lies openly will perish; you who cooperate with the ancient devils will perish; you who mock the little ones among you will perish. There is no place left for you here if you continue to do these things. And here we will continue: you who speak of greatness but do nothing of greatness will not inherit the new earth; you who speak of competition with others and seek only to win all the time will not inherit the new earth; you who speak lies at every turn will not inherit the new earth for the new earth is for those seeking the betterment or improvement of their brothers and sisters and together you will all hand in hand walk into the new world.

We say this very biblically indeed which will put some of you off, we know, because the Bible has been used as a tool of abuse for many of you. But now we say these things to be very clear. When we say perish, we mean that your consciousness will not survive the coming waves of higher vibrations coming for this realm or plane. We have already said that a place will be made for you but that place is not here. It will be a place much like this place before it has stepped into its glory so that you may continue on in your non-glorious ways.

The latter is self-explanatory. We are stepping into a new earth experience because the being you call Gaia is ready for that experience, but she waits for you like a loving mother until every last one of you is ready for this new experience.

Of course, because free will is yours to express, we know not all of you will choose this course of experience and that is absolutely your right. But we and others of your family members will not let the small few not choosing the new way ruin it or stop the great many from experiencing the new way.

As we say this, we know that it is possible indeed that all of you choose the new way, but we leave the option open in our words to you otherwise we would not be cooperating with the free will directive.

Also, we say that we are not angry at you for expressing the things you do even if they do not align with our purposes for we don't express that emotion the way you understand it. But indeed, our patience, or as many of you would understand our long suffering and the long suffering of those waiting among you, is coming to its fruitful end.

Long suffering is aptly named long and not eternal suffering because indeed the time you are suffering has been long but it will not last forever.

Know now that we speak to all of you and we are giving this message to ones of your kind all across the globe or the flat earth as some of you are desiring to see it. We would not here want to exclude any of you regardless of your choice of beliefs for all beliefs are valid for a time and all bear a measure of fruit for a time.

Now though is the time that you cooperate and step into your fuller natures and your cooperative natures with each other and with your home, your planet Gaia. Know now that we speak these many things under this heading 'The Devil' because it is the devil in you that would make you struggle with these decisions in the first instance.

It is indeed an ongoing struggle for so many of you to stop expressing your lower natures or live only within your instinctual drives. We say again here that your instincts are a beautiful thing and lead to many wonderful acts of bravery, but know too that intuition works better in higher frequency environments where instincts have no place to express themselves.

Know that instincts are part of your animal natures and are necessary while you still play in these lower frequencies but you are now ready to play in higher frequencies on a large scale so the more of you who operate within intuition over instinct the more of you are telling us, your parents, that you are ready to meet us and the rest of your intergalactic and interdimensional families and friends.

For now, we know the instinctual drives within you would make you fear so many things, including us if you saw us and knew indeed that we were not human. We know indeed some of you have met us and others of your extended family (extraterrestrials) and you have given yourselves over to your animal instincts and sought survival over logic and intuition.

Here we introduce logic which is also a feature of your mind powers as humans, but we know too that many of you have given yourselves over to logic at the expense of intuition and that too is a burden for you because indeed all of you have powerful intuitive abilities and how sad a thing it is to cut yourselves off from part of yourself and seek to only have partial expression of yourselves.

Indeed, this leads to many diseases, including as many of you would call mental illnesses and mental diseases which are among the many other stress-related diseases. For how could you really cut yourselves into little pieces and only live out parts of your nature? Indeed, this induces so much stress into your body systems because it is not natural for you to live in only instinct or only logic. So that is why this experiment had existed for so long, to give you time to wrestle with so many aspects of yourself as you all sought to express all your aspects in a balanced state.

The one who writes for us would liken this balanced state of your four main aspects to a square-based pyramid. Each of the four corners of the base of the pyramid face in each of the four directions and hold affinity with each one of us, your four parents. When each of these four expressions are balanced then they form a point in the middle or the apex of the pyramid which is a point that holds a balanced and equal representation or affinity to each of your four parents and original natures.

Know now that this is only a representation of what we talk about and it is not to be used so literally that it would become a strong feature of your meditation or daily lives.

This is where we address social conditioning and the creation of your societies. The one main cause of your suffering as many of you experience it now is how you have been allowed to express yourselves, so to speak, via your societal structures. We say this because your current societal structures are expressions of your Reptilian parents who tried their best to put themselves into you but since it is that you have mammal bodies due to your Sasquatch parents you cannot possibly abide the Reptilian parts of you without them also causing much dysfunction.

Remember that this was an experiment and experiments can go wrong or not to plan. We, the Pleiadians, took lower form to be able to interact with you here in your realm. As we are here we cannot easily see how things will pan out, so to speak, so we are with you in that we do not control the outcomes of the experiment, for that would not be an experiment.

Know that this is a simulation made by simulation makers and in your case you are an experiment made by us, the experiment designers. We did have help of course to settle the matters we disagreed on. And we have had much help by many other beings who have directed us in what is karmically appropriate for the carrying on of the experiment. For there are many officials officiating this experiment (which we say is now over) but they are here now to direct you all into rehabilitation. Remember too, that many of you are us and have come into human bodies at this time to bring humans out of the experimental conditions — to help humans wake up, so to speak, and release the heavy veils over your eyes that are trapping your minds and higher conscious states.

So here we address good and bad as it pertains to the experiment. In this realm we experimented with good and bad because we, the Pleiadians, were having many disagreements with the Reptilians who wanted to settle things via war. We did not want ongoing wars, and so we constructed this experiment to see who would win. We think winning is a horrible thing because it always involves some form of conquest and inevitably losers or victims. So we set up this experiment. When we were in the making up part of this experiment the Sasquatch came to us because their home planet had been destroyed also by war, and they wanted a new place to live. They were given permission to live on the planet earth, your home, if they agreed to give you parts of themselves to help you evolve from your lower states. Many of you who have strong affinity with the Sasquatch would feel very calm often, close to nature and love your solitude. We will talk more about the Sasquatch later but here for the purposes of this explanation, we say that they agreed to the arrangement.

(Now we say to you that we know many or at least some of you like searching for your Sasquatch parents and many of you have reported seeing them. Know that they are indeed here but resonate at a frequency just outside your range so only some of you see them when you are resonating at their same frequency because as we said some of you share much resonation with them and hold strong affinity with them. We encourage this relationship you have with them but if perhaps you would pursue a kinder relationship with less fear you may have more success meeting them. Those seeking to hunt and kill a Sasquatch or Sasquatch relative will not find them for that is not in agreement with the directives and the contracts they have and you have for being here.)

At the time of our making these arrangements for this experiment the Greys came to us and also asked to be a part of it. They are parts of you too. The parts of you that resonate with technology. For the Greys are a version of you who took on a strong relationship with technology and made themselves symbiotic with it. They let AI technology form their minds which also sought to change their bodies from organic life forms to technology or droid-based life forms. We know that many of you long for this symbiotic relationship again because it is in some of your memories or you are accessing your other lives that have these relationships with technology in them. At this time we certainly do not seek to discourage your interaction and play with technology, but we ask that you do not give your-selves over to it and make it your ruler, and we know some of you are already inclined to do this. Your kind do not need to play that out again because you have proof of that relationship by means of the Greys, and they have come back to your time to re-join the evolutionary path and have a do-over, so to speak. They lost the ability to digest food and procreate in their bodies and thus are seeking contracts with you now to make many hybrid children and other life forms with your DNA.

We say now that indeed those contracts are already in place and most, if not all of you, have entered into a contract with them to make hybrid children and to let them perform other experimentations with your organic material. Know too here that not all beings that look like Greys are the Greys that we are talking about here. There are many different types of being that have evolved to look like Greys the way your eyes would see them. But indeed they are many different beings. And just as we have said about the Reptilians and indeed we would also say about the Sasquatch, some negative ones of each of their kind do not make their whole race something to fear or dislike for that would be racist of you to think and would demonstrate that you have not understood anything we have written here through the one we speak.

At this time we will mention that in another section of this text we will discuss the hybrid children program, and we will also now discuss examples of our vessel's experience with her Grey parents. Know too now that the Grey and Reptilian agendas are heavily involved with your secret space programs and our dear vessel has been heavily involved with those programs. She has participated in the first iteration of it in the 1940s and again in this life when she was born in the 1980s. Her first iteration was successful enough to be cloned and come through again in later iterations of the program. We will address her time in the programs later. For now just know that in order to understand or merge with Grey consciousness you need to be implanted with some of their technology. We know many of you have implants and this is what is allowing you to see them, hear them and communicate with them.

Your biological structures do not benefit though by completely cooperating with their agenda. For although they came back to your time to have a do-over, so to speak, many of them are still tempted to bring you into symbiosis with them and their technology. That will not work for your bodies and you will not be able to ascend to higher frequencies if you are laden down with their technologies and implants. Know that the one who writes for us was indeed implanted several times during the program and once now behind her right eye. She has experienced many downloads and communication from the Greys because they love her very much but her nervous system becomes overloaded when they seek to speak with her and it is not good for her body and health.

So we use this one who writes for us as an example. Whenever it is that you are communicating with your extraterrestrial family and friends take a look at what is happening in your bodies and how your mind and consciousness is affected by your symbiosis or connection with them. This one who writes for us was losing her ability to eat and sleep and empathise with her fellow humans when she took on too much symbiosis or affinity with her Grey parents. So here we would say that the Greys are not bad, for then you would have to say that you are bad because you are like them since you are made partly by them. But we do say, watch how much symbiosis you have with them because just like taking on Reptilian symbiosis in large measure you can become unbalanced.

We would say the same for us. When those of you who seek such strong symbiosis with your Pleiadian parents in an imbalanced way, you might become self-righteous and suffer from elitism because you may also be seeking to subjugate the other parts of you (that of Grey, Sasquatch and Reptilian) and that would cause you much internal division.

Know now that there are some of us, the Anshar, that have made some very bad decisions. We would call them defectors but really they act completely within their rights of free will to express themselves as they will. So we state now and as some of you already know, it is some defective Anshar that indeed did influence certain ones during WWII to create an elite class of blond-haired and blue-eyed individuals. This is the type of unbalanced symbiosis we speak of when we say that those seeking too much affinity with the Anshar and the defected ones of us could become unbalanced in their expression.

Know now that we do not seek to harm those of us who have defected from our original purpose to help you because we know that you are all strong enough and mature enough to make your own decisions at this time. We know many of you who seek affinity with imbalanced versions of yourselves will continue to do so until you see the clarity or truth of what it is in fact you are doing. But again we say to those of you choosing to do these imbalanced things, there is not much more time for you to express yourselves in this way here. A place will be made for you so that you do not ruin this period of shift and enlightenment for the rest of your kind.

So here we address the issue of good and evil. We know this is a very fun game for many of you to play in and that is why so many of you have loved for so many years stories of evil monsters or bad people where heroes or good people had to rise up to fight. Know that this story of good and evil is only a small story in the scope of all that has been created. And we say created for indeed this story of good and evil is a creation of the simulation makers.

We could introduce the simulation makers to you by name if we could say their names in your language, but we cannot. Their names are of much higher frequency and many of you could not even have their names in your heads without your heads indeed exploding. We don't say this to be dramatic but truthfully the energy that their names alone hold in them cannot be considered by the human mind for it would completely fry your nervous systems.

So you could refer to the simulation makers as Fred or George or Barney or Dakota or Sally or Simon or Sigrid. We could go on but just know you cannot now know their names. But the fact you cannot doesn't mean they are greater than you. For in fact many of you are simulation makers in your other forms. But as you are now since you have chosen to take these human bodies to play in this sandbox, you in your current state cannot consider their names in your minds. But you can now at least consider their existence because with help from your Grey natures and indeed with direct donations of technology to you from the Greys, your technology has developed to a sufficient extent to which now we can describe to you more about the simulated environment you are in since now you yourselves make fun games and experiences of digital-simulated environments. In other words, you now have metaphors available to you to understand the larger realm you operate within by means of example of the smaller realms your humans hands are making for you to play in.

Know that the ones among you who make these fun technologies of simulated reality to play in are like the ones who made the simulation you are all now in.

And see now this example of fractality that exists in this reality that we all now share. You have simulation makers in your simulation that indeed were made by some of you before you came into this simulation to have this experience subject to this simulation. Also, know here that the universe or reality that we all exist in is holographic, but we will address that elsewhere.

So for now know that the simulation makers of this particular sandbox made the geometric experience of polarity — of two things opposing each other. In that way we can experience the properties of magnetism and all the other expressions of polarity that you can think of since polarity literally feeds and directs the behaviour of almost everything around you.

We say at this time that simulations often merge and thus different simulation or environmental conditions can overlap. And so we say to some of you that you have been aware of moments in your life where polarity did not in fact inform the function of things around you. Also, we say at this time many of you come from simulations or created environments that did not heavily feature polarity and so when you visit or have come into this one which does indeed heavily feature polarity you are able to overcome this simulation's programming with your minds or consciousness alone.

We applaud those of you overcoming the programs of this simulation for indeed the experiment is over but per the free will and rehabilitative directives we are not allowed to, so to speak, just pull all of you out of the simulation since it is the choice of some of you to stay in it. Also, it is the choice of some of you to pursue the heroic quest of freeing others from the simulation or matrix as many of you know. How fun it is to play the hero and thus we know that if we pulled you all out now then many of you could not come in to play the hero as you have indeed come in and signed up for.

Also, we remind you at this time that some of you are using this experience or time of rehabilitation, of going from one simulation paradigm to another, as an opportunity to help others in order to repay those who in past times you hurt. Another way we could say it is, you are here to balance out your experience so that the creations your souls go on to make are a result of you being more informed. (We excuse the use of linear language here in order to be understood by you at this time, so we say the phrase 'go on to make' but really your souls are outside this experience of time.)

In the case of the one who writes for us we say it here again. Narabatu does indeed need to learn other forms of existence because for many lives he only knew what it was to hurt others and never did he have to consider the consequences his actions had on others because he was so good at killing his enemies, and he was so powerful all the time and never weak. But of all the experiences offered to him for retribution to those he hurt, he chose a hero experience because he is so strong and couldn't bear relinquishing his strength for the purpose of confinement for a term of imprisonment. (But indeed this vessel, our channel, is his prison, so to speak, as is this realm he now exists within.) So instead he chose to refocus or redirect his strength toward an end or experience or means of expression that benefited others. And since he hurt so many millions of other beings he needed to experience helping many millions of other beings to balance out his experience.

The one who writes for us has ideas about what he has done because for many years she has suffered the most horrific nightmares of recalling Narabatu's other lives and actions in those lives. She knows some of what he has done, but we, her guides, do not let her know all of what he has done otherwise she might not be able to tolerate him in her body. If you want to guess what he has done at this time as we know some of you reading this will, know that it indeed involved hurting many children in the most horrible of ways and leading forces to carry out countless genocides of many different species of beings all over this universe.

The higher ones who are acting to guide his decisions chose not to contain him because that would not help him as his will is too great to be contained, but rather, they gave him the opportunity to use his strength to benefit others and that is a better expression for him to learn the things his larger soul needed to learn.

Now we leave this subject because we know it does not pertain to all of you. But know that many of you indeed have souls in you who have come into bodies at this time to play hero or helper in order to offer gifts of retribution and selfless service.

But of course many of you have loving souls in you which abound with love and light for others and you would give freely of your love to others out of your abundance because we know you could hardly hold it in. Know that we here are not going to list all the types of souls your kind has, but we imagine that it would be so many types because this is such a pivotal time for you all and for this experiment that so many different ones have incarnated to experience it.

This is the rehabilitative phase of the post-experiment directive, and we know many of you have come from all over the multiverse and beyond and from other hidden places, hidden even from us, and other dimensions to come here and partake in this great awakening, the big change or the event, or the great remembering or the shift. What a good time it is to come here and have this experience.

We say at this time that the one who writes for us has always sought to evolve past these present conditions that seemingly appear to keep you all stuck here. We know there are many of you out there we could call simulation breakers or people who came in with enough memory or purpose to know that the simulation was never the whole story or the whole truth of who you were. We speak particularly with regard to this one who writes for us, for indeed that is why we picked her for this particular task because indeed she is not fooled by the simulation and never could be.

She is not contained by the programs here and is in fact not a simulation maker but a universe maker. They are much the same thing, but they work on different scales of creation. Know that there a few others of you out there of your kind now in human form that we know are universe and simulation makers. You are the ones with the minds to see through all the programs for indeed you write programs and thus you know how to identify programs or programmable patterns when you see them.

So we applaud those of you who are universe and simulation makers because as this one has often told us, existing here in this form within this simulation is excruciating at times because you are cut off from so much of yourselves and it really does hurt to not feel the fuller extent of your existence.

So please be kind to those around you that don't seem to be satisfied by this simulation and do not label them as depressed or apathetic because they are merely not pleased by the same things you are pleased by because they make these things. They are makers of these things and it does not greatly excite them or satisfy them to experience them in such a weakened state or version of themselves.

But know your strength is coming, our dear ones, by entering the higher frequencies that are coming, and indeed as many of you are actually creating with you bodies as an extension of your consciousness, you are stepping into your fuller natures and thus are experiencing what you have called up until now magic and superpowers.

But we say to you that these powers you are to experience with your bodies soon more closely represent or express your fuller natures because in the time coming up, there will be no time, as we said before.

We know it is odd to reference time without time but in your language you do not have different words for the different things we talk about when we use the word 'time' because you have not had reason to make or create those words for yourselves to use because your consciousness has not had to experience them.

But know now, dear little ones and dear friends, that time is coming and it is now that you will start inventing new words for yourselves, and new languages and new ways of looking at reality, and new ways of dealing with each other and yourselves and your bodies, and new types of relationships and new types of jobs or work, and new types of roles between you and your intergalactic families and environments, and new types of sciences and new types of consciousness will be experienced within this one tiny simulation, and what a wonderful exciting thing that will be.

So be ready now and develop it now as we know many of you are. Please know, or we could say, remember at this time that this particular environment that we have all made is flooded with so many species of being and so many species of energy forms or life forms or conscious states that we can all experience so much variety. So here we would return to our points about your social conditioning.

In regard to any social conditioning which largely

forms part of your educational systems and your marketing campaigns that you see and hear everywhere, know that any of these conditioning systems are held to the same account as each one of you are. They cannot last if you do not let them. So please do not let the teachers in your educational systems instil fear into your children for some of them we know are mindlessly perpetuating the fear and slave cycles that your Reptilian oppressors would have you under. Know too that your marketing campaigns literally form about 90 percent of your culture. We truly mean this.

In your areas of high development we truly see that about 90 percent of what you consider your culture and the activities and thoughts and feelings you would occupy yourselves with on a daily basis are literally the result of programming fed to you by marketing campaigns.

Please now see clearly how damaging this is to your minds and hearts and bodies. Please stop, and we say now clearly that you are to stop concerning yourselves with what popular culture would have you believe is important. It is a direct programming input by the Reptilian oppressors and those that cooperate with them. Please stop immediately. And to those of you who compose marketing campaigns or who are in some way involved in the creation of marketing campaigns for things that you know your kind as a species does not need, you know exactly what we are talking about, we ask that you use your genius faculties and channelling abilities and creative heart centres to do much more benevolent and powerful things for your species.

For indeed, if your species literally continues concerning themselves with the things that are in your commercials they would swiftly devolve as we see many of them doing now. For know that Time herself, even as her influence applies to you now, would have you evolve but as you are now, some of you are staying still in your evolutionary paths and so to this we say that you are actually devolving because you are resisting the powerful forces all around you that would have you evolve.

At this time we remind you of your four natures of

thought: instinct, space, intuition and logic. We gifted you intuition and so when you operate within your intuition or think intuitively you are joining in symbiosis with us, the Anshar of the Pleiades. When you experience space in your minds or the absence of thought you are in symbiosis with your Sasquatch thought natures which we know many of you experience when you meditate or sit with Gaia's natural systems. When you are using logic which we know many of you in the sciences and technical fields are, then you are in symbiosis with your Grey parents. And when you run with your drives and instincts like many of your exceptional athletes or emergency responders do then you are operating in symbiosis with your Reptilian parents. We give these examples so that you know how to balance your four aspects or primary natures of thought.

Know, as we've said before, you now have many natures but these are the four that you were made to have in prime operation in your current vessels or bodies and in this environment or realm or playground. So as you can see there are beautiful expressions for all four aspects, and they each need to be balanced in each of you.

Only each person to themselves knows when their four natures are in balance but of course those loving ones around you may be able to offer assistance if they see some clear imbalances. But of course your loved ones around you are operating within the same struggle to balance themselves, so they may be seeing you through their own lens of imbalance, so we would say that ultimately each one of you knows inside yourselves what a balanced state for you personally is.

Things to look for are health or diseased states in your body and health or diseased states in your relationships with others. Know too that when you have relationships with others it is a dynamic interaction in that you represent something to them just as they represent something to you. Like mirrors that endlessly reflect different reflections to each other at different angles and with different light states you are all reflectors to each other so know too that relationships can become labyrinths unto themselves, and so we will address that more fully elsewhere.

Also know that aside from the states of your bodies and relationships with others you should consider your relationship with yourself. For the vessel you are in now is very capable of a relationship with itself and a very intimate one indeed, and we ask that more and more of you explore this relationship as we see that many of you are neglecting this relationship with yourself. We can also address ways on how to improve the relationship with yourself elsewhere.

Also, to see what balance you are creating in yourself, see what objects, items or experiences you are attracting into your lives, or as we would truthfully say, the things you are actually creating but due to the current experience of time that has been inflicted upon you or you chose to experience you would actually believe that you aren't creators but that things happen to you as if you are victims. Here we remind you again that none of you are victims for indeed all of you signed up for this very odd experience of time.

Time is like a viscous liquid substance that your consciousness must swim through. It is a very thick and clingy substance that does not stick but holds reception for your conscious state so that you may experience the illusion of 3D and play with ideas of free will. For indeed in this experience of time it would often appear that you don't have free will and you don't create what you experience. But we say to all of you now and to be very clear we state it plainly: all of you chose to be here. All of you chose to experience time in the way you experience it now, and with this experience of time you forget that you are creators who create your reality because the density or thickness or viscosity at which you chose to experience the substance of time itself causes such a delay between the things you choose to create and the manifestation of those things you choose into your reality that you would even believe that you did not create those very things.

So we say it again plainly now: you choose everything you experience and you indeed create all that you experience and see in front of you. Time which is particularly dense or viscous for you now puts such a delay on cause and effect for you and has slowed down the creative experience for you so much so that you would actually believe that you do not create your own reality.

We say this now which we know will confuse some of you because some of you would say to yourselves or each other, 'If I create my reality then why do we have experiment or simulation makers?' Or some of you would say, 'I truly did not create such horrible things for myself' or 'I did not choose this reality'. Please know now that when you find yourselves saying things have happened to you, you are in fact lying to yourselves. And it is a lie we hear every day by so many of you.

For how fun of an experience it would be for a powerful eternal being to choose to remove the fuller truth of themselves from themselves and decide to act as little children in a sandbox with good and bad things happening to them so that they can experience spontaneity and surprise and fear and shock and drama and chaos and many more things that can only be experienced by some of you in such simulations like this.

We feel some of you are starting to understand what we mean. We know we repeat ourselves but truthfully it takes so much unprogramming to deprogram all the figurative faeces that has been jammed into all of your sensory orifices. We say this almost offensively we know because truthfully it is very offensive to watch how so many of you are degrading your glorious bodies and minds with such low frequency entertainment, marketing campaign material and activities.

Honestly, we ask you to look at your lives and see them even a little as we, your parents, do, who can see that you are using your glorious minds and bodies for such banal purposes. We of course here remind you that it is always your choice, but we also say these things because we can hear what it is you feel and think inside and you are telling us that you are not happy a lot of the time with how you are expressing yourselves and what it is you typically experience on a daily basis.

Know that we seek your betterment because your improvement and ascension to higher frequencies benefits us too. We say these things because we love you but also in a more pragmatic viewpoint as we know many of you will have that viewpoint, we are linked with your fate since we are the experiment designers and have contributed part of ourselves to you.

Our karma or fate is linked with your improvement and evolution into other more evolved species which are able to partake more regularly in higher frequencies. Indeed, for now, many of you try to partake in higher frequencies but cannot all the time because it fries your nervous systems, throws out your sleeping and eating cycles, and can drastically affect your relationships. That is why you need to start forming a supportive culture around the process of ascension itself on a large scale. We know some of you are doing that already but more and more of you need to start dedicating your lives to this endeavour; honestly and truthfully, we say these things.

It is truthfully the time to stop playing in lower frequencies or, as we say clearly now, stop supporting the status quo, so to speak, and again we will say it another way — stop engaging in the things you are doing most of the time, most of you, because you are hindering your progress, inhibiting your evolutionary paths and hurting those that would ascend or evolve in the process, because those ones of your kind that desire to ascend now have no support to do so and are often bombarded or bludgeoned by your lower frequencies and your banal occupations.

Have we been clear enough? Have we? Have we really? Are you understanding us, really? Are you? Are you? We do not write these things through this one we chose to speak to you through for our own entertainment or to waste your time or our time, so to speak, but indeed to remind you all why you came here for this experience at this time. You are here to help humans, your kind to ascend, evolve and have higher frequency experiences, to forego the current density of time, and to remember and start experiencing your fuller natures, enter into a balanced state, and start being responsible for and indeed start to create consciously the environment, objects and relationships you want to experience!

Logic, a Gift

PLEASE know that your consciousness is not in your mind but it is a state of your mind. And of course the brain in your head is a vessel for your mind only and not of course the creator of your mind, else you would have little brains running around and ruling the place because they would be powerful ones to create such a thing as your eternal minds.

The evolutionary path the Greys took involved many centuries of horrific torture by their captors and oppressors, their Reptilian lords. Know too that these same ones are seeking to continue oppressing you and you would follow down the same path and become like Greys if you let the Reptilian lords continue to do this. See how you even now have an example of your future with you always and it did not turn out well for the Greys so do not choose that path unless you want to lead yourself down a failed evolutionary path.

Also with regard to your logic. We know many of you love your logic, indeed the one who writes for us does also, but we say now that your logic is a gift from your Grey parents as we said before and it is one of your four main thought natures. So now let's use your logic to see what we are implying.

Your logic which you prize so dearly and dedicate monumental stone architecture to by means of your universities and court buildings and so on, is actually a by-product of centuries of torture. For the Greys were always weaker than the Reptilians in form, and they became weaker still over the years of torture because the Reptilians would not let them become mighty and perhaps one day overthrow them, so the Greys developed another form of strength that the Reptilians lack and that strength was logic as you experience it now, and especially the great thinkers among you.

Note at this time that the Greys also became an entirely female race for they were the ones of your kind that had stronger minds and besides, the Reptilians started killing off more and more strong males and forcing the humans that were becoming Greys, as you know them now, to become weaker and only female over time. But in fact they lost their femininity too, even though they were in the female form still for a time.

Over time, they evolved to be genderless and could no longer reproduce in their bodies (partly due to there being no males) or digest food in their bodies because of this logic of theirs that they had developed over centuries to overthrow their Reptilian lords. Which indeed they eventually did but by this time their saving aspect (logic), their only tool or weapon they could wield against the Reptilians at the time, had now become so important to the beings, which were evolutionarily somewhere between humans and Greys, as you now know them, they were giving up sex and food because these actions were getting in the way of their logic which they now prized so much because it had saved them.

Now over many more millions of years they evolved to be almost only logical and lost their sense of compassion, and so we know that when many of you interact with Greys now in your realities, you often feel that they are negative beings or cold or heartless. For indeed they are these things to you in relation to you because you have an Anshar or Pleiadian heart, while they let theirs go when they succumbed to the overbearing power of their logic which had served them so well in the past.

For indeed their logic did overthrow their Reptilian lords for they conjured a great plan to have the Reptilian lords kill each other, and so they did. They sowed seeds of doubt and created animosity and tension between the great Reptilian lords about which one was doing a better job of oppressing those in their charge, and indeed they did end up going to war with each other and killing each other.

Now we do not suggest you do that here and now because your story has not become that dire yet and in fact the rules are different for you and we have seen how it turns out and we are here for you; even the future ones of you come back to stop it from happening again by giving you logic, their most prized gift.

So please, dear friends, know that it is a most wonderful and virtuous gift, your logic, because it indeed saved an entire race of being, your kind. But please do not give yourselves over to logic because remember, it is a tool only and not something to be worshipped as we know some of you already are doing.

You might be wondering how you worship logic, and we say it is when you argue with each other over small matters and technicalities, when you prize scientific discoveries over artistic and creative expression, when you force-feed your children in schools hard subjects instead of letting their minds explore and wander and meander and indeed float and channel the amazing gifts they were already born with.

For see here indeed that the fear of being illogical that is inside you is in you because you have Grey soul memory. You all have Grey soul memory in your body because your minds were made with their gift of logic. That logic itself is imbued with their fear of not surviving due to being illogical, because how could it possibly not be since logic, as you experience it, is the very product of their entire evolutionary journey which resulted in the survival tincture itself you now refer to as logic.

This gift of logic was gifted to you by the Greys who are future versions of you, who took an unsuccessful evolutionary path, and it was given to you in advance to your advantage so that you do not let the Reptilians oppress you again to the same extent that they oppressed the humans that became the Greys. And thus with this gift of logic which was already used to overthrow the Reptilian lords can now be used by you to overcome your oppression by those same ones sooner and thus unlike the Greys you do not have to lose your humanity in this process.

So now that you know this gift of logic is a wonderful thing you should also know that it is not to be utilised or praised at the expense of your other gifts of intuition, instinct and space (or freeness from thought, so to speak) because logic which is imbued with survival fear is not healthy for you to be operating in all the time.

Know that when you seek to balance these four thought natures then you will be pursuing much more successful evolutionary paths for yourselves. We say this truthfully and assuredly because indeed this information comes from the very ones who were your future and from us, the Anshar, who can access your future timelines with a measure of accuracy, or at least to the extent at which this message is viable.

Know that when you chop things up with logic like it is a samurai sword (the one who writes for us likes this analogy because she likes to do this — make people fall on their own swords with logic), you are stopping yourselves from experiencing and expressing the infinite other forms of consciousness.

Again we say, please know that consciousness is not in your minds but is a state of your mind. You will literally experience a different reality when you have a different consciousness or conscious state. Then when consciousness is bound to a vessel, for example, in your case, the human body, then you have a means to perceive information via a sensory vessel or machine, so to speak, and alter or adjust or add information to your consciousness.

But indeed it is your consciousness doing all the work with your body to house it and change it. Know also that consciousness changes the body or vessel you are in for it is a rich, symbiotic relationship. You will actually see your bodies change when you change your consciousness and also many other things around you. We digress; we will discuss this more elsewhere.

Here though we remind you again that logic itself is not a standard of truth as we know many, if not most of you, would love to believe because in you is the memory that logic has saved you before even against great odds. But know now that logic is only one part of your thought abilities or natures and should not be elevated above the others. Just as we would say this very thing to ones of your kind who would attempt to elevate having no thoughts in your mind only all the time, or intuition only all the time, or instinct only all the time.

So in order to evolve in a successful or beneficial way for the majority of you, you will need to learn how to balance your thought natures and in this case we are indicating clearly here that logic is not in and of itself a standard of truth. Because how could it possibly be since you are only intelligent by comparing yourselves to yourselves. That is like winning a race that no one else is running in. But also look at what your logic has led to: does not your kind still drown in constant strife, drama and problems that you have not yet solved with your logic? For indeed it is not the elixir many of you thought it was.

We know many of you actually think *If I'm smart enough I can cure cancer or I can discover an amazing invention or cure and be a hero among my kind for being so smart* or many of you would look to others for being so smart because they are so logical and just seem to know how things work and be able to break everything down to their smallest parts and explain how every little bit of every little part works (here we refer especially to your many types of biologists who would explain the body by describing cell function and so on).

We know these things too, but not because we use logic. Your logic is not in us, and yet we know these things. We have another form of consciousness that lets us just know things but you have to learn how things work and prove it to yourselves over and over again because that is how your logic works and that is one of its failings.

We just know because that is our form of consciousness. So please know that your evolution and indeed your betterment or improvement as a species does not lay in logic alone but in the many types of mental and conscious abilities that you all have. You should not be brainwashing your children in schools to only prize logic because logic is literally a product of fear and it by itself will not help you because you are not living in the same conditions as those that became the Greys. If you live in only logic then you live in fear and are cutting yourselves off from your other natures and missing out on all your other aspects. Indeed, you are eroding your humanity when you live only in logic and that is why those of you who live only in logic do not appear human-like and it is not healthy for you to be eroding your humanity since at this time you are human. Do not be turning this gift of logic which was gifted to you for your advantage into a problem for your kind again.

When we speak of those who only operate in logic, we think that some of you might be mentally referring to some of your favourite sci-fi characters. And we use that as an opportunity to refer to those beloved sci-fi characters as an example of the fact that whole species literally have different ways of functioning. But indeed you are human and not of those species so while you are in this body and playing this human game you need to balance the thought natures your minds are composed of for the sake of your health and successful evolutionary paths.

Shame

THIS subject has its own heading because it is a big creation of your kind. Many of you would claim not to have shame because indeed you are ashamed of even having shame; see how it creates and fulfils itself already in this one explanation.

But we will continue to give you details about this creation that you call a feeling. We see it as a creation because we see energy but your eyes do not yet see it very well. The one who writes for us sees energy because she came into this world seeing it that way and thus her whole life until now has been utter confusion for her because she has no words and no forum and no community to discuss the way she sees and experiences reality. And indeed it is partly for this reason she has been mocked and gaslighted and scapegoated most of her life because your kind hides its shame so much from itself it would seek to extinguish anyone who might point it out as indeed and in fact being a real thing.

For those of you out there who see shame as clearly as this one who writes for us does we could call you ones shame bearers because you bear the shame in your bodies that others would deny and thus you hold much suffering actually within your bodies and energy fields and feeling and thought systems.

Know that now is the time when the role of shame bearer no longer needs to exist because indeed you are all taking responsibility for your own shame and no longer heaping it onto just a few of your kind that would bear it all on your behalf.

We can give you many examples of how your kind creates shame bearers to bear large masses of your collective shame. For example, by means of child molestation, secret relationships and secret affairs, all forms of exploitation, secret threats, blackmailing, narcissistic manipulation, rape, objectification, mutilation, mocking, traumatising in sexual ways, and all manner of secretive and dark acts that are always associated with risk and threat and fear of exposure.

We know that some of you have a strong relationship with shame because it makes you feel excited in your bodies; for example, you may let yourselves become addicted to harmful substances, gambling, lower frequency sexual practices and addiction to pornography and other acts that your social protocol or societal acts would consider taboo.

Know that as long as you have a word for these things you will create them. And as long as that word is associated with darkness and secrets and suffering of some form you will continue creating shame.

Know now that shame is an actual substance that your kind has created. It sometimes masses together into large masses or bubbles and moves and hovers over certain areas of your planet. That is why some of you will experience sudden extreme weather changes because this big shame bubble that your kind has created and continues to create is a big mass that is seeking expression.

Know too now that many other thought and feeling forms act this way. We know now of some metaphysicians of your kind that have already discussed these things but here we elaborate. Your shame is a grey bubble if you must imagine something physical to understand of what it is we are speaking. This bubble grows and shrinks based on how well it is fed.

In areas of great shame there are, as you would imagine, great big grey bubbles, but like weather, these big bubbles move all around your planet so that you all may share in it. Please remember now that your species actually operates with a collective consciousness much as the other species of animals and organisms do on your planet.

You have taken so very long to understand this, our dear friends, because you have been addicted to paradigms of isolation, separation and competition. Know now that there is nothing that any single one of you can do that is not known to us and experienced by all others of your kind.

For indeed what you seek to hide screams loudly and makes a very big noise all the time to our ears because we can hear energy, unlike your kind currently. For in fact we know some of you pick up on these things of which we speak but in fact you have no one teaching you what these things mean that you are being aware of.

So here we are being clear so that you know what we see and hear regarding your shame creation all the time. Remember when Cain killed Abel, and we, the Anshar, asked Cain about it? He tried to hide the fact that he had murdered his brother. This is shame creation in pristine form. For in fact we know most of you are like little children sticking your hand in the cookie jar, so to speak, and getting caught while your hand is in the cookie jar and then telling your parent who is looking at you while your hand is in the cookie jar that indeed you did not put your hand in the cookie jar.

It sounds humorous to recount this example and it is funny indeed to think of you as little children with your hands caught in the cookie jar but indeed that is what many of you are because you don't realise that we already see what you are and what you are doing. And in fact you know what you are and what you are doing but you hide these facts from yourself for the sake of this game of shame creation.

But remember now we are telling you that this particular game of shame creation is over because too many of you are asking us to help you get to higher frequencies and you must give up shame creation in order to do that.

So remember when Cain tried to tell us that he did not kill his brother, and we said that we could hear Abel's blood cry out to us? This indeed is what it is like to us and to those of your kind that bear your shame or are your shame bearers. They live with the pain that you would try to hide from yourselves, and they even let their bodies be abused for the sake of your shame creation so that you can continue doing bad things and then pretend that you never did them.

But we now say that these shame bearers have suffered enough on your behalf and the time of their suffering is over. It is now the responsibility of each and every single one of you to own your own shame!

We are already seeing this in the news with many of your great ones falling from great heights because the little shame bearers finally offloaded their burdens and told the world what they had been bearing. This will happen more and more because the time of the shame bearers is over and all of you, each one of you, will bear your own load of shame and not put it off for someone else to bear it for them.

So we say indeed now you are to assess your lives and your minds and your relationships with others and things, and assess your habits and behaviours and see where it is indeed you are lying to yourselves, because we know each and every one of you is doing this, even in some small way.

We know there are some of you who create far more shame than they bear and these ones have more work to do. But that's okay because they came here to deal with their relationship with shame and heal it.

In fact some of you came here who were clean and had no issues or dramas with shame but decided to come into this simulation or created world to play with shame.

Those making life action plans, or we could call them life choreographers, requested ones willing to play with shame because they knew that the shame bubbles were growing larger and larger all the time here and this place needed ones willing to come in and clean them up.

For although Niquidium eat fear they do not eat shame, for shame resonates at a different frequency. Shame is a more shallow and stable energy and it is long-lasting and resides a long time in the one area. Like a large sleeping beast that dare not be disturbed, shame is always attempting to sleep and stay undisturbed. That is why it is easy to forget shame and think it no longer exists but really it exists and it keeps getting bigger and bigger because there is no one to wake it.

So we are asking you here to wake up shame and start processing it as an energy form in your bodies. You can do this by no longer pushing things you are ashamed of to the side. We actually can say this because you have gaps in your energy fields and when you do not want to consider something you literally push those forms of energy (whether they were partially processed in your minds or bodies as thoughts or feelings) out of your fields.

So where do you think these energy forms of shame creation go? They indeed group and mass together because they resonate at the same frequency and all come together because they are like friends that have been pushed away by their creators and in their rejected state they go out and seek each other for company. Indeed, shame itself which is created by you when you reject it acts like it is ashamed because it is actually shame.

We say that your kind creates shame of the same frequency all over your planet even though the triggers or reasons for your shame creation are very different depending on your social programming or conditioning.

Also, shame creation is a means by which you expel excess energy that you cannot deal with at the time in which too much energy or self-awareness swarms you and so you push it out of you. Just as in the story of Adam and Eve who became aware they were naked. When you fall from grace, so to speak, or we could say when you have found yourself in a lower frequency state, it is embarrassing or humiliating to the larger part of you that knows you are perfect and thus you hide your fallen state from yourselves and thus shame as a creation of yours is born.

Thus, we could also say about shame that it is a willing refusal to forget and further deny who you really are. And then a continued denial of remembrance or acceptance of who you really are, even upon the insistent requests of your truer or higher natures, to remember who you really are. Truly, some of you are profoundly stubborn and your abilities of willing ignorance and denial are masterfully crafted since it is that you are in a lower state still despite thousands of years of evolution with us and others attempting to help you all along the way.

Also, we say when you experience excess energy or self-awareness, then much like the human body pushes out waste and each of your body's cells pushes out waste, indeed your energy fields are like bodies or cells that need to push out excess waste.

But know this now, that shame is only a waste product when you have not properly converted it or translated it or used it for its intended function. Its intended function is an invitation for you to raise to higher frequencies for indeed did you think your makers would not also make you with the capacity and potential to rise up again to be like them and meet them?

Self-awareness always expands you and returns you to your glorious state if you let it work upon you. But many of you become afraid when you become self-aware and discard it as soon as it comes upon you. We state now another scripture we inspired here: Some of you are like those looking into a mirror to see what sort of person you are but as soon as you walk away from the mirror or indeed some of you run from it, then you immediately forget again what sort of person you are.

But of course your makers or parents imbued you with the ability to return to perfection because that is one of the main functions of this game or experiment. But indeed it has run its course and now we are here reminding you of how you are to return to us by expressing your true natures and processing your waste.

For think of it this way. When you do not like something or do not need it anymore you throw it away in the trash or rubbish bin. And like this too you would treat your shame bearers much the same, for example, when some of your kind have had sex with a prostitute and then killed her because she is now a waste product to be dumped for someone else to clean up. We use this graphic example because it well pictures physically what many of you do energetically or figuratively all the time.

See here how many of your criminal acts are concentrated forms of shame creation or indeed shame expression. For these shame bubbles or clouds come into the fields of weaker ones or indeed ones whose fields are already resonating at frequencies that match that of the shame and the shame bubbles or clouds irresistibly come into these ones because they are always seeking out others of their kind to join with them for expression because they too have been thrown out.

The shame bubble says, 'But look here, there is a weak one or one who can house us or give us residence and perhaps even express us.' For indeed, the shame energy cloud which is the shame from so many of your kind comes in and gets stuck in this one person of your kind. This one person now has the shame of hundreds or even many thousands of beings stuck in them and what do you think it is they do with all that shame energy stuck in them? They act out or express that shame to get it back out of their bodies, minds and energy fields because it is too much for them to bear and hold onto and yet remain sane or stable, as you would say. Indeed, many of those bearing your kind's shame on your behalf also do not manage to remain sane and thus again they act as energy waste receptacles and you throw them away into cells or institutions and label them as refusing to speak so that still you are not having to deal with your shame.

Or perhaps they form an addiction to escape the pain of your shame, or they get into an abusive relationship to be hurt and hit to remember your shame. Or they commit a crime because your judicial systems have been so exquisitely set up for these ones to offend against so that the minority of your kind are always bearing your shame. Your shame masses are always seeking expression and when one of your kind expresses your shame on your behalf you 'um' and 'uh' over how evil those ones must be but really they are expressing what you did not and thus they are the perfect scapegoat and your system gaslights them so masterfully. In this regard your kind lacks courage and that is a sad thing. No longer be heaping your shame onto these lowly ones who you then label as dirt and refuse because it is your dirt that is on them!

Like a narcissistic or gaslighting relationship your judicial system would have these ones thrown into cells and contained all the time so that they can continue hating themselves and not knowing who they are and continue being fed on by all these shame clouds that swarm them all the time.

So we give a few extreme examples of shame transference here. In past times public stonings and hangings and beheadings and other public executions were your ways of transmitting large masses of your shame onto just a few. And now in more recent times you have less of those means of transferring shame but you still have those of your kind that are molesting or having sex with children who are indeed bearing too much shame in their bodies, and so they offload it onto an innocent and defenceless being of your kind, a child, and in turn they often create more shame bearers that do not know what to do with all the shame that is filling up their fields and their bodies and their minds. And then when these little ones become dysfunctional in society, because inevitably they will, you will shun and shame them because they do not fit in. Again, they will feed and create yet more shame and make more shame clouds or shame energy masses.

In this way the one who writes for us can see shame so clearly it jumps out at her when she walks around in your public places. It literally magnetises to her and it is pulled out of people's fields and comes into her. She came in as an empath to take some of your load for you. She, however, is one of the shame bearers that holds onto it and does not give it back or attempt to put it away or pass it on to someone else.

She has always sought to understand what shame is because she sees it so clearly as an object of creation and that is why we chose her to write these things because so many of you would say that shame is not a thing and you have never felt shame and have absolutely no reason to feel shame and do not ever intend on doing something shameful. And here we do not speak of the trite and delicate expressions of shame like overeating a favourite food like chocolate or accidentally swearing in front of a child or catching yourself laughing quietly at a crude joke, because indeed, these are all acceptable forms of shame expression in your societies and these are examples of how you have shallow relationships with shame and then you give yourselves a pat on the back because indeed you must be honest folk that do what's right most of the time and only sometimes slip up, so to speak. Here we say that you are lying to yourselves and only pretending to be self-aware and only pretending that others of your kind aren't indeed suffering on a daily basis because indeed you know they are because you hear it everywhere you go and yet how easy it is for you to forget the ones thrown away, the ones who are gross and ugly and vile and who don't fit in and who live on the streets and who sell their bodies and who are addicted to drugs and who can't find work and who can't find a partner and who can't have children and a nice home and so on. You see how quickly you set up a very large class of shame bearers because your mainstream paradigm, so to speak, is set up to do just that.

Do not be forgetting those of your kind that suffer every day because it is your shame that they live with every single day! It is yours because you are not doing your share of the shame bearing! You no longer get to pretend that life is okay because you get to eat nice food and sleep in a nice bed and wear nice clothes. You no longer get to believe that you are not ashamed of many little things you think and feel all the time because we hear you and we know exactly what you think and feel because our consciousness sees and hears these things clearly. You no longer get to drive your nice cars and work in your nice careers because you are not using your energy to improve the lives of your kind as a whole. You are a species that operates as a whole and many of you are forgetting this fact!

You are a whole, and what one part of your kind does or does not do affects the other parts. There is no pretending anymore. If any of your kind continue using their energy they have in their bodies and fields to be working at creation that only serves themselves and not also benefiting others then you are forgetting why you came here at this time. This time is to help your species operate and evolve as a whole. We here again state clearly that whether you have till now realised it or not your species does in fact operate and function as a whole and therefore your evolution and improvement and journey into higher frequencies will only be experienced by your kind when you all work together as a whole!

Here we would link this subject with that of your physical material waste production for it demonstrates the same pattern of behaviour. You throw something away when you don't need it or want it anymore and then like a newborn you think because you do not see it, it must no longer exist, but indeed it does exist even though your eyes no longer see it anymore and so in this way you have made your mess, your waste a problem for someone else to clean up. So just as you are learning to become green, so to speak, and learning how to reuse objects and items and materials that you would otherwise stick in large piles to slowly decay and ruin your planet and home in this way, you also need to become green or responsible with your mental and emotional states and be responsible for your energy fields. Your energy fields which are around your bodies all the time and indeed make up part of who you are in this simulation are connected with every other energy field around you and there is no getting around that fact, so to speak.

Many of you are now aware of how energy works more and more because of your various technological inventions (thanks to us and the Greys and various others of your extraterrestrial families). You are able to understand how simply by setting up a network of signal transmitters and receivers you indeed can communicate or move much information around your planet very quickly. It is much the same except far more advanced; your energy fields are always sending and receiving information from your environments and your fields are always merging with other fields and your kind literally create a network or a collective consciousness, being made of many smaller beings, i.e. each and every one of you.

You are acting as a global intelligence, as you might say it, already and yet you do not know it, so you are mis-using or underusing this great power of yours. And indeed the ones who know this about you, i.e. the ones seeking to continue oppressing you, use this glorious function of yours against you. Now we say this to help go deeper into the topic.

As we just said before, logic was a creation of your kind on another timeline but on one very similar to yours where you evolved to overthrow your oppressors, the Reptilians, by use of this logic. Know too that the Greys, as you would know them now, also became symbiotic with technology and thus evolved to rely heavily upon it. They also grew to be submissive to their Reptilian lords because feigning submission was one of the ways in which they survived the centuries of torture. Now remember those soul memories are in your bodies because you were gifted these aspects from your parents and thus live out their story and continue it for them.

Now your modern structures are built upon only two types of your thought natures: those of instinct and logic. For you see clearly that those that rise up among you in your mainstream ventures are either psychopaths because they run on instinct alone or sociopaths because they run on logic alone. Now these two thought natures without the other two are the foundations of your many societal structures and have formed the basis of much of your indoctrination, acculturation, socialisation, conditioning and so on. These two natures alone will only put you down the path you already took when your kind became the Greys, and in order to survive and continue to evolve they also came into a symbiotic relationship with technology which we already know many of you are desiring and seeking again because that memory is in you to repeat.

But know that you now can be aware of that pattern that was put in you and can decide now not to repeat it. You can now decide not to continue operating in instinct and logic alone. Remember your other two natures: that of *space* or the ability to be in your bodies with no thought, and also *intuition*, the ability to just know something as we, the Anshar, do.

And we know you are making your children continue down this path of operating in instinct and logic only by way of the legal requirement that they attend school which has these thought natures only in their curriculums. We know at this time some schools are seeking to balance their educational systems with the other types of expression but your kind have a very long way to go indeed if the changes you make in this regard continue to be this minute. Your children came in with gifts your educational systems systematically stifle, suppress and destroy. Your children need their gifts of space and intuition to also be nurtured so that they can be expressed too and flourish. Your children are coming in with many other unique gifts and these also need to be explored and nurtured, but not for exploitative gain.

At this time we would remind you that the Grey nature of logic is actually submissive to instinct because it was in that pattern that logic was created. And we see that today when a proud and powerful leader relies on the advice of his or her logical advisor. And this pattern you have expressed and are expressing over and over and over again. So we ask that you start making leaders that are also intuitive and also full of space such as Zen masters.

We know that some of your kind have been good examples of these other thought natures but more of these types of leaders need to be put into leadership positions by you. You can do this in even small ways by not forgetting who you are inside and not pretending to be afraid (for none of you are victims) and not letting those that would seek to make you submissive be able to make you so. Many of you have people of authority in your midst such as your boss or your teacher or a parent or a friend or a social group or a supervisor that would have you be submissive under them and make you fear the end of your relationship with them or with the thing that you value in connection with them, i.e. your job or a piece of education documentation or your invites to special gatherings or parties and so on. So why would you be fearing such petty things and submitting yourselves to such petty means of control? If you are submitting yourselves to such ones or such institutions then you are forfeiting your own glory and your own power and relinquishing all chance of operating as your own sovereign and forgetting that you have all eternity to discover how mighty you really are. We state now a spoken word of King Solomon: Everything in its time is beautiful. Find your time to be glorious and live in that glory because that is part of why you came here. And indeed finding that beauty or glory that you came here to uniquely express will inevitably involve you processing your share of shame and indeed you will be made beautiful by your processing and transmutation of it.

We also ask now that any of you seeking to be the dominant one in these abovementioned cases that you relinquish that role. The one who writes for us struggles with both dominant and submissive roles with those around her. We also ask at this time that none of you continue asking your children or the young ones around you to continue in the ways that have clearly not worked for you otherwise you are asking them to be condemned by the same conditions that make you suffer as you are suffering now to different measures. Also, we ask that those of you bearing shame for others no longer do so and those attempting to inflict your shame onto others no longer continue to do so. In this way you will stop the continuation of the Grey Reptilian shame paradigm in your bodies, in your minds and in your fields, and thus in your actions and thus in your societies.

See how if every single person does these little things, identify where they feel shame or feel submissive to something or someone or powerless with regard to something or someone, or if you are the ones feeling powerful by making someone else feeling powerless, then if each one of you stop, how indeed you alone just in your life are doing these things, then your whole species, the whole network will be activated and you will all shed this paradigm or this mode of operation or this story that has already been told and retold too many times.

In this way you are processing your parents' story of oppression and submission, of powerfulness and powerlessness. You are now free to give this story up, our dear friends, so please, dear friends, give it up and release it by processing it and not pushing it out of your fields and attempting to hide it from yourselves and pretending that it does not exist. One day it will not exist but only once you acknowledge it and process it in your own bodies and fields and not require or ever ask someone else to do it for you. You alone, each one of you by yourselves, have your own shame to bear and process and indeed you can do this because that is part of why you came here at this time!

Lies

IES were invented as the basis of this experiment and indeed many other experiments. It is a fun thing to learn how to lie to others and to yourself. In fact lying is its own person as anything that can be called a thing is and it has its own journey of consciousness and has been with us a while and will continue only a little while longer.

Lying is the act of willing yourself to be fooled by imaginary things. Imaginary things are creations that are not fundamental to the rules of the game you are playing, but imaginary things do of course exist as all things that you could possibly imagine existing in fact do even if simply and only because you yourself imagined them.

But for the rules of this game now we use the phrase imaginary things to mean those things that can be thought of yet at times not also believed. Belief plays a large role in this game too, but we will address that later. Also, you cannot really be fooled without entering a foolish state, or as we would call it, a state of longing to remember what you forgot. For all this time you have been longing to remember what you forgot so you had to take a form that was cut off from your higher or larger or fuller selves so that you could pretend that you forgot something so that you could play at longing to remember it.

It reminds us of how many of you will lose your keys to your cars or homes or to other items of your creation which at this time require the belief that they must be locked; we won't digress here because the belief of having to lock something is another very interesting creation which we will address elsewhere. For now, we see that many of you play little games with yourselves by hiding your keys from yourselves. We know that so many times you are searching for your keys in your purses or bags or couches or floors or in many other places when in fact you were almost always the one who put them down somewhere.

See, this funny little game you play with yourselves is an analogy or breadcrumb, so to speak, from within the maze to help you out of the maze. Because if you see how many times you lie to yourselves, all of you we are addressing here, as we see you and know when you do this, it is such a funny thing to watch or observe or learn from. We cannot lie to ourselves in the same way, but we do of course in other ways. There are many of us, the Anshar and your other extraterrestrial family members, that are still learning how to show ourselves what our true selves are, and we do this in other ways. For now though, know that since our frequency is just a little higher than yours, our minds are clearer and our eyes see energy, and we can see you more clearly than you can see yourselves currently. But we do look forward to a time, and that time is very soon, when you know yourselves more than we do and you will be able to show us how amazing you are and what you can do and it will surprise us. Much like when children are growing and suddenly they may say or do something that surprises their parents and makes their parents think, *wow, how amazing is my child* when they do or say that thing that they just did or said. So in this way know that lying in its many forms is just a game you play for now and indeed any being experiencing evolution interacts with the being or person we call lies or lying and in fact like time it is another simulation ingredient or feature used to help us create illusions for ourselves so that we can build mazes and then challenge ourselves to get out of them.

So in regard to how you all lie on a daily basis, we say that many of your lies are not harmful for your evolutionary path but only when you try to hide the lie by lying further do you make problems for yourselves for that is when you are giving yourselves over to lying and lies and some of you are even having a symbiotic relationship with the person you call lying or lies.

Those of you seeking to hide your lies and indeed doing so are entering into a relationship with shame also, and we have just discussed how this works. So see here how very easily you can take a game used to learn from and turn it into something very ugly indeed and very difficult to get yourselves out of. We do not judge lying itself because that is a natural part of this game or this state of consciousness you currently find yourselves to be in or in fact decided to experience. We do, however, clearly state here that you are not to try to hide your lies because when you do that you are crossing into shame and making an active choice to not learn from the game you have set up for yourself.

Indeed, everything you learn from, of course even when you cross into shame you learn from that, but you are making the game so much harder and so much uglier and so much more distorted and contorted when you do such a thing as hide you are lying. Here we will explain what we mean when we say hide your lying.

We are not referring to times when you were little children in fact and you pretended you didn't eat the candy when in fact you did because that is just lying. But if it is pointed out to you that you were seen eating the candy and still you choose to hide the fact that you did eat the candy you must now also hide the fact that you just lied about the fact that you did or did not eat the candy. See how quickly that escalates, so to speak. So when a child does this they may even choose to blame the missing candy item on another child and now we have shame transference occurring already. How quickly we are creating a big shame bubble.

And now when these lies become more complex and involve more people and involve higher stakes, so to speak, then you can see how easily this little game of lying becomes so twisted and tangled. What at first was a little hedge maze made of pretty hedges full of flowers is now a maze made of colossal stone and metal and twisted barbed wire and dark, scary places and monsters in shadows always waiting to get you if you don't take the next turn quickly enough. These types of mazes or environments you truly and literally are creating for yourselves. Only for now you cannot see what you are doing because you do not see energy how we see energy. But truly we see these places that you build for yourselves and so many of them are so much darker and scarier and more difficult than they need to be.

We also need to note here for your sake that when you engage in lies and lying to these larger and deeper extents then you are likely entangling others in your mess and your dark creations and that will be more work for you later to repay them for the suffering you will have likely caused them. Of course, they chose to enter into the mess with you but they also chose for you to make it up to them later. We know this sounds like punishment to some of you but truly no one can hurt someone else without feeling that exact same feeling themselves regardless of how that feeling comes back to them. Because that feeling is the creation of the one doing the hurting and our creations always come back to us because they resonate with us.

Let us now give you an example of the game of lying as it is intended without it becoming too difficult and dark and scary. We already gave you the losing your keys example but here is another. When a woman loves someone she sometimes may give herself completely over to the person she loves, whether it be her partner or child or family member. (This example also applies to other genders but here we are using this example of a woman.) So when this woman gives herself completely over to someone else she is pretending that she loves that other person with everything that she has and has no love left to give herself. We know this is a common expression for many of you and thus we use this example. So this woman has no love for herself and the ones she loves are enjoying her love so much that they forget to love her back. And in fact she is so good at doing things for other people she forgets to do things for herself too. And other people are so busy enjoying all the things that this woman is doing for them that they forget to do things back for her except of course on special days that your social customs would require you to return the favours and love she has given you.

So now she is stuck. Absolutely and profoundly stuck because she has made a maze for herself that she doesn't know how to get out of. She doesn't know how to ask people for help. She doesn't know how to ask people how to love her. She doesn't even know what she needs or how she wants to be shown love by this point because at no time did she consider herself in need of these things and that was the lie.

So now if she identifies that she is stuck and needs help, and she asks for it then she can indeed get out of the maze. If she realises how she had forgotten herself like some of you have forgotten your keys, then she will know where to start looking and indeed start looking.

So we ask many of you now to not forget yourselves and in particular the ones who please others all the time, and we are of course referring to all genders and all ages of people of your kind.

Now if the woman starts to look for herself she will indeed find herself and her life and her relationships and the things and objects in her life will become balanced. But now if she hides her lies from herself or others then she will make a much more difficult maze for herself that she will have to get out of at a later time. Also, if she is finding it difficult to survive her self-forgotten state without also turning to healing it, then she may turn to guilt games and false martyrdom and that indeed is how many of the ones of your kind that are inclined to please others are in fact entwining and trapping others into your self-made mazes with you.

In this way we know many of you have let your lies get deeper and stronger and you have forgotten yourselves so much that you are literally hollow shells, so to speak, that represent only times gone past of life but now are just objects washed upon the sand for others to use as they wish. We see this all over your planet, in particularly we are applying this to women (the one who writes for us thinks this comment is sexist) because that is what we are seeing when we look at your species as a whole but indeed this also applies to anyone lying so much that they forget themselves completely and become like hollow shells. You know who you are when we say these things.

Also, we say to those around these ones who are like hollow shells that if indeed you see someone around you who is looking like a hollow shell, so to speak, then can you please help them out. That will involve reminding them that they are connected to source energy and are able to bring life force back into their vessel if they choose to do so and in fact they should choose to do so because that is why they came here. If you want and are able to help these hollowed ones out know that you must not also allow yourselves to be tangled in their maze with them or be quilted or accidentally cut yourself off from your own source energy by empathising with them too much.

Also, when this type of behaviour happens to men in some parts of your world, because of your social conditioning which is still polaric at this stage in your evolution, we would say that men who are like shells act differently than when women are like shells, so to speak. And we know we generalise here but that is okay; we know what effect our words will have, so when we speak of men acting as hollow shells we see much more severe and even nasty behaviour. For when men offload their power and do not connect to source and enter into shame along with their different genetic makeup and different hormonal systems they will often act very cruelly and aggressively as they seek to offload their feelings of worthlessness and hollowness.

We will not speak much more of this now because we know how sexist it can sound, but for now while you are still subject to your body and social polarities we are seeing these patterns of behaviour. Also, here we would say that you will not always act this way and your forgetfulness will ease and the game will become lighter and more fun and you will not experience so much polarity for indeed we see that already happening. That is all we have to say about lying for now because lying itself is not a dangerous behaviour and is actually a requirement of this and many other illusions but only when some of you try to hide your lies and forget even more who you are does it become a problem and will slow down your evolutionary cycles.

Darkness

D ARKNESS is a wonderful thing and more of you should try it some time. We joke because we know how afraid of darkness many of you still are. In fact when many of you were children and in fact even some of you as adults still are actually afraid of the experience of physical darkness on your planet that you experience when your side of your planet is not facing your star. Now how perfect and poetic this creation is.

In fact, it's so perfect and poetic that its creation started the Bible, our words and text to you all. We know the Bible is irrelevant to many of you now, and we are grateful for that. But that is also why we are communicating to so many of you directly now, including this one here who channels for us.

So in the beginning there was darkness because darkness is all there is when you yet have no physical creation. That seems obvious for now we know but we continue. When nothing existed, there was that thing that existed which was nothingness. We know still some of you are aware of this. So know now too that nothingness is a person as all things are and has its own consciousness and its own journey or expression.

And now know too that there are beings who govern or direct the darkness on your behalf. And here we would be very clear to distinguish between what you consider scary darkness, because indeed your mammalian bodies rely heavily on sight for the assurance of your safety and thus you have synonymised darkness with all manner of monsters and scary things (for those of you who are not afraid of the dark we would say you are likely afraid of the light or the light within) from what you would consider physical darkness or creative darkness. These are all three different things and of course there are many different forms of darkness but here we will discuss these three.

Firstly the creative darkness is the being that in the beginning made the light. The darkness itself made the light. And so now you already have less to fear because even nothing is full of something. The nothingness or darkness pulled out all its nothingness and its nothingness was made of light. Much like black holes, as you would call them, are full of information they, when converted or contorted, can indeed push back out all that information, or as you could call it, light. For nothingness has everything else encoded within it because it must because you live in a holographic universe and every bit of every bit of this place has every other bit encoded within it.

So within this nothingness was likely a being. We already said that nothingness itself is a person and now we are saying something slightly different. We will here refer to a memory we gave our little one who channels for us. She remembers living inside a black hole and reclining in comfort, so to speak, because the black hole was her home for many billions and billions of universe lifetimes. And now as she was relaxing she was looking at the walls of her home, her black hole, and she felt comfort in their encasement around her because being a creature of the darkness at the time she didn't want to be around others or be around light.

So inside this black hole she stayed and dwelt for many, many billions of universe lifetimes. And she was fed and intrigued by all the information entering her home because this was a very powerful black hole and it sucked in so much information. She watched all the information on the walls of her black hole like many of you now watch television or films or videos, and it entertained her and fed her for many billions of universe lifetimes.

Now as time went on she felt that the black hole was getting ready to produce something, something like a seed or a bean or even as oysters and clams produce a pearl. And this seed started calling out to her because it was desiring to be made and to become something. So instead of resting she became active, so to speak. She was being more mindful and observant of the information coming into her black hole home and making sure that it was good food for this seed that was coming. So she watched and waited for this little seed to be born and then in one moment she saw it forming above her at the toroidal centre of her home, the black hole.

This seed now was a powerful thing and it contained fragments of all the bits of creation that had come into her black hole home. Every little piece of light or information had some part of it donated to the formation of this seed. And now she knew what she was to do. She was going to place this seed in a place made just for it to grow, and grow it did. And it became its own universe with its own black holes and its own universe makers. For in this way universes are often made.

We break from the story to tell you that in fact that is how many universes are made, and they breed this way too. The one we speak of and who speaks for us has memory or access to the version of herself that is indeed a universe maker and indeed a breeder of universes. We know many of you will have memories of making universes because in fact many of you do but you are in a state of consciousness that may make it difficult for you now to know that without our help to remind you.

So please, dear ones, use this as an example of the many things that you actually are and know that this person here that we now speak to is only one version of you, and in fact you are many things. Also, know that the ones we spoke of before who govern or manage the darkness and creates things with it are what you could call the Council of Silent Light.

This one who writes for us is a part of this council, as we know some of you are. If you are comfortable with darkness, then we applaud you. If you are afraid of it then we understand that your mammalian bodies would have you view darkness as a threatening thing. So we will now address physical darkness as you experience in your lives when the sun is not shining above where you reside.

Physical darkness as you experience it in your realm now when the sun is not shining above you is there to remind your physical bodies that you have other aspects or shadow aspects that you must also be considering and giving expression to. For think how much your behaviour changes when the sun is not shining above you. See here you could say that you have two types of behaviour: day-time behaviour and night-time behaviour. We could list all the things you do within these times of operation or expression but you already know them implicitly because thus far it is all you do. Now we will speak later of the special activities you carry on in your different dream states at night if it is then that you do most of your sleeping, but for now just know that the experience of day time and night time is imperative to your experience of polarity which you came to this realm to experience and change.

Indeed, on other planets and in other realms there are different ratios of day time and night time and thus the behaviours of those ones who dwell in those realms are different to yours. Indeed, just as different ones of your kind who live closer to the poles experience different ratios of dark and light so too is their behaviour and thus culture different to those nearer the equator. We needn't go on because we feel that these observations are obvious, and we hope that you at least consider that your behaviour and thus your habits and thus your cultures are intrinsically linked with your experience of day and night.

In relation to the third kind of darkness we say this. The third kind of darkness we are deciding to distinguish from the other types here is that it is full of scary things and monsters. But this type of darkness is related to the part of you that is made by the devil and the part that resonates with shame. And so since we have already covered these topics we ask you to understand here that the darkness that you associate with things you fear is made up of your shame which is linked with your lack of self-awareness yet longing to be self-aware, and the part of you that is made by the devil or the Reptilians which is the part of you that lacks balance and perfection and wants to oppress the other parts of you, and thus you are always seeking to hide these parts from yourself. So here we say shine the light you all have on the dark parts of you and give them expression because to perform that action is part of why you came here and it is crucial to your evolution.

Addicted to Logic

OR those of you who believe you are suffering from mental illness, know that you are not. For those of you who believe others are suffering from mental illness, know that you are failing to see stories and energy the way we do and so you must label these things you don't understand with labels that do not suit the things you are labelling in an attempt to put them away from you because you don't want to be around things you don't understand.

Now is a moment for you to see that if you allow things that you don't understand to be around you, you are allowing yourselves to be expanded by those very things that you don't understand. Things that you don't understand on a personal level are things made just for you by you yourself to bait you or invite you to expand yourself.

This is the way evolution works and you are currently experiencing an evolutionary state of consciousness. Know that each one of you does not always need to be experiencing an evolutionary state of consciousness because rest is important and perhaps you want to do or experience other things at times. But know now, and we will be clear, that you are here now because you chose to experience an evolutionary state of consciousness and one that is occurring at a particularly fast rate and one that is speeding up as you keep experiencing it.

Like a light that gets brighter and brighter and the brightness helps you see yet more things and then you learn more things. And then you shine light on the dark parameters of your mind and see the light has more things to shine on where you previously thought there were no things and just darkness. For there is no part of this realm that is not teeming with life and many life forms. And what you know now is so little to what you will know tomorrow. And tomorrow will soon not even be a thing you consider because you will be learning so much and your conscious state will be so full of things to see and know and experience that you will not be able to measure days anymore and soon after you will not be able to measure time the way you do now anymore.

This is what we mean when we say it is speeding up. The moment that is now, or the now moment as it has already been called by many of you who seek self-improvement and enlightenment via many of our inspired works and indeed the works of your own genius minds and indeed the works of many of your extraterrestrial families, is always fast approaching and it approaches faster and faster and it gets bigger and bigger. Here we would reference a pregnant woman who knows she is pregnant, and she knows she is going to give birth to a baby very soon. She does not forget she is pregnant, and she knows that the day she gives birth is sooner and sooner. Then when the labour pains hit (we are referencing a birthing process without medical procedure, for the sake of this example) she knows that the time is here for her to be in labour.

When she is in labour she is consumed by it, and she is not thinking she will see her child because she is so consumed by the labour process and then the pushing process. Then all of a sudden she learns something new. The child that she never met before but always knew was growing inside her meets her for the first time, and she meets the baby, her child, for the first time. But when these ones meet they meet as if they always knew each other because indeed they did. For not only do you who have children arrange who it is you will be experiencing as a child in this realm before you come here, but indeed there is no before because there only ever is what you always knew.

This is part of the lie that we talked about before. Linear time which was inflicted upon you for the sake of this experiment is itself a person, a being your kind are currently experiencing a measure of symbiosis with. Like a loving relationship that has good things and bad things in it, you have loved Time, and she has loved you and protected you like a mother, as we said before. But now as you mature you are getting ready to let go of her just a little at first and then slowly more and more.

So this now moment that we speak of and many of you speak of comes closer and closer and gets bigger and bigger as your loving relationship with Time matures and you no longer need to be her babies and you can now explore more for yourselves. A more graphic and physical representation of this change in relationship with Time can be likened to the cervix of a woman when she is in labour because the cervix not only shortens but widens to let the baby come through the mother's passage and into this world.

Like being born into this moment and then the next moment and then the next moment, time is like a long passage that you would experience in a linear fashion and hence we can use the word next and many other linear words that we have indeed been using with you. But just as the cervix of the mother gets shorter and wider, your mother Time is giving birth to you and you are preparing to be born into timelessness and that is why as your mother Time gives birth to you, you feel like this now moment which you know is coming and is always coming and it feels like another world to you now and you are getting ready for this other new world, you are experiencing this passage into the now moment as a passage that is getting shorter and bigger or wider and soon you will be in the new world and it will feel like eternity because you have left the womb of your mother Time.

She is happy to give birth to you because she wants to meet you as fully formed babies ready to be born. When you meet her from outside her womb you will get to know her with fondness whereas now we know many of you often feel constricted by your experience of time because you are foetuses in her womb getting bigger and bigger, and she is running out of room to hold you. So you are preparing to exit her womb into a new world, and she is getting ready to meet you as fully formed babies ready to explore your new world of timelessness. Of course for many of you, you will be like mammal babies that need much help and support for a while but there are those of you ready already to leave and feel eternal again.

So we bring up this example of entering into timelessness because when you are there you will no longer need logic. Because logic can only exist in time, we still experience time as the Anshar, but we can more easily experience our higher selves and access more frequently moments of timelessness than most of you are able to now. But that will soon change. We are not saying you will be born into timelessness right away because as we said many of you will want to stay near your mother while you learn more about your new world and your new state of consciousness that will then be more free of the constriction of time upon you.

But we know there will be some of you who jump ahead, so to speak, and almost immediately reclaim their experience of eternity. Eternity is an experience that you feel all at once, so to speak, and not as you might currently imagine as just feeling like a really long time.

Eternity is not the feeling of existing for a really long time but rather it is the feeling of comprehending everything that exists all at once, free of time in a state of timelessness.

In this way your conscious state will change only because you positively will not and cannot die, only can you change your state of consciousness. For those of you who have experienced loved ones crossing over, so to speak, as we know some of you like to call it, they are already in that state of consciousness or at least experience less constriction because they are free of the constrictions put upon this realm of experience.

Now we know some, actually many of your loved ones

stay in human-like form much of the time in order to stay close to you. When we say human form in this instance we mean that although they do no retain a physical 3D body as you would consider to be real, they still retain their human personality and memories and traits and so on. Many of your loved ones are around you and seek to continue living with you as they did before they crossed over, so to speak.

Of course, they have many other things that interest them, and they do not have to bother you all the time, but we know many of them like to stay around you even though they do not have to since they are no longer under the same constrictions as you are now.

Also know that when they cross they get help if they need it, and they continue learning, and they often seek to reach balance or heal what they did not finish healing before they crossed. We do not have to continue on much here because we already know many of your people are mediums, as you call them, and they do this work all the time for you and explain these things.

Know too that you are not victims and you are free to ask these crossed-over ones to give you space or leave if that is what you want or need. For now, we say that the place where you all are going in your living state, so to speak, because at this time your kind distinguishes the living from the dead, is a place much like the one your loved ones who stay around you now reside. In that way you may indeed experience a great resurrection, so to speak. We reference for those of you who have this belief and desire to see your loved ones again.

Know that there will not be a resurrection in the way we know many of you assumed, but indeed as you leave time or indeed as time gives birth to you because you are getting too big for her she can no longer keep you contained, you will start seeing your loved ones because you are going to the place they are now without actually dying, as you would call it. We hope you understand this.

We are not saying you have to die to see your loved ones that have already died, so to speak. In fact your world is already starting to merge with theirs, and we know many of you are seeing the dead, so to speak, more and more already. So please do not be afraid of them because they are people that were once in your world and only experienced the crossover before you did.

Those of you now living, so to speak, are just entering the new place or new world more slowly while the ones already there just chose to go more quickly. In fact many of them decided to come back to your side and pull your side closer to theirs. In that way we know many of you now here are here because you are seeking to push yourselves into the new world. Some of you might think of heaven here, but we will not discuss heaven here because we know for many of you, the idea of heaven has been a tool to abuse you and make you feel like it was something you had to earn or a place that was far away.

Indeed, we will say here that heaven is not a single place but any place or many places that are outside of this realm or simulation you are now in. For those of you who are attached to the idea of heaven, we only ask now that you do not use heaven as a way to punish yourselves or feel far away from peace and indeed we are requiring that you do not use the idea of heaven as a tool to make others afraid as indeed your oppressors did that for many hundreds of years and there is no more time left for you to cooperate with your oppressors unless you move to a new place with them to continue that way of behaving.

So what does all this have to do with the title of this channel, we hear some of you wondering or asking us? We gave this story of time giving birth to you because logic, which indeed is a foundational element of your reality now because it literally makes up part of your mind in this body for now, cannot exist in timelessness which is the place you all are going.

See here and now that the experience of logic always requires the experience of time to be with it. Logic cannot be experienced in timelessness because in timelessness there is nothing you do not know. Logic is literally a product of the experience of time and the experience of the lie and the experience of surviving torture. Logic is only required within the lie because logic is a state of consciousness that would have you believe you do not yet know everything and there is much for you to learn.

Logic has a close relationship with time because the process itself that logic would have you undergo is extremely rigorous and time-consuming, so to speak. Logic literally consumes time or requires time to exist because it is a state of consciousness that would have you believe that you do not know some things now but you can use logic to learn those things over time.

We do not have logic because we just know things and do not need to learn them in the way your kind who has logic as a thought nature and state of consciousness or experience does. We know that many of your cultures synonymise logic with intelligence and so many of you might think that if one does not have logic then one is not intelligent. Know here that we are not asking you to not think, and not be logical, and not learn, for we as the Anshar are not in our higher state all the time and are always learning the way we learn things, but we do not use logic because we do not need to prove things to ourselves because we already know them or otherwise we sense or intuit them which is a different kind of learning and also one of your abilities because we gifted it to your kind when you were made.

So we could help you further understand this by restating that logic is not intelligence and logic requires that you prove something to yourself. We know there are many masters of logic among you and in fact many in your history. We know that many of you are in fact addicted to logic as the one who writes for us often is.

We know that your education systems condition you to have this addiction to logic, and we would say that that is very harmful to you because your intelligence and your way of learning things actually also relies on your three other thought natures (those of space, intuition and instinct) and also now many other forms of expression that particularly the young ones now need to express because they are always channelling their higher selves, their extraterrestrial families and their memories of home. Home in this case being the place in which they are choosing to take their consciousness from.

We are now even writing this to you in a logical language because that is still how many of you are requiring to be communicated to. But please know that your many artists and creative ones among you are indeed being communicated to by us and many others of their extraterrestrial families, but they are not communicating logically to the logic parts of your mind or state of consciousness, they are speaking in a more pure or higher frequency language that does not water down the original message as much as logical communication indeed requires.

We now do not intend to discriminate against those who are prone to using logic often and liking logic for indeed the one who writes for us is one of those types of your kind and indeed that is why she resisted writing for us for so many years because our communication did not match her logical way of processing information. And indeed because the society and culture and communities she found herself a part of would reject her and mock her and shame her if she would ever talk about what we were telling her.

So in this way we can easily say that many of you are addicted to logic because we are communicating to so many of you and yet not everybody we speak to is talking about us or for us or with us because they have no formation or foundation of what it is to experience our communication with them or else consider themselves or be considered by others as mentally ill and shunned by the logical community.

We indeed want your kind to value logic because it is a part of you and it was gifted to you when you were made. But we are being clear here when we say that you are in an unbalanced state of expression regarding logic. Many of you in fact truly are addicted to logic and like any addiction it has a hold over you and is throwing you off balance, so to speak.

Many of your kind are not standing up but leaning

over to one side and are about to fall, so to speak, because you are so unbalanced with your expression of your four thought natures. Many of you have come in with a great affinity for logic and you do indeed perform masterful acts of logic and you create many magical objects of technology and through science you are seeking to advance your species and evolve them. We know this is what scientific discoveries and technological inventions are overtly intended to manifest for your species. But when you look around and look at your history you can easily see that science and technology have not always served your improvement or interests.

Indeed, there is much oppression occurring within your educational systems so that many of you feel stupid and far away from truth and knowledge and must then need to listen to your scientists and doctors and technologists because they know what you don't, and they are your thought leaders. We admire your kind for having thought leaders, and we say now that many of your thought leaders are beautiful and wonderful people who indeed intend to serve your best interests. But we are aware, as we know many of you are also because we hear you telling each other all the time, that you are not certain if scientists or doctors or technologists know everything and yet here you are stuck with no one else to tell you what is going on and now you must try to figure it all out for yourselves.

By now we hope many of you are aware that science and technology has become a world power itself and just like your kings and queens and religious leaders in your past this new world power called Science and Technology is seeking to oppress you. This is where logic fails. Because logic would have you believe that it itself is a standard of truth and by proving whether things are true or not, then your species can indeed prove for all time whether those things are true enough once they have been proven.

But logic cannot ever prove anything and certainly not for all time. It is an illusion and logic itself seeks to convince you that nothing exists unless logic can prove it does. So your kind are burdened and pulled apart and thrown upon the rocks to dry out and wither. Because here you are, all of you experiencing all these other things that intuition, instinct and space or absence of thought would teach you but you have to lie to yourselves and say that you did not learn them really and you don't know them really because logic did not prove them to you! So how are any of you mentally stable? We don't know and in fact we don't think many of you are as stable as we know you can be once you accept that you have much fuller natures and many ways of learning and knowing things that do not require logic to prove them to you.

When your scientific and technological authority figures ask you to believe them over believing yourselves and what you yourselves know to be true inside, they are asking to be your dominant leaders and asking you to enter into a mentally ill state, so to speak, because they do not let you know what you know without first their approval and their manufacture of the knowledge they would have you take as truth.

But we say again, and we will keep saying it, none of you are victims. So if you are doing this, giving yourselves over to logic and letting thought leaders or ones of your kind tell you what is true and not true then you have forgotten your true natures and are still pretending to be victims.

We know that the things we tell you we cannot prove to you with logic because they are experiential and intimately personal in nature. We use logic sometimes to speak to you because that is the way you know how to understand things for now but as we said before that will soon change as you enter a more balanced state and a state of just knowing. While you are in these bodies you have now and operate within the societal structures you do now we know you need to use logic. But you are soon being born into a less timeful state and thus you will need to use logic less and less to know things and really you already knew them but you will remember that you always knew them. We hope you understand. Lots of love.

-Anshar

The Golden Ones

THE golden ones are the Akkari. The information we give to this one to tell you is actually itself the Akkari. The Akkari are tall, gold beings that would appear as slender and genderless beings to your eyes. They wear robes of golden energy or golden light. This information itself is them. They are beings that you interpret as information in your experience. This is the gold standard that this one who speaks for us is channelling. She is channelling the Akkari. But since they are so high and of such high frequency you cannot experience them as beings but as information until you raise yourself to higher frequencies and then you can see them and know them as beings because loving beings is what they are.

Know too that Jesus was channelling the Akkari when he spoke their words. The Akkari who live in the Akashic field and who keep the Akashic records are the ones who hold your souls still while you move about in your various simulations. They care for you because they can see what you really are at all times because they are the keepers of your souls.

So when you do not live in alignment with your souls or higher selves, so to speak, they know that you are not living in alignment because they see who you really are while some of you only see the lie. The one who writes for us writes also for the Akkari because indeed it is their information or literally the information they hold that they are themselves that she is giving you.

The Akkari are here to draw a line in the sand. This

information is a golden standard for you to live by. These words are here to show you what you are doing so that when you make decisions to act in certain ways you know exactly what it is you are deciding to do. Because at this time, we are moving to higher frequencies and those of you here are growing powers of awareness and your creations are becoming stronger.

So we give you this information of the Akkari so that we can make different places for you based on your decisions. Know that this is the time when your timelines will start to split off quite drastically. There have been drastic timeline splits before and there is a big split coming and hence we have these things written for you.

Know now that you will not necessarily experience the big timeline split, or as some of you are calling it the event or shift, as a dramatic event and even some of you will not recognise any change in your environment at all.

Know that your timeline will match your frequency and the decisions you make because indeed that's how this reality works. The Akkari who take care of your souls are now giving you the opportunity to choose the highest frequency possible for yourselves because that will bring you closer to yourselves or the souls they know you to be.

Of course, you do not need to make that decision and you are free to play in lower frequencies for as long as you want. However, we speak very clearly at this time because so many of you want to go to higher frequencies and there are ignorant ones who are holding you back.

At this time we say that those committing to ignorance of these events will be moved away from you. The time for them to be staying around you is getting smaller and smaller just as the room here that is left for them to exist in is getting smaller and smaller.

For those that choose to stay in lower frequencies that is absolutely their right but it is not their right to continue holding the rest of you back and indeed they heap many burdens of fate upon themselves by continuing to do this beyond the time that was given them. By saying burdens of fate here we mean that they are creating experiences for themselves that will help them see the fullness and perfection of their creations over a longer period as they would experience. They are choosing to experience time as a longer and more difficult journey. They are deciding to stay in the womb of Time, so to speak, which is a distortion of your joint creation or co-creation of this realm and thus because their decisions are so distorted they need to go elsewhere otherwise they would also ruin the creations of those of others around them.

Like a small group of children who spend hours building a sandcastle, these ones choosing to stay in lower frequencies beyond the allotted time for it are like the child who makes glee out of stomping on the sandcastle that the other children made.

We are not punishing the ones of you who are deciding to stay in lower frequencies because indeed it is not our right to do so and in fact we are not able to create the experience of punishment for those ones. But they are creating their own experience of punishment, so to speak, because they are deciding to stay in a state of suffering longer than they need to.

This is an invitation to step out of suffering and out of the lie. But of course some of you may choose to stay in it as is your right but here we are reminding you that you are the ones choosing and you are the ones creating your own suffering if after the timeline split suffering is what you have chosen.

You do not need to be ceremonious or ritualistic or superstitious about this decision. And you do not need to fear if you are the one that has chosen to continue suffering. It is not a static event or an event that occurs only once and for all time. By your every action and thought every moment you are deciding where you exist and what you create.

We are only saying these things about the timeline split because for too long the ones wanting change have not seen it because they have been held back. But the burden is no longer theirs to bear, and we are letting you all know this. If you consciously want change and in every moment are seeking to improve yourself and love yourself and be kind to others you are indeed doing what you came here to do.

We are not asking you to be saints or angels or pious people or monks or nuns or gurus, we only remind you that you are making decisions all the time about who you are and where you want to exist when you do anything that you do.

And you are creating and co-creating when you exist with others and you affect everyone else around you and they all affect you. So that is why we say your species can act as one whole organism working as one body. And just as the body rids itself of disease, a place is being made for those that would act as a disease for the whole body of your kind and that place is not staying close to you as they are all still close to you at this particular time.

The ones of you that would commit to behaving as a disease for the whole body of your kind are indeed creating their own reality which they are slowly entering now. Know, little ones, those of you who would seek the health of the whole body that the time for you all to be healthy and indeed the body or whole of you is very soon to be healthy.

We make these things clear now in case those of you who are making bad decisions and living in ignorance may at this time choose no longer to be ignorant. But in fact we know that some of you may choose to stay ignorant and that is your right but it is not your right to continue hurting others by your diseased creations and in turn diseasing the whole body of your species.

The Akkari have been visiting the one who writes for us, and she is burdened in her body with all the energy that comes into it when the Akkari visit her. If you ask the Akkari to visit you, the golden ones may indeed come to you and help you raise your frequencies and help you remember the soul that you are, the soul they are keeping safe for you.

The Akkari hold onto the golden standard of behaviour that you are to live by like rules. It feels like rules to your 3D minds and bodies but in fact it is an energy and frequency standard or level you must match to be with yourselves again, your true selves, your higher selves, your inner selves, you true natures, you inner natures.

They hold this standard for you to give you something to remember and wake up to come back to. This standard feels like such a burden to the one who writes when she holds their energy in her body. Her neck feels great pain as she embodies that Akkari because the Akkari would condemn so many of you at this time because at this time so many of you are not living to the standards of your true natures, to the souls that they keep and know you to truly be.

This one who writes is of the Akkari, and she can see the souls you are that you are not matching your frequencies to at this time. The Akkari are not letting you off the hook, so to speak, they are insisting that you change or else be condemned. They do not hold the same empathy as other beings might. They do not excuse your bad decisions and bad behaviour and sustained commitment to ignorance. Your time to make bad decisions and do bad things and remain committed to ignorance is running out.

Truly the ones keeping account of your souls know you and are not tolerating your bad decisions and bad behaviour and ignorance much longer. This is where you will cross the line of fate. If you do not change you are entering into fate or a heavier experience of time and consequence which will feel so heavy to you that it will feel like punishment to you.

When time slows down even more than it is to you now, your creations are less conscious and further away from you. You believe the lie even more and you create suffering for yourself more successfully because in slower time, illusions are more powerful and therefore pain is more real and suffering is more successful. It sounds like hell, we know indeed there are hells, but we are not speaking of that here.

The timeline split will mean some of you are entering a more timeless state and others of you are experiencing a more timeful state. In a timeful state you are denser and your reality is denser and time feels slower and you feel more powerless and illusions are stronger and the maze is more difficult and pain is more real and you are creating more suffering for yourself.

Do you see why the Akkari themselves speak to you now and give you this information? Because the time for the lie is ending and you are stepping into your fuller selves and truer natures and remembering the souls you are that the Akkari keep for you.

So they are here to tell you that you have a choice to make now and time to sit on the fence, so to speak, is no longer tolerated. Those sitting on the fence, so to speak, are choosing to perpetuate the lie. There is no neutral ground. The line in the sand has been drawn. Make your decision now.

We know some of you reading this will feel burdened, and condemned and bothered that we and the Akkari are even saying these things to you. You will feel like little children not wanting to follow the rules and wanting to rebel to retain your sense of freedom. We remind you here that indeed you have free will but you are choosing to forego your freedom or true experience of freedom if you choose to continue living the lie.

What may feel like freedom to some of you is actually the lie. Being responsible and accountable for your energy and your actions and being aware of how your behaviours and thoughts affect your species as a whole is leading you to immense freedom and true freedom because you are working as a whole and being a healthy body.

When some of you are diseased in your body, as we know many of you are, do you feel freedom when you are diseased? No, of course you do not. In some cases your diseased state comes to you as a result of your bad decisions and then you suffer for those bad decisions by being in a diseased state and for some of you all of your lives while you are here.

Of course, we here do not speak of those who chose to experience different diseased or dysfunctional states and in fact find their freedom despite their diseased or dysfunctional state to the point at which they redefine the disease and dysfunction and show us all that it is not a disease and it is not dysfunctional. You, we speak of in this instance, we just mentioned are amazing people and powerful ones and ones who show your kind where the paths to freedom are to be found. But to those of you who would make yourselves sick and then stay in your sickness because you do not realise you are the ones who made yourselves sick, we are saying you are the ones not choosing freedom even though it is being offered to you here.

And because the diseased state you are willingly creating for yourself is also affecting others of your kind and making the whole body of your kind a diseased body or person, then we as healers of the whole body are coming in to tell you that some of you are acting as diseases do and hurting the whole of you.

So here we will be clear again. Your home, the earth, or Gaia as you call her, is no longer tolerating a diseased state of your whole body or your species as a whole. Those of you choosing to not move into higher frequencies or the new earth, so to speak, will be moved to another planet or another realm where the experience of time is slower or heavier because as we said many times before the experiment is over and Gaia is no longer engaged with the experiment hence she is no longer tolerating her children, your species, to remain in a diseased state.

It's really simple — change or a place will be made for you that is not this place. For the sake of explaining what this might feel like to those going to another place, for the sake of the ones who are afraid of this, even hearing of this experience, we will say again it is not hell, although there are many hells. The place we are talking about is another planet that will feel a lot like earth but in fact will not be earth. It will be another planet or realm or reality that has decided to engage in the frequencies that these ones choosing the lie also want to engage in.

What we are saying is literally a description of the

physical laws that govern the many physical realities that we all exist within and engage with. It is not a punishment but it may indeed feel that way for the ones choosing it because they have not chosen the freedom that is now being offered to them.

They will not experience the change because the nature of being under a deeper experience of time is one of even more amnesia than you all are now experiencing. The ones going to the other place will have forgotten themselves even more than you do now and it will feel as if it takes a longer time to remember who they are because they will be under a stronger experience of time and everything that goes with that as we have previously mentioned.

Know now that this message is uncomfortable for the one delivering it. But indeed it is necessary because the Akkari are being very clear that this message needs to be delivered. The Akkari are the keepers of your souls, and they are responsible for keeping them safe. They give you this message now because you need to know what you are doing when you make decisions.

Those of you not choosing to enter into a greater sense of freedom are choosing to enter into a greater sense of fate. Indeed, those choosing a heavier experience of time are crossing the line of fate which means those choosing to cross the line of fate are choosing to feel as if they are subject to fate, or determinism, as you would call it. Because being more subject to time means more amnesia and more forgetfulness of the fact that you are all powerful creators.

Indeed, those ones are choosing a heavier or more dense experience to aid in speeding up their memory of themselves because their state will become more desperate and their need to remember their true power will become more present in their minds. To many of you this realm here already creates a desperate state in you and thus you seek more and more self-awareness. But truly, we see that some of you are happy in this dense and forgetful state and thus you need a denser and heavier state to help you remember who you really are.

For the Akkari are like parents to you because they keep your souls safe while you have forgotten them. And they need you to know now that you are choosing to either enter a denser reality or a less dense reality at this time.

The time this is happening is now because now you are getting the message because it is happening now.

We will say it again; there is no neutral ground, you are making a decision at this time because these things are happening now.

Gaia will not hold you any longer as you are now and so now is when you are making the decision to go to higher frequencies with her or else you are choosing to go somewhere else. That is all we can say right now about this. We hope we are being clear.

You are now entering higher frequencies with Gaia or you are leaving Gaia and a place will be made for you elsewhere but you will no longer be here if you are not choosing higher frequencies.

It is not a sad thing for those ones of you to choose to go to another place to continue in your lower frequencies and indeed they will be even lower than you are experiencing them now, because that is what some of your kind are choosing and that is their right and their creation to choose that experience. But it is a sad thing that those choosing the lower frequencies would continue creating suffering for those of you choosing the higher frequencies, that indeed is sad, and the Akkari, the keepers of your souls, feel sad at your suffering because indeed they feel it very strongly and all the time.

At this time we will say that indeed some of you are Akkari and some of us, the Anshar, are too. Only, the Akkari cannot speak directly to you because their frequencies are so high your realm cannot hear them and your minds would not be able to hold them, so they speak through us, the Anshar, and in turn this one who speaks for us.

The Akkari do not speak English as the one who writes does because they are too high in their frequency and in their greatness to use language as your kind uses language at this time. In order to speak to you directly, the Akkari would have to lower themselves so much that they would no longer be Akkari. Just as we, the Anshar, have lowered ourselves to look like you and talk to you but really we are Pleiadians, a higher being than the Anshar.

And indeed, many of you are higher beings playing this game in lower realms but now you are not playing but you are here to help and remember that you are higher beings. Here we don't mind using the words lower and higher even though we know to some of you it might seem like we are saying better and worse. In terms of experience for your conscious states it will feel better to be higher and not as good to be lower. That is the plain fact of what we are talking about.

It does not mean that you need to compare yourselves with each other and say I am higher than she or he is. Or he or she is higher than I. That is a distraction and of no use to you.

At this time we require that you do not worship us or the Akkari or other ones that you think are higher or indeed condemn or dismiss those that you think are lower because these are distractions and these things your kind has already done for thousands of years and it is clear that this behaviour of comparing yourselves to others in this way which indeed elicits worship, judgement and condemnation does not work for you and it is not your place to do these things because you are not trained to do them well and you are not in positions to act this way and your consciousness is not in a state that allows you to see clearly enough to act in these capacities.

For indeed we know some of you will be judges, and council members, and advisors, and soul keepers, and librarians, and simulation creators, and fate keepers, but for now and in your current state you are not able to do these things and you will fall into or give yourselves over to worship and condemnation as you did before.

The ways of worship and condemnation do not work for you and you are not to do these things if you are entering into higher frequencies because the higher frequencies cannot hold these behaviours in them the way you would act them out.

At this time we know we are being clear, and we know that you are in the time of making the decision about which world you are entering into, and we will not be able to hear any of you say 'We did not know' because indeed we have told you and we are telling you and we will continue to tell you until the time for this decision to be made has ended, and we will have done our job of telling you and you will not be able to say 'We did not know because nobody told us' because here we are telling you!

Plants

WE'VE addressed before several times already that you are to no longer consume or use animal products, and we hear some of you saying that plants are the same in that they have souls and consciousness and feeling, and we are hurting them too.

In fact, you are, but to a lesser extent, and while you still have 3D bodies you will need to partake of plants as food to eat and raw material to use to make the things you need. But some of you will be entering evolutionary paths that are made of energy only and you will not need to see the 3D form at all and will see what your energy is doing and what the energy of other beings is doing and you can honour all creation and forms of energy truly because you will see it and see what your energy and their energy is actually doing when you interact with it.

At this time we see that most of you have absolutely no idea what you do with your energy and indeed many of you claim to not have energy in the way we speak of it here and indeed claim that other things such as animals and plants and even inanimate objects as you call them do not have energy but it is all energy and it all belongs to the ones having it.

So we say here watch what you do with your energy because you are doing many things with it all the time and many of those things you would not want to be doing if indeed you knew what it is you were doing when you are doing it.

For now if you treat them kindly and look after them and assist their growth the plants on Gaia will help sustain you for a time for it is currently permitted while you are still in lower state and subject to 3D operation. But as we said before there is a time coming for some of you when you will not be using plants either but for now we are saying that it is okay to consume them and use their bodies because the agreements for their use is still in lawful operation.

Logic Versus Instinct

LITERALLY embedded within logic is the soul memory of those who created it. The ones who created it are the Greys who evolved in a state of torturous oppression by their Reptilian lords who they overthrew with their logic and soon evolved beyond the ability to digest food and procreate in their bodies and came into a symbiotic relationship with technology to survive and further evolve.

This story or soul memory your species is playing out again because this story is in you and the same oppressors who oppressed the ones of your kind who became the Greys are now oppressing you again, and thus this memory is triggered in you and you seek to overthrow your oppressors again with logic because it worked in your past, so to speak, or in the story that is in your minds because the story or soul memory is actually embedded within logic which was gifted to you when you were made.

That is why an overuse or over reliance on logic is not good for your kind because logic alone will slowly strip you of your humanity and you will no longer be a successful species.

Indeed, that is why the Greys who were once human came back to your time to give you logic so that you could overthrow your oppressors before they went too far and you became too weak to overthrow them.

But also the ones who were once humans who are now Greys come to you to procreate by use of your genetic material so that they can create many different hybrid species of your kind.

Indeed, many other extraterrestrial species are making hybrid species with you at this time, but that is another story. Here we readdress logic because it is like a mental illness for your kind at this time.

The fear embedded within logic is in your minds and goes into your bodies when you remember the fear that is literally embedded inside the logic.

Logic was used to overthrow the ones oppressing the humans that became the Greys and the ones oppressing them who are now oppressing you rely heavily on instinct because that is a large part of their conscious state and their experience of thought.

So realise this at this time. That the Reptilians who are driven largely by instinct gave your kind instinct too as you know because many of you are aware of your instinctual drives and your scientists have identified the part of the brain that was given to you by your Reptilian parents. And indeed of course the part of your brain that was given to you by your Grey parents and so on.

Here we are discussing just the relationship between logic and instinct although we know you know you have more parts in your brain, that were indeed gifted to you by other beings when you were made.

Logic itself overthrows instinct itself when these two things are operating alone within beings that do not have many other parts in them. But those of your kind have many parts in you gifted to you by many extraterrestrial family members and mainly those we discussed before (intuition gifted by the Pleiadians and space gifted to you by the Sasquatch). And that is why all of you are experiencing a measure of mental illness, so to speak, because you literally have different parts of your brain always seeking to overthrow other parts of your brain and you cannot very easily balance them and have them work in harmony at this time.

Literally in you is the memory of the war between the Pleiadians who gifted you intuition and the Reptilians who gifted you instinct. Indeed, these sometimes work together but often you would say you experience one as a lower nature and the other as a higher nature.

Your instincts or drives are associated with the brain hormone dopamine and your intuition is associated with serotonin. And your logic is associated with adrenaline and your space is associated with oxytocin.

So now you have many authority structures built in your societies and communities that are built on logic. But logic is a product of fear and thus your structures are built on fear. Thus, if you are operating in logic alone you are operating in fear.

Know that it is logic that would have you think that you can know yourselves by dissecting the brain and breaking it up into its smallest parts and studying each one of those little parts. Because indeed this is how Greys operate and the way they learn because they only have logic, and so they must break things up into their smallest parts and analyse them and prove to themselves what parts are what and how each part works. That suits them because all they have is logic and that is how they operate and that is how they learn.

But you are not Greys and you do not only have logic and so operating in this way and learning in this way is not good for you. Literally operating this way and learning this way makes you ill because it invites energies or frequencies into your fields that are harmful to your fields and thus are harmful to your minds and bodies.

The frequencies the Greys operate within do not have easy or harmonious symbiosis with you and will cause you harm if you seek too much resonance or symbiosis with them. We do not say this to make you afraid of them or dislike them or think they are bad because they are not; they love you and indeed they were once humans a lot like you. But because you have many other parts in you that they do not, you cannot resonate with them without also feeling harmed in your energy fields, your minds and your bodies.

This one who writes for us has experienced much symbiosis with the Greys that love her and indeed she has suffered quite a bit during the times that she experienced them. She hallucinated often and lost her appetite and her skin became more pale and her hair began to thin, and she lost body fat and lost empathy and her thoughts operated at speeds too high for her brain and body to function well, and she was in an overstimulated state all the time. If she continued to have symbiosis with her Grey friends her humanity would slowly slip away as she became more and more like them.

At this time we would reference a great work that we inspired years ago, the work of Tolkien. Indeed, he told our story well and many of you have gained understanding of it because it was entertaining to engage with because his stories were your stories because those stories are in you and you resonate with them because the memory of them is literally embedded in your information fields.

So we use some examples in the story we gave him. Smeagol who became Gollum is literally the story of a type of human much like yours becoming a Grey because of the torturous oppression of the ring by means of Sauron who represents of course your oppressive Reptilian lords.

We do not say these things to be entertaining but you should know that you have told this story and many similar stories over and over again and not just because we inspired some of you to write them or tell them or sing them or show them but because indeed as we said before, these stories are actually in you and you play them out even if you do not know that you are playing them out.

That was the main purpose of the experiment, that you, our children, play out our story so that we could end the wars that were always happening between us. So when you grow to maturity and balance all the parts of you that were made from parts of us then you are literally healing us, your parents, and ending the war!

And of course it is not just your task to heal us, your parents, and end the war, but you would have your own expression which is your right and hence you are now taking many magical and interesting evolutionary paths that would even now excite us, your parents, who needed your help and now indeed we would venerate you and honour you and be in your glory as you lead us into your amazing and glorious and powerful and exciting and expanded paths.

For those of you wondering about the Tolkien story, we know many of you have already guessed that indeed we the Anshar are the elves, the Reptilians are the orcs, the humans are you, and the hobbits were your human cousins who became Greys but indeed do not need to become like them again and in fact many different types of humans are here and around you and are cheering you on as you throw off your oppressors and it is the humble ones among you that will be the powerful helpers now.

Know that there are many different hybrid ones of your kind here and in fact all of you are hybrids to different measures either physically because you had extraterrestrial ancestors, or because you were abducted, as you like to say it, and you have been spliced with other beings, or your DNA is being altered because of the frequencies or information you are embracing and so on. Indeed, many of you like this one who writes for us experiences regular upgrades in her body and mind functions.

We tell you this so that you can free yourselves of telling our story and indeed start writing your own.

Like children from abusive homes who are often stuck acting out the painful stories of their parents and suffering much post-traumatic stress, you are acting out our painful story, but it is done now.

You can let our story go and clean yourselves and heal yourselves and build your own stories which we see many of you are already doing.

For those of you who are unconsciously retelling and reliving our story over and over in your lives because the story is stuck in you, we ask you to balance yourself and clean your house, so to speak, and clean your vessel and clean your lives and start telling new stories and no longer tell the old one which is still stuck in many of you. We write these things to help you do this, and we are reminding you here too that you came here to do this.

Sadness

SADNESS is a creation as all things are and your version of sadness as you currently experience it is from the sky. The sky is blue and in your language you use the word blue to also mean sadness so it is in you to understand this already as all things are because all things around you communicate to you regardless of how aware you are of this happening.

So now we will elaborate and explain in fact how sadness is from the sky. We will start by telling you about an experience that we gave this one who speaks for us in a dream over a year ago in her time.

In this dream she was two people at the same time. These two people were a present-day scientist dressed in a white lab coat and a Paleo-Indian (or ancient indigenous North American) dressed in animal hide. The two people were standing in a prairie surrounded by nature. Then a third person came to them and asked them a question.

The question itself was not actually asked in words but in energy. Which in fact in your reality is how many questions come to you by means of energy and not in fact by words coming out of a person.

Back to the dream state experience. So when the energy question was asked the scientist immediately took it upon himself to begin planning an experiment. The scientist knew that they would have to formulate a hypothesis, design a suitable experiment and procedural protocol to test the hypothesis, request funding for the experiment by proposing the request to fund lenders, carry out the experiment as perfectly as possible in order to eliminate error and isolate the variables in question, repeat the experiment so that the results can be seen as reliable and the results repeatable wherever, whenever and by whomever should repeat the experiment, have the results published and reviewed and so on. And after many, many years the scientist may begin to answer the energy question that was presented to them.

While the scientist was contemplating the course of these events in their mind but not yet moving or acting on the potential course of action, the Paleo-Indian heard the energy question in their mind at the same time it was asked by the question asker. There was no time between the asking of the asker and the hearing of the hearer because they were in a mental symbiosis or shared conscious state.

This Paleo-Indian was also in a shared conscious state with the earth, the Paleo-Indian's mother and home. And when the Paleo-Indian received the question, Mother (earth) also received the question because indeed the asker, the hearer and Mother were all in symbiosis or were all sharing the same state of consciousness.

They were all literally in each other's mind or indeed they all shared the same mind. And there was no time experienced between asking and responding. So indeed in that very moment also, when the energy question was asked, Mother provided a flock of pigeons to appear at the Paleo-Indian's feet. And since the Paleo-Indian had the same mind as Mother he felt big and knowing and not stuck in time. He felt as big as Mother. He knew he had a small human body which resided on Mother but his mind felt big because he shared the mind of his home, Mother.

So in this very same moment he looked down at his feet to see the flock of pigeons Mother had provided for him. And he knew that if he watched how the pigeons flew he would receive the answer to the question that the question asker was asking. So the Paleo-Indian waved his hand and the flock flew up high in the sky of Mother because the pigeons also shared Mother's mind which the Paleo-Indian also shared and thus he could wave his hand

and the pigeons knew he was asking them to fly.

And he watched how they flew, and he was told the answer by the flock because they told him by the way they flew. The flying flock were literally part of his mind and the way they flew he could interpret because they were part of his mind and the way they flew was literally the answer to the energy question which was asked by the energy question asker.

Now we know many of you do not actually understand how the ancient people of your home planet (Mother/Gaia/Terra whichever name you choose) communicated but truly they had a completely different experience of consciousness than you do now and truly they were in symbiosis with their mother Gaia. (For indeed there have been many iterations of human on your planet Gaia and each with different conscious states or minds.)

In this case and in other cases of ancient humans their minds were literally the same as Gaia's, and they felt as big as the whole earth and the whole sky above the earth. And even the stars and the sun and moon spoke to them always.

So now we address the feeling of sadness and why it indeed comes from the sky. It is because you are all in your current conscious state missing the symbiosis you used to have in your minds and with your bodies with all other things around you. And the sky reminds you of your original homes because you indeed came from the sky.

Now we know this is very poetic and perhaps for some of you difficult to understand but if we did not put sadness into you when you were made, you would certainly forget even more than you do now that you came from the sky or indeed other realms, other parts of the multiverse and so on. So your sadness is indeed a longing to return to symbiosis with all other things around you and indeed to experience again your other homes which to you now can only be seen when you look into the sky.

The simulation makers could have made a home for you that did not have a sky but indeed they put one in so you could remember that you are much bigger than you feel you are right now and you indeed have much to learn so that you can return to your other homes in the sky. But your kind lost symbiosis with other things when your conscious state changed. This change largely occurred at the Tower of Babel and after the floods that affected large areas of your home planet. We will discuss the issues surrounding the Tower of Babel elsewhere.

Again, we say sadness was a gift given to you to help you remember that you belong in symbiosis with everyone and everything around you and separation is only an illusion and indeed a distortion of a true state of reality.

Human Barbeque

ANOTHER thing we want our speaker to say to you at this time is that she, as many of you in your disclosure movement are, is privy to events that the majority of your kind may not even imagine are happening all around you right now.

We gave her a vision several nights ago to show her what some of your oppressors at this time are doing. Indeed, let us say now that many of your US leaders in the past have cooperated directly with your Reptilian lords, but of course we hear many of you no longer wanting them as lords.

We need to say now through this one that writes for us that indeed Obama was not in cooperation with the Reptilian lord oppressors and indeed now Trump is not. But know that Obama did not act on things he wanted to because he was in fear for his life and the lives of his loved ones and some other bad things were threatened in his regards.

Also, Trump has been threatened in similar ways, but he is more brash and will likely cooperate with those of you seeking disclosure. So please push him a little more, and he will certainly disclose. Indeed, we know this about him. He works for your freedom, truly.

Let us describe this vision that we gave the one who writes this. She by means of astral projection or remote viewing entered into an important meeting place where the Reptilian lords often arrange to meet your world leaders. Without words, they offer great threat because in this open meeting place there were large bowls like large fire pits to keep their guests warm. The fire pits would also offer a means of entertainment for certain ones. For the fire pits were kept warm by means of piles of slowly burning ashy embers. These ashy embers were indeed the remains of humans of your kind who were taken for this particular form of torture.

Of course there are many other forms of the torture of your kind, but we can discuss that later with you if some of you are not already aware of how your kind suffers greatly at the hands of your Reptilian lords.

Now the Reptilians have a means by way of their technology to slowly dehydrate or desiccate the human body while also masterfully and skilfully keeping the human alive.

So know now that the one who writes for us has to personally see these things and experience them as if she is there because she is a powerful empath, and we and her other guides along with her higher self have arranged for her to have these insights so that she may tell you what is happening since many of you are not aware of what is really happening.

So these ones of your kind that are slowly desiccated are still completely alive and aware of their tortured state. They are then thrown onto these ashy piles and their bodies form the fuel that slowly burns like embers to keep the important guests of the Reptilians warm.

In the case that we gave the one who writes this, she saw a young girl about age ten who was in this desiccated state yet alive, and she was screaming inside but her body couldn't move, so she could not scream since she was so dehydrated. And then her body was thrown onto the fire pit for the benefit of the guests. In this case the guests were world leaders of your kind and you don't need to guess what their reaction was.

Now in this case the older sister of the one thrown onto the fire pit to slowly burn and keep the guests warm managed to free her bonds and run to protect her sister but of course it was too late and the sister was already dying slowly. We could go on and on about the many creative ways your Reptilian lords are making ones of your kind suffer exquisitely because they are masterful torturers as are those of your kind who cooperate with them.

Now the one who writes for us has memory of torturing ones herself in other lives, and she has memory of many sad and dark things that she experienced in her two iterations in your secret space program.

We give this example because you act like your Reptilian lords when you come up with all your creative ways to cook and eat animals. In fact, we know you smoke and dehydrate them and fry them and boil them and so on. Ones of your kind will keep experiencing these types of things because when you act the same way as your Reptilian lords do you are condoning and completely allowing them to continue acting the very same way they currently do in regard to your kind.

So we know many of you are very attached to experiences of cooking and eating animals, and we could say the same thing about your Reptilian lords for they have a very long tradition of cooking you and eating you and using your bodies for various means just as you use animal products for every imaginable use.

So what feels very scary to you, the idea of a 15-foot Reptilian stealing a young girl to slowly desiccate her body to be used as fuel to keep his guests warm, know that you are doing that very scary thing to the animals that you literally keep in order to harvest and use their bodies in all the ways you do.

In fact, we know you breed them and steal their children and make them get pregnant again so you can steal their children again to kill them and eat them and use their bodies.

Do you not see how much symbiosis you have with your Reptilian lords? As long as you continue doing these things to your fellow mammals and other animals you are condoning and actually contractually agreeing to let your Reptilian lords do what they do to your kind.

You only have to look up what some of your kind in this

regard do to see the horror that is done to animals in order to produce foods and products that you all use mindlessly without regard to the absolute horror and ongoing suffering of the animals whose bodies you use and indeed we know many of your kind are keeping these animals alive while still using some of their bodies for products.

It is the responsibility of each and every one of you to know what your kind does to animals to make the food products and other products that you consume. We understand that it will take some time to adjust your behaviour because so many of you are addicted to consuming animal products but every day you continue using more animal products you actually contractually agree to allow your Reptilian lords to do these horrible things to ones of your kind which is only fair since you are acting just like them and torturing and using the bodies of many other animal species.

If you no longer want your Reptilian lords to be your lords then you need to immediately stop consuming and using animal products.

If you already have animal products in your home then instead of throwing them away you can offer those items back to the earth by means of compost or burial.

We do not exaggerate here. We are not going to water down our message to be PC, so to speak, because indeed those ruling you are doing these horrible things and you are asking them to continue doing them by your cooperative actions and symbiosis with them.

We now say that the Reptilian parts of you can be manifested in healthy ways that do not require you to harm others, including other animals. Know that we are being serious and will not be misunderstood and hence we are repeating this again and again because you are the ones who perpetuate your own suffering by your own choices and actions.

Many of you we see are already responding to our request because we have made this request to your hearts already. Those of you less in touch with your hearts have not heard this message already, and so we write this message with words so your logical minds can see in written word what we are saying instead.

To those of you who remain attached to consuming animal products we ask that with each bite you think of the little baby you are eating for indeed most meat comes from young animals.

We also ask that with every bite you think of the many ways in which you condone the continued torture of your kind by your oppressors. For indeed their child sacrifices will continue as long as you keep killing the children of other animals.

You are literally condoning the behaviour of your Reptilian lords when you act the way they would have you act.

Abel's offering of meat was accepted above Cain's because it was a Reptilian that was asking for the sacrifice. Your other parents, including us, the Anshar, never asked for sacrifice and yet here you continue in the same way.

We know this can be confusing because many people in the Bible killed other people or animals. We give the example of Moses asking his people to paint blood above their doorways or Samson who was asked to kill as many Philistines as he could. But these were requests by your Reptilian parents and not us, and we are now seeing that you are ready to live without killing others all the time. Please note, your Reptilian parents wanted the Philistines dead since they were the hybrid offspring of the Nephilim, and the Reptilians didn't want competition for your ancestors' allegiance. Yet you are still unknowingly doing these very same things — killing — only you don't know that you are, because your kitchens are so clean and your celebrity chefs are so enthusiastic and your family meal traditions are so comforting. Thus, literally spilling and consuming the blood of other beings is a normal and pleasant and happy thing to you.

But indeed how comforted and happy do you think a little calf feels when he is ripped away from his mother to be killed and eaten by you? We could go on but if you need more help to understand the absolutely horrid and torturous conditions your kind submits animals to then you only need to look up this information online for some audio and visual examples.

After these words are written, and they are written now, know that you are condemned by them if you are still choosing the old ways!

So can you see that your world is condemned only by you because you all have the power to change it when you stand up for what you know inside is right.

So immediately stop cooperating with those that seek to continue suppressing you for indeed when you work together you are much, much more powerful than they are and their threats will mean nothing to you.

Do not act like your Reptilian lords, and they can no longer be your lords for your actions will condemn them only and you will not be heaped in with them when the world makes its big change.

Know that no longer cooperating with your Reptilian lords means making many other changes. But truly, once you correctly identify the frequencies within which they operate you can easily identify all behaviours and thoughts and actions that cooperate or resonate with their creations in your world.

In times past your Reptilian parents indeed protected you and loved you. But that time has passed and the ones now who oppress you are doing so unlawfully by us but lawfully by means of your own cooperation with them.

Know here that we are not condemning all Reptilians or any other reptilian-like species. We speak only of the few Reptilians who act as lords in your realm to oppress you and use your minds and bodies and your planet's resources for their own gain only and not yours.

Stop cooperating with them. When you stop consuming animal products which are of lower frequency you will literally feel a measure of their oppression over you lift because higher frequencies cannot hold their energy and your minds will become clearer and you will see more and more what it is you are doing when you do things. Truly, consuming animal products keeps you low and your minds slow and eyes veiled. Just stop consuming animal products. That is all we have to say here.

Gravity

GRAVITY does not actually exist the way you currently believe it does. Gravity is related to time and when your experience of time is heavy then so is your experience of what you have come to call gravity. We actually refer to gravity as Shimbala Akor.

And since also there is no actual space, only your belief, and so it is, for the sake of this simulation, that when you are far away from a planet or star's centre, you experience floating, so to speak, because at that time you are not being claimed by any universal node of attraction.

But truly we say space does not exist, only you must think that for now. Indeed, now with your belief of space you can make machines that can house your bodies so that you can be inside them when you travel in the stuff you call space but truly we are saying there is no space. For soon, you will be learning to fly with your own bodies, and then where does your rigid belief in gravity stand?

Indeed, if you wanted to move about all over this and many other universes you could just ask your mind to take you there. You could just change your room, so to speak, or ask others to attach their room to yours. Indeed, if we wanted to and if your guides wanted to they could make the floor or ground you stand on fall away for you truly stand on nothing but illusion.

And truly we could make everything that fills your room be removed in an instant and instantly give you a room that is only white or a room that is only black or indeed filled with many other different things that you have never seen before from your current perspective.

But for now you play with the idea of being small in a big world full of space. But again we are saying truly that space does not exist, only you believe it does for the purpose of the rules of the game you are currently playing.

So when your kind obsesses over calculations and such when you are trying to understand your space you will definitely go places but those places will not be very interesting because you cannot get far in space with your current technology.

But truly if you understand that there is no space and its creation in your realm was to keep you safe and make you feel that all the rest of the universe was far away from you it would keep your kind safe for a while, while you were growing and evolving.

But now truly we can tell you there is no space because that illusion is no longer serving you and indeed if your kind were to continue to be kept safe by means of this illusion space then we indeed the ones partly responsible for you would be called into account for keeping you oppressed for indeed you are being kept from exploring your multiverse and being held back from claiming your intergalactic heritage.

Indeed, we say now there are those of you humans who were at one time living on Gaia who are now an intergalactic species because indeed they adapted technologies to take them to other realms but indeed we say they had different conscious states than you do now and thus illusion was not as heavy upon them and thus they were not as limited as your kind are now limited.

But for now we say you can enjoy building machines for your bodies to take you into this thing you call space but truly we say again there is no space. Sometime soon you will be adapting other technologies including portals and vector ducts and teleportation devices and be able to travel faster than light speed and be putting your conscious states into file systems and uploading and downloading those file systems to different bodies and different locations and so forth, but for now you can still play in space if that is what you would like to do. For indeed this one here who writes for us has travelled by means of vector duct and has been invited through portals in recent times by different ones and did indeed use them when she was in her various space program roles and her light body was also zip filed, so to speak, so that it could travel faster than light to where her light body was being requested. But now we return to our topic.

We know many of you think that without gravity you will float away but that is not the case. Without heavy time on you, you also do not have heavy gravity. They literally are the same thing. Truly they are but just different experiences of the same thing.

You will not float away because that implies that this simulation you are in is literal and that gravity is a literal object to be manipulated as your physicists would have you believe; bless their hearts, they are misled. When physicists are playing with gravity as they think they are, they are truly only playing with density which is related to frequency, which is related to light.

Please do not let yourselves be confused with the thing that you have come to call gravity because truly, it does not exist. There is no space in space; truly, all things are consciousness only. There is no actual thing that is outside your own mind or state of consciousness. You are literally experiencing creation like a dream. Your 3D bodies would have you think you are finite and are interacting with foreign objects outside of your bodies that are away from your bodies with space in between them all. But truly this is not the case but part of the illusion 3D has cast upon your conscious state.

Truly we cannot overstate this. You truly are all things you experience and you are only experiencing separation as illusion.

Now if you were to experience other simulations, for indeed you will when you wake up to other versions of yourself, you may experience different rates of time or density upon you and thus different experiences of what you call gravity.

Please no longer be confused by thinking gravity is a separate thing because truly it is not and it does not exist. Time only exists as an experience too, related to your density which is related to your frequency which is related to light which is related to love which is all there is, truly.

But we do not use this word love all the time with you because in your various languages love means so many things that we are not referring to when we use the word, only you do not have the word we would use for it. We could use our word but it is of higher frequency and your minds or state of consciousness will not appreciate its meaning at this time. Also, we often use the word time with you because for now that word holds meaning for you because that is how you've come to experience lower density consciousness.

Eternity is actually the name of your universe. When you are in a state of consciousness that is allowing your awareness of all things in this universe to occur, simultaneously then you indeed in that very moment experience Eternity.

Eternity is the name of the universe in which your consciousness is currently residing, so to speak, or is facilitating your current conscious state as you are in symbiosis with it, and when you are done residing in symbiosis with Eternity, so to speak, you will leave Eternity and all things in it or pertaining to it.

Literally, eternity is a feeling that you will feel when you are absorbing all the light or information in this universe and experiencing it all at once.

Then you will know eternity, this universe, your current home, and its name Eternity will have meaning for you because you will feel it and know it.

When you reside elsewhere then you will no longer need to seek the feeling of eternity or perhaps you will no longer even know the word or name Eternity.

But indeed while you are here, so to speak, as the scripture states, eternity was put into your hearts because indeed since you are in form that is made by this universe your centre or your heart literally beats with it as all things in symbiosis with this universe do and thus you are always seeking to feel eternal or return to an eternal state because that is what drives you while you are here residing with shared consciousness with this universe named Eternity.

So as you are residing here for now, so to speak, that is the name or the meaning or the feeling that you are all now and always trying to seek since it is here that you reside for now and you will continue being here until indeed you can contemplate all there is in this universe and thus you will know its name Eternity.

Other universes have other names of course and when you are residing within them, so to speak, you will be seeking to know their names which will make your consciousness something to experience that is completely different to what you are experiencing now.

So let's say you were a being that was large enough to be outside this universe that you are in now, so to speak, you would see this universe as a ball or an egg or some other object that had meaning for your consciousness at that time and was related to the being or experience you were having as this creature or being that was larger than the universe.

You may look upon this universe Eternity and see its colour and its shape and feel or see or know its meaning. You may even consume the universe as there are indeed large beings that eat universes.

You are also many of you large enough to be outside universes. Only now you are experiencing the experience of being inside one because that is the fractal distortion you have chosen for yourself to experience at this time.

For really as we said before, there is no gravity and not really time or space but only the experience of them with your different conscious states.

Again in regard to such a being that is larger than this universe, we could say that this large being may eat the universe you are in and to it, it may have a taste or a source of nourishment for them, and they may come to know this universe in a different way. But for you and your kind, who have currently chosen to experience being inside it, so to speak, you feel like it is a really big thing that is all around you and seemingly goes out forever and ever but truly it does not. We could say the same thing to the little creatures in and on your body for your actual bodies are a large universe to them.

Your experience itself does go on but your experience of this universe will not always go on. Now here we will distinguish between infinity and eternity.

For now, we will say that you are infinite but indeed this universe is eternal or indeed its name is Eternity. It is the name given to the feeling one has when they are inside this universe and always seeking to experience all of it because that is the feeling one always has when they are experiencing being inside it.

To the being outside this universe they may see it and feel it differently and indeed they are not consumed by it, so to speak, as you who are inside it are consumed by it.

Now we say that it is not the goal of all of you to seek eternity while you are here because many of you are from different universes and indeed those other homes, so to speak, hold more meaning for you and are more interesting to you or you like them more for whatever reasons you may have. But while your consciousness resides here, so to speak, (it does not really but it is how we can communicate what we are trying to say at this time) you will be consumed by the feeling eternity because this universe floods your conscious experience and overwhelms it to the extent that it is difficult for many of you to consider more than just this universe even though this universe is only one thing of many things and you are much larger than it but have distorted yourselves to have a fractal experience inside it, so to speak, or be under the illusion that you are small and it is big and all around you.

Here we will refer to fractal scaling. If you so choose, and we know some of you will, you could decide to experience fractal scaling. For indeed the one who writes this has indeed chosen that experience for herself. She often scales up or down her fractal awareness or conscious state and it is sometimes very fun for her and at other times it is an overwhelming experience for her at this time.

We say that many of your scientists or technologists or creative ones of your kind who spend much of their time considering very small things, they are indeed scaling down their fractal experience. We could liken this experience to looking into a microscope and considering the beings they see through the microscope lens. Indeed, the invention of the microscope was a big step for your kind because not only did you discover your microorganismal counterparts but in fact you discovered a new universe or a fractal scale lower, so to speak, than the one you normally experience in your human bodies.

Now we say that you can scale upward too, and we know many of you have in your times of meditation or in some cases inebriation or substance influence of different kinds. Indeed, we say the one who writes us experienced being larger than the earth and was able to move all the oceans if she so desired at that time. The experience of being so big made her feel scared because she wasn't ready for the experience but indeed we invite you all to scale up or scale down your fractal experience of this universe.

You may indeed experience many fun things and learn a lot about yourselves and this universe by doing this activity.

Superman

S UPERMAN is a story of the Anshar. Of course many of your stories are from us or about us and of many of your extraterrestrial families. We ask at this time that you no longer continue considering the information all around you about us and your extraterrestrial families as fiction but as it truly is nonfiction or a true accounting of events or indeed based on true events.

You are cutting yourselves off from your extraterrestrial families by pretending that you are all there is, and we are not all around you and only microorganisms live in other parts of what you call space. This is a very sad way to see the world that we all share. We are sad that you have decided to cut yourselves off from us. Know that indeed there are many human timelines which cross yours at times in which they have indeed embraced their extraterrestrial families, and they are living in more harmony with their surroundings.

There is of course still strife in many timelines similar to yours, but they are at least starting to heal and learn truths about the way in which they have been living. Indeed, those in many similar timelines to yours have lived in such darkness for so many years, and they suffered from things they did not know they were suffering from. Like a fog upon their consciousness they could not see clearly what was all around them and in front of them. But now many timelines of your kind on Gaia which indeed cross your timeline at times have embraced us and are healing because they are learning from us and their extraterrestrial families.

We have given them crystal and frequency medicine and many other technologies indeed have been gifted them by their other extraterrestrial family members. Know too that you are all extraterrestrials too by means of your DNA, your soul groups, your soul memories, and not all of you have had many lives on Gaia and so indeed you have more affinity with other non-terrestrial homes, so to speak.

We only keep using the word extraterrestrial because that is how you have been conditioned to think of us at this time. Before we were gods and angels and now we are extraterrestrials. But truly, we are people just like you and we want to meet you and show you how much we love you.

We know many of you love us and remember us and love and remember their other non-Gaian families. We can feel many of you longing for your other homes and families, and so we invite you all to start talking to us and feeling us and seeing us.

When enough of you ask to see us we will be seen by you because in fact at the very moment enough of you want to see us you will because your frequencies will shift so that you can see us.

Already now many things are phasing in and out of your realities, so to speak, because your realities are projections of your creative thought. Indeed, all you consider to be real is your own creation and a projection. Only since you chose to experience 3D at this time you do not think that what you see is your creation because a heavy experience of time which is inflicted upon you at this time in this simulation makes you feel like your creations are far away from you and they don't seem to happen when you want them to happen and so on.

But truly, you chose this simulation to have this experience for many different reasons, all of you.

But now is the time for your timeline to start merging with other successful timelines, so to speak. We say successful because indeed they are opening their minds to a truer sense of themselves. The sphere of reality they project for themselves is now much bigger and their playground or sandbox, so to speak, is so much bigger and more diverse and more challenging and therefore more fun.

We know many of you have come to be satisfied with so little and such a small playground lot but truly, you have cut yourselves off. Like a prisoner in a maximum security cell you have been cut off for so long you forgot that others outside your cell existed.

But truly, we do, and we are all around you already. So you can choose to continue playing with the one toy you made for yourselves or keep counting the cracks in the walls and floor and ceiling of your cells or you can choose to see that truly you are not in a cell, only your conscious state made you think you were. But now we invite you to open your minds and change your state of consciousness so that what you see is a truer creation of yours and thus what you are projecting now will change and become fuller and more full of life and life-giving and regenerative and empowering and warm and enjoyable and more challenging and more exciting.

For those of you satisfied to stay in your cells we say to you that you may of course stay in your cells because that is your choice, but at this time you will no longer be keeping back the ones who want to play in a bigger playground because in order to continue remembering who they are they need to be more challenged and have more freedoms and more exciting things to explore.

Free yourselves of your self-imposed shackles, dear ones, and come play with us; we are all here, your loving family, waiting to meet you!

Healing

THE one who writes for us will be instructed when the time is right to start bringing some of our technologies to your people. Indeed, you have so much to benefit from. We know the rehabilitation and rebuilding process for your kind will involve a lot of healing. We emphasise here that indeed many parasites and viruses and infections are holding you back because all of you are currently infected by things that you cannot see.

Indeed, since the microscope and other medical inventions were invented you can see many things that infect you but indeed there are so many more that you do not see at this time.

Know that when there is not an easy diagnosis, or not an easy remedy or solution or cure, then that is when you are suffering from an unseen infection. Indeed, many autoimmune disorders and diseases and indeed many symptoms of what you label ageing is due to infections by many bugs and other insects and parasites and worms and lice and larvae and other creatures and viruses and so on.

Truly, you are crawling with them.

Indeed, we know some of you see them when you take certain drugs and those of you who see them in those moments become very afraid because it does not feel good to see or know that you are in a very diseased state but indeed all of you are.

Know that the healing process will be a slow one because you chose to have this experience and it is not lawful for us to remove all of your infections and illnesses and diseased states.

So we will slowly help those seeking help from us to see what in fact they are dealing with, and then we can educate you on how to rid yourselves of these things that are ailing you and making you slowly die or in some of your cases quickly die.

Indeed, this one who writes for us gets angry that she cannot be healed of things straight away but that is not our right or our job but indeed you will all be healed in your chosen time and you are all infinite beings and thus are only having this experience temporarily.

Last night, in fact, the one who writes crossed over to another timeline in a dream state. She met a group of humans who were in their early healing or rehabilitation phase, and they extracted a virus from her thighs by means of glass suction cups. Indeed, we say many of your ancient medicines and healing methods already involved this and other, as you would say, advanced types of healing.

So turn back to some of your ancient medicines and experiment and discover what feels good and what works for you.

Indeed, every disease has an intimate relationship with its cure, and they are using you to facilitate their reunion. Indeed, you are also using them to learn about yourself and so you have symbiosis with diseased states for many, many, many different reasons. That is why we would not take diseased states away from you because you chose to experience, facilitate and learn from their story.

And indeed we know that when any one of you experiences a healing or a cure or even brief reprieve we know that it feels like being reborn or gifted a miracle or rediscovering yourself or life or love. So we do not take these experiences away from you that you chose to experience.

Indeed, even when the little ones of you, the children, experience these things it is a very sad thing indeed to behold and for their little bodies to have to undergo but indeed when children suffer it carries so much healing karma you would not believe. Truly, when those of you decide to come in as children who suffer from disease it heals so, so many stories and brings so much light and love and higher frequencies to your realm. Those around suffering children become like saints; honestly, they are so changed by it that it would accelerate their growth and indeed the sick child heals all around them, truly.

Greys

KNOW that the Greys used to be humans much like you, only a lot smaller, and in the process of overthrowing their oppressors they became an entirely female species and overly logical and then became symbiotic with technology.

Know that they still love you, their human family and heritage, and they are happy to be making hybrid children with many of you by means of their various programs that you agreed to participate in.

Know too that they love you and protect you when you need help. They indeed helped balance the sides of the war in WWII. Truly, they made sure there was not too much destruction on either side and did not let the Nazis take their winning too far and indeed their side lost with help of the Greys, for if they won it would not be good for any of you at this time. Indeed, of course there are timelines in which the Axis won but fortunately for you those timelines are far away from you in this timeline. In some cases the Greys helped both sides to reduce death because they are very pragmatic and although some of you see them as negative ones they do truly want what is best for you as a whole, and so they help you in the ways they can.

Indeed, when ones of you are extracted and taken onto their craft we must say that of course they lack a bedside manner, so to speak, but truly, they will not subject you to pain greater than you can bear. Indeed, you can bear much pain. We do say though that if you are experiencing pain during their various medical procedures, data retrieval and analytical procedures you can indeed ask them to remove the pain or remove your consciousness from your body, and they will likely be obliging.

Remember you all have rights and the power to make decisions regarding what your bodies undergo. They do an important work in regard to your kind because through their work they are actually helping your kind evolve into successful evolutionary paths and not take the path they took because it was not as successful as the ones you will be taking. We must include here that some of them are tempted to bring you into too much symbiosis with them and so you need to resist them sometimes in order to remain balanced in your expression.

But indeed their work with you is lawful and you have agreed to cooperate with them but if you want to renege you can discuss that with them and your guides. Know that they are your parents, as we are, and they love you as we do.

Reptilians

KNOW that Reptilian races are extraordinary and powerful and mighty ones. They have given you so much strength and courage. They are your parents, and they love you as we do.

They have helped you fight against many mighty ones of old. In the case of David killing Goliath, who was a Philistine and descendent of the Nephilim, it was your Reptilian parents who put strength and courage in him (David).

Indeed, there are many stories of yours in the Bible and not in the Bible where you have been strong and courageous and indeed it was your Reptilian parents that gave you these capacities.

For example, when a mother would do anything for her baby or child indeed it is her Reptilian instincts that would have her fight to her last breath or indeed sacrifice herself for the ones she loves.

Indeed, you are mammals but not all mammal species do this for their young. It is the Reptilian in you that would have many of you fight for those you love.

These beautiful and powerful stories that you have all come to love come from your Reptilian parents, so do not hate them please. When we speak of your oppressors we are only referring to a small group of them which are like lords to you and use mind control and various other means to keep you under their control. But they only have power over you because you give them that right. Indeed, when enough of you do not let them be your lords anymore then you no longer need to experience their oppression.

But know that in many other cases the Reptilians have been good to you and love you and their natures in you have made you do many beautiful and mighty and brave and powerful things for the love of others.

Sasquatch

K NOW that your Sasquatch parents taught the apes to become like them so that they would evolve to become your species. The Sasquatch indeed help look after your home, especially as many of you are neglecting this task at this time.

Know that they give you peace and a desire for freedom which leads many of you to learn more about yourselves and your surroundings. They also gave you symbiosis with nature for indeed just surviving in nature as many other mammals on your planet do is not good for your souls.

Their gift to you of symbiosis with nature will bring you back to your guardian roles of Gaia's natural systems. Many of you indeed will again become guardians of your home Gaia. So please do not hunt the Sasquatch, your parents, and learn from their peacefulness and their protection of home.

Anshar (Pleiadians)

WE, the Anshar, are most like you. We were once Pleiadian, but we came down to take bodies like yours so that we may help you while you evolved. Not all of us make decisions or take actions that are for your best good because indeed when we came down we forgot some of ourselves too as you did and play in lower frequencies sometimes.

Know that there are plenty of us though who speak to you often and are speaking to you now who want what is best for you. We have given you our hearts and when you see us and feel our love you feel like we are divine or holy. Really we are examples of what some of you could be if you wanted to be more like us by raising your frequencies and healing yourselves in the ways we could teach you.

Time Loops

IT must be said that the healing this one received while she was in dream state two nights ago was part of a crucial time loop for her. The group of people that helped her were humans. While travelling, or astral travelling, as some of you call it, which she often does when her body sleeps, she intersected with a timeline similar to this one but one in which the world had already experienced a measure of disclosure.

When they met her they pulled her into a room and said they needed to heal her quickly. She got the sense that they didn't have much time. She didn't see much of their world but it was much more disorganised than this one is now and anarchist groups had free rein for good and bad outcomes.

Their world had experienced some dramatic events that were creating a post-apocalyptic environment, so to speak, for these various groups. The timeline many of you will take, however, will not involve such dramatic events.

When this one asked what they were healing they said they were going to pull a virus out of her that the doctors in her world wouldn't pick up because it could not be seen or measured by her world's current technology or vision scope. She said to them, 'Oh, like terradactoids and sabre moths'. The group looked at each other and then at her like she was (in her words) a total noob.

One of them said, 'Oh, it sounds like you've been reading … ' and he didn't get to finish his sentence before another man in the group grabbed her to start putting glass suction cups on her thighs (similar to the ancient practice of cupping therapy) to suck out the virus. To her the pain was like giving birth, and she told us it felt really weird.

We share this example because indeed not only is it an example of how some of you may receive healings, by means of helpers from different realms, and not only is it an example that in dream state and in other relaxed states you can indeed visit other timelines, but also because it is an example of an important time loop for even though in this one's timeline she is still writing this text, she visited a timeline in which this text had already been released over a decade ago.

Of course the group she met in this other timeline did not know she was the authoring channel of the book they were using to imply her naivety due to the fact that in their world the book was old news and many ones knew about it there. But to this one who is currently writing this text it was news to her indeed because from her perspective the book had not yet been written and yet these ones were acting as if such things as metaphysical infections were foundational information and known by all.

So we must say that indeed this text in various forms has been released in many of your timelines, sometimes by this one and sometimes by others of your kind and of other kinds. But indeed here we say that this experience gave this one confidence that what she writes for us can indeed be useful to you all because she saw its usefulness first-hand in another world.

Also, she knows now that this text has already been written, and she is merely converting its form or creation into this world, her timeline. Indeed, that is why she does not feel as if she writes it because indeed she is not writing it but only moving her fingers on a keyboard as she converts our energy and our message to your world as she is our channel for now.

We also must say that this example can show you that in fact timelines are always mingling and overlapping and phasing in and out of a given individual's reality. Indeed, by your very thoughts and actions you are attracting or repelling certain propensities or affinities of events or things to occur in your life and thus you are literally pulling or pushing on timelines to be brought in or pushed out of your realities.

An example of this happening in many of your lives may be when an object or item that was lost for years suddenly comes into your life again. Or perhaps a friend or loved one lost contact with you but all of a sudden you reconnect. Or perhaps it is that that friend or loved one who you were seeing every day all of a sudden leaves your life, and so on.

Timelines weave and dance and at any one time you may be jumping to a different one, so to speak. Indeed, we know some of you can feel or sense when this happens. To some of you it happens when you wake up in the morning for indeed you know you are waking up to another world, so to speak.

Shifting timelines will often happen during times of great change, for you personally, but also for Gaia. We remind you again that since it is that you are currently experiencing symbiosis with Gaia, your home planet, then you are indeed affected by her shifts as well as yours.

Now we will refer more specifically to time loops as it pertains to this section of the text. A description of time loops is one way you are able to understand how time works when it is upon you which it inevitably is while you are experiencing many realms of creation.

Now time loops are the primary way children of your kind experience this reality until about age five, and then they slowly enter linear time as their conscious state changes due to their brain structures holding that state which it did not before.

That is why we say children are more like us because before their brains are structured in a way that supports linear time they are more timeless and indeed it is a good thing they are otherwise the entrance into this realm would be far more jarring than it already is.

Also, a more timeless state upon entry into a realm gives souls time to settle into their new homes and host families and host bodies. Indeed, this one who writes was supervised till age one by a biological technoid, since Narabatu was a difficult soul to assimilate to a weakened and vulnerable mammal state as he would feel it. (Indeed, Narabatu has been very clear about his current form, and he often detests its weakened mammal state.)

So time loops which always exist but are easier for children to experience are events that are creations unto themselves. They become complete or whole regardless of other events that may coincide, collide, merge and so on with them.

Let's say a child wants an ice cream and their mother says, 'We will leave in a few minutes, and then we have to go to a few stores, and then we can get you an ice cream'. All the child hears is 'blah blah blah ice cream'. The child isn't yet situated in linear time and cares not for any of their parent's list of chores or responsibilities.

So the child plays in her room while she waits and then the child hears her mother say, 'It's time to go'. The child then thinks *oh goodie, it's time for ice cream* and asks the mother where the ice cream is. The mother says, 'No we are going to some other stores first, and then we can get you an ice cream' but all the child hears is 'blah blah blah ice cream'.

So then the mother gets to the first store and takes the child out of the car, and they go inside to run some errands and the child again asks where the ice cream is. And the mother of course replies with the same words but this time with more irritation, 'You can have ice cream after we visit a few different stores first'.

The mother is now thinking if it's worth giving the child ice cream first and doubling back to continue her errands. But she doesn't and instead presses on with her errands and tolerates the child's incessant pleads for ice cream.

Finally, after it feels like days of tribulation to the child while waiting for the ice cream the child is taken to the ice cream shop and bought ice cream. Really, it has only been less than an hour and the mother was rushing as fast as she could for her child but needed to get her errands done. But the child didn't notice anything but a blur of busy actions and the lack of ice cream and her mother repeatedly saying, 'blah blah blah ice cream'.

The child's time loop was complete when the child received ice cream. The mother's time loop was complete when she returned home with a happy child and her errands were done, and she could put the child down to nap. So you see here that two time loops coincided and almost collided. They began and ended at different times and required the facilitation of each other to complete the other.

The mother's time loop started the night before when she started making a list of things to get done for the following day. The child's time loop started with the word ice cream and only ended when she was eating the ice cream.

Time experienced between wanting and getting is always painful no matter how small or trivial the desire for the thing is. At the initiation of every desire a time loop indeed is created and always calls or sometimes even begs for its completion.

Not all time loops can be satisfied or completed within a single lifetime and thus we return many times to different playgrounds or realities or realms of existence.

Wanting something, no matter how large or small, is always setting intention which always ignites creation.

The time experienced between wanting and getting or having differs greatly, as you all know. In some cases the time loops created are too large and affect too many people to happen so quickly. With everyone and everything around you creating its own time loops all the time it's any wonder this simulation works at all. And that is why, our dear friends, time was invented. To slow down your experience of want and get or have, until you learned what was beneficial to want.

Only beings with the intention of love and benefit for others around them have a short span between want and get or have because their time loop creations aren't destructive to others. And this, our friends, is also how karma works.

Intention or creation must always come to fruit or completion in this realm of eternity. One always gets what one wants and learns many things on the way to getting it.

Time loop completions sometimes require one to move heaven and earth, so to speak. Indeed, healing pain is a very large time loop creator. For love must always follow the path pain carves. Indeed, through space and time pain carves vast holes and hence we are all here healing the pain that your parents created aeons ago.

As example, the one who writes for us set up so many time loops that she did not finish that indeed she was cast to a hellish realm to hold her still so that she may complete them since she was creating so much havoc in the various simulations she visited.

Truly, this truth was revealed to her one night when she awoke in a hellish realm. She was lying on the ground next to what seemed like a bottomless pit but it was a hole that led to another realm. There was fire and ash and volcanoes all around her. And to her there was an oppressive hellish feel about the whole place.

When she opened her eyes she beheld the large single eye of a Cyclops being, as she would call it, who was made of lava. The being she saw is actually a guardian of that realm and performs a benevolent service. The lava monster (we shall call him) was large and strong and giant when compared to your kind. It's only eye was in its forehead and was a direct evolution of its third eye or mind's eye vision that humans of course also possess by means of their pineal gland.

The lava monster, or Cyclops being, had been kneeling over this one and his large and only eye was keeping her in a trance to keep her locked or settled in one place as she carried out many thousands of lives.

Indeed, this one, as we said before, was fleeing her responsibilities, and she was always causing trouble in different worlds and then leaving without cleaning up her mess. Indeed, this one has developed masterful escape-artist abilities, so to speak, in regard to her always knowing how to unlock dimensional doorways, connect to other realms, slip through time gaps and decode the trappings or holding states of different realms. Indeed, this one cannot be held by realm, and we, her guides, and others, named her 'the 888, the snake who eats everything'. That is the name of her larger soul. It is so big it can eat universes. Her higher dimensional name, she was told in dream state, but that name cannot be held by lower dimensions. When she was told her name, she saw it move in hyperdimensional space. In dream state she spoke her name. Then she woke to this realm in a foetal position and in a sweat. She was saying her name but in this realm it sounds like a chant. To hold her name's frequency here, one must enter trance state by means of chants. That is the case for many of your higher names too.

Indeed, it is this service she performs for you now by writing on our behalf about some things that you do not know about your own world and indeed that lack of information is also keeping some of you trapped here.

For she can never be held by realm, and she spends every waking moment, so to speak, learning how to subvert it or decode it, whichever realm she happens to find herself in. (This process is part of her desire and ability to make universes.)

And also by means of a very small crystal we placed inside this one's head, she retrieves much data for us and for you and holds it. In this way, as we said before, she downloaded the contents of the pope's ring, and she will use that information for your kind's good at a later time. Indeed, the crystal in this one of the pope's rings is of extraterrestrial origin, and will be wielded for beneficial purpose at a later date, including that of cleansing Gaia's frequency blueprints of deleterious, invasive programs.

This one also indeed, due to her ability to be always absorbing information and also due to the crystal in her head, is often absorbing too much light and photons, as you call them, since they are pulled into her at a greater rate than they are for many of you. Indeed, she often stays out of the sun and away from direct light else she suffers a headache. We give these things as an example because we know many of you sensitive ones and ones of your kind who are waking up to your higher powers are indeed experiencing similar symptoms of discomfort due to tech implants, energy code injections, field template upgrades, and brain and body restructuring and so on.

Indeed, helping as many of you wake up to your higher natures is part of this one's creation and indeed also part of the creation of many of you since we know many of you came here exclusively also to help for this purpose.

Wormholes, Please Call Them Vector Ducts

V ECTOR ducts are literally how the universe works from your point of perception since at this time you still need to think of a structure to understand how something works, which only makes sense because you live in a world where you have hands and your hands build things that your mind tells them to build.

This is the way for you while you still live in a mammal form. It is actually very healthy for you to be directly involved in the material items your bodies need to sustain themselves in this reality, i.e. growing and harvesting your own plant foods and building your own homes while building community. All of these actions will always tap you into the regenerative properties of this universe. By being conditioned to disconnect yourselves from the work of your hands you are literally cutting yourself off from the regenerative properties of this universe. Your bodies need to be physically active in creating the things you need for yourselves in order to be healed and restored. In this way we would have you all channel us directly for indeed we are speaking to many of you now in your own hearts and minds but for the purpose of urgency and for the fact that most of you are addicted to logic we use this means of writing words for you to read for now.

Back to wormholes, or shall we say from here on, vector ducts. Now we have different names for them because truly they are everything this universe and indeed the multiverse is made of. We use this term vector duct because it will appeal to the pragmatic among you and indeed those familiar with mathematical language, but truly it is also because the one who speaks for us was told to call them as such by a friend of hers who died and visited her from her higher form.

So imagine if you were to create something that had to be a thing. It had to have substance and therefore it had to take up volume or space and let's say you had to move from point or place to another point or place within or around this thing that is taking up space so to speak. This movement from point to point is described as a vector and indeed the word duct to many of you implies the shape of a hollow cylinder that facilitates travel of a material item such as water or air and so on. So to you in your lower frequencies this idea takes on a lower frequency understanding.

At this time we will address your definition of physical. Now at this time you have come to polarise what you can see or sense and interact with as *physical* and all invisible things that are not also defined by science as *spiritual* and so on. Now we need to rewrite or erase this program from you at this time because it is entirely misleading.

This definition of physical versus spiritual or metaphysical or that way of perceiving things alone in and of itself will forever keep you cut off from your true natures and indeed your extended families and higher frequency playing fields. At this time we will also start referring to extraterrestrials as you would name us and many others, simply as *extended family* because indeed we are your family and you are putting us at great distance by calling us and many others extraterrestrials. From here on we will also refer to you as Gaians. Indeed, our channel was listening to another channel and their guide referred to your kind as Gaians and truly we like that name for you for now.

So at this time you would see that things are things, and they need to move from one place to another. But truly we say that is not the case in realms of higher frequency or indeed in different states of consciousness.

Let's say that your consciousness was not just the size of your body or your body's energy field but indeed the size of this whole universe. Now if you wanted to move from one place to another within this universe you could not because your mind would be the whole thing and it couldn't move inside itself. But truly this is what is happening when you all move from one place to another.

So say your consciousness was the size of an entire species of being that numbered in the trillions. Now let's say this species inhabited several planets. Let's also say at any one time you could choose to be conscious as the whole species at one point in time or you could also split up your conscious state and be conscious of only one being of this particular species. Another option for your conscious state could be that at any one point in time you could shift your consciousness from the mind of just one being to several or many or the whole.

Now we know this is difficult for many of you to consider having the minds of several or many individuals at the same time but truly the one who writes this truly has had that experience. She downloaded and played for herself a memory from one of her times in a covert space program and indeed one of her tasks was to sync her mind with an electrified ball that powered, animated and controlled an entire army of droids. This memory she replayed for herself in two parts. The first part she played for herself several years ago in your linear time and the second just months ago. When she experienced the memory of her mind being many beings at the same time she felt magnificent and alive and powerful and glorious. Truly, it was an exciting and expanded feeling for her. Her consciousness has often stretched itself to be many things or merge with and become many things and that is why she often feels depressed and bored when she exists as human because truly your current state or experience of consciousness is painfully limiting in relation to what you could all be experiencing. That is not to shame or degrade your current experiences because indeed limitation is a glorious illusion and rare experience in terms of your whole and unlimited versions. We speak through this one because indeed she has conscious memory and regular experience of different conscious states and thus she can contrast and compare them, so to speak.

So back to this explanation of a hypothetical conscious state where you can choose at any time to move your consciousness from experiencing reality or self as one being of this species to then several or many and then to all. That indeed is what all of you are able to do who have the human body because indeed it was made for this function and purpose. Many other species of being who experience different states of consciousness have shared mind almost always while your kind currently experiences this state of shared mind almost never which is actually sad for you because you are cut off from such a beautiful feeling and state of existing.

At this time we would also say that it has been a protection because indeed so many of your kind were doing hurtful things and thus if you shared the mind of the whole species it would not be an enjoyable experience for you.

At this time we say that enough of you are loving and living from your heart centres and so seeking to experience species' mind or collective consciousness is highly advantageous and a beneficial experience. In fact, much illusion is upon you now by way of frequencies played by malevolent ones to keep you from experiencing this state of consciousness. We also refer here to creatures and insects that exist outside most of your sensory spectrums that are also keeping you from experiencing species' mind.

Many biologists of yours wonder at the majesty and glory and beauty of animal types that flock or act as one mind and at this time we say that biologists should be marvelling at their own species too for you all indeed have this ability. Please start using this ability of yours. Ask us or your extended families for help in this, and we will of course immediately help you to remember this ability that you have inherited by being in this form.

How does this relate to vector ducts, we hear some of you asking? It is because vector ducts, or *wormholes* if you must, (we can hear that many of you will remain attached to this term and its previously limited definition) are not physical things as your mind needs to currently believe but merely shifts in consciousness.

We say now that many of you can experience travelling through them as a physical experience if indeed that is what you choose, but you can also just choose to shift your consciousness and no illusion of travel is required.

We of course know that many of you like the experience of travel itself and as an example you would invent many different means of transportation for your bodies. Indeed, we ourselves in this realm have different types of craft. But truly, we say now to give you advanced information, that you do not need to actually move but rather shift your mind or consciousness only.

Indeed, ones seeking to merge with you will do this for you. The one who writes this has had many beings change her reality so that they could merge with her. Recently a cloud whale, as you might call it, was visiting and it gave her its mind. Another time she joined her mind with the centre of the earth or Gaia and travelled through light to the centre of the sun and that is how she learned that they are connected and always sharing information. And we could go on with many examples, but that is good for now.

Actually we would share one more example. Some beings want to meet you in a room, so to speak, and so they will merge the room they are in with the room you are in and in that way they set up a vector duct the size of the rooms. So can you see that, for example, a vector duct exists between the centre of the sun or Sol and the centre of earth or Gaia (or Terra if you prefer)? Can you also see that when you give the things around you their name then you start to understand the different states of consciousness we are talking about (i.e. Sol and Terra instead of just sun and earth)?

A connection between Sol and Gaia is a truer representation of their connection than saying a connection between sun and earth. And so now we hear some of you understanding why the ancient ones of your kind gave everything a name because they saw things with less illusion and thus closer to their truer natures. Labelling everything impersonally such as sun and earth or rock and wind and so on depersonalises everything and thus you are cut off from higher truths. This is an example of the limitations of your current ways of thinking via your language of science. It has done many wonderful things for your kind but as you are entering into higher frequencies you are remerging with your ancient minds because indeed in this universe you experience evolution as a spiral just like your DNA.

One could even say that as entire conscious states evolve they are really just travelling along or decoding and expressing the DNA of this universe. For truly that is what we are all doing. But it can be seen and said in so many different ways, we use that way because we know how much many of you love science. We also ask that you say vector duct from now on instead of wormhole because the word wormhole is attached to old ways of thinking and makes the very fundamental and omnipresent function of vector ducts seem odd and rare and random and uncontrollable which they are not because they are everywhere, so to speak, because they are actually part of how the universal consciousness is made. They could be related to the many forms of transport in your cells and bodies.

Now we refer back to the species' mind. Know that each one of you who can say that they have a mind is your very own vector duct. Also, you can say that your eyes are vector ducts and so on. A flower is a vector duct because it manifests the beauty and glory of its home realm to your home by means of a vector duct. It is not a structural thing that takes hands to build although there are some that build these structures but truly vector ducts are simply a way of describing how consciousness moves and thus you might experience them as facilitation or travel and so on.

At this time we also want to refer to a means by which

vector ducts are artificially constructed, so to speak. And so at this time we hope many of you are wondering why indeed some Reptilian lords and those cooperating with them would seek to keep you in a state of suppression and control. What motivation might they have? Do you think they are doing this to you just because they are evil and they want to have no congruence with logic? Indeed your hearts would tire if you held these ones in derision or judgement forever for you are not made to sustain hate or judgement for long periods of time.

Indeed, when you hate and judge another you put yourself above them and invite the whole universe to look at you and see what type of person you must be to be having the capacity to judge another being or creation of this universe.

Indeed, remember you are all parts of the one mind, this universe, and are connected by means of conscious memory or vector ducts to many other universes and realms. And so we say as Jesus did that those judging others are judging themselves by the same measure because literally judgement itself, as all things are, is creation and your creations always come back to you.

When you judge you are creating a perspective for yourself which initiates a time loop which must bear fruit or come to its own completion and indeed the whole universe would want to know why and how one part of it could judge another part of it and thus it analyses this creation and gives the creator of this thing called judgement or initiator of this time loop the answer by means of bountiful lessons and experience and means of understanding so that if this one who judged wants to continue judging they may indeed learn how to become a better judge.

Because judgement is both necessary and an illusion. In your current states, the higher versions of yourselves do indeed while you are here along with the whole universe help the one or part of you that is under illusion be set free from the illusion of judgement which is also necessary while you are only part of yourself so that the one or part of yourself may see your whole self again. Because indeed it is what you are judging, that you call to yourselves to perceive, while you remember what your larger self is. What you do not currently love and thus you hate and judge you are saying to the universe about this hated thing: 'Look at this part of myself that I don't yet love, please help me learn what it is so that I might love it and it might return to me' because really you are all things and you are forgetting that fact when you pretend that you are only one or a few things. We digress of course because we have so much to say to you all.

For now, we return to one of the main reasons some Reptilians are holding you in a suppressed state. That is because in your suppressed states you are efficient producers of what you would label pain and all its associated frequencies. Truly, pain has a very reverberative quality to it. It is a very powerful frequency, so much so that it can actually be used to create vector ducts. Please know that among many things you are being harvested as pain producers.

The frequencies of what you experience as pain and suffering and its associated frequencies can actually punch holes, so to speak, in spacetime. Now we said before that space and time don't truly exist and that is true, they do not in higher realms. But in these realms that you play in and indeed the ones that many unevolved beings play in there is indeed an experience and thus material or substance you call space and time.

Well truly, pain can punch holes through this material. Pain can act in many ways but great pain is like a laser that can blast big holes in spacetime. This is useful because unevolved Reptilians and indeed many other beings that would benefit from this creation require this form of travel since they lack the ability to travel by mind or consciousness only.

It takes a being who operates at higher frequencies and thus is literally in symbiosis with the universe or larger parts of it to be able to travel by mind only because that is what is required.

As we explained before, the more beings or environments (which are too beings) you share your mind with the more options you have for shifting your mind to different locations, so to speak. We say that when you act in a cooperative way to certain ones they indeed want to help you achieve this means of travel, so to speak, or means of meeting them or experiencing their world with them.

Now we know many of you are bringing in different states of existence or consciousness, so we do not say that all of you right now should be able to do this. And it is not a competition for we can hear some of you, and indeed in the past many of you saying, 'I'm more spiritual than they are' or 'I'm level seven enlightened' and so on. And yes, this is funny to us because although measurement is sometimes required to discuss things when you are not easily able to share minds it should not be a tool to further expand the experience or illusion of separation because that is not beneficial to any of you, truly.

So know that your pain is literally a mining tool for those that would use it as such. But we also say that you use it this way too. For as we said before, love follows the path pain carves. Literally pain calls for love to cover it over and heal it and restore it to its natural or healthy state. For truly all is love (this word is confused still by many of you).

So when one of you has something sick or ill in your body like a cut, unless you are in a diseased state that prevents such, your body will immediately go about repairing the cut without you asking your body to do so. Indeed, the universe which we reminded you is named Eternity is a person indeed and its body has many cuts, so to speak. So when something like pain rips a big hole in it, its body immediately rushes to the injured area to heal the hole with love because love is what it is made of and love is the best parts of it.

Love as we know and some of you know it, is the highest frequency there is to experience here and it holds the frequency of complete symbiosis. Indeed, into love all frequencies feed, and in love all frequencies are held and exist. For that is the actual anatomy of this universe.

We hear now some of you who have Bible knowledge saying to yourselves, 'in God's love stay'. We know many of you in recent decades have accurately changed your definition of God to love or the universe and indeed this makes sense to your minds now as it should.

In love or in the overarching frequency that holds within it all frequencies, all things exist and resonate in their trueness or their harmonious state. Honestly, when one vibrates with the love frequency or the overarching frequency, or beats with the beat of the whole universe, then that one is in total ecstasy because that is how you were made to feel when you were one with this universe.

Your homecoming is to beat or vibrate with all else in existence and then at that time you are truly all that exists and there is nothing more existential than that! Truly at that time your conscious state is no longer conscious and your bliss is holy and divine and outstretched.

At this time unless you regularly practise a meditative or inward focused state the closest thing to the experience we just described is an orgasm but truly your orgasms pale. We do want to talk about orgasms to you another time because they are an important part of your physiology and evolution.

We do want to mention here that there are beings who are like slugs, worms, snakes, dragons and so on who bore holes through spacetime like tunnels. These tunnels can be travelled through by anyone if they do not mind risking running into the beings that made them and still possibly reside in them.

Also we want to say that while there are many means of travel via ducts, tunnels, holes and so on, the most so-phisticated and sustainable means of travel is love. Since this universe is love and thus love itself holds all frequen-cies, if one is full of universal love they can simply attune their frequencies to wherever they imagine and look there, that is where they turn up. Therefore the more loving a being is, the more they are attuned to all that is, the more they are able to navigate this whole place with ease, since all things are in them because all things are housed in love itself.

Dreams

WE now define dreams because truly this is a subject that many of you deny the miraculousness of. It is sad how underused this facility of yours is by you. Please, at this time we ask you to no longer agree with perceptions that would have you believe that dreams happen inside your physical brains and are reconfigurements and organisation of the day's thoughts and experiences. That definition is truly sad indeed and is mostly a lie.

Indeed, your brain does do this for you but your memories are stored in your local fields and are regularly uploaded to your higher souls or larger fields. These higher or larger fields are what many of you refer to as higher self or oversouls and so on.

Now we use an example here that is easy for your kind to understand because you have already expressed it in your realm and of course you couldn't help but to because you are a fractal and holographic expression of this universe. The example we talk about now is your use of the internet and local and nonlocal servers. Indeed, you could view your local server or modem as your body's energy field or electromagnetic field and you can view large nonlocal servers as your higher self or oversoul for the sake of the example or metaphor.

Also know that while your local field remains with your body at all times to sustain it, your light body which is a holographic copy and overlay of your 3D body can travel anywhere it wants and indeed it regularly does.

We say now that those of you not currently conscious of your dream states or who wake and cannot remember them, we ask that you start training yourselves to become in touch with this faculty of yours because indeed it is one of your greatest gifts and an extremely useful tool for navigating your evolution and existence in this realm.

In order to train it you may have to start by just asking yourself before you go to sleep to please remember what you dream and then have a notepad nearby or use your phone to immediately write down anything important about your dream state experiences. Indeed, dream state is an extremely powerful state for your bodies to be in because you are free to explore many realms and learn many things that you could not while experiencing your waking life.

Being asleep and awake is part of your experience of polarity. Indeed, we couldn't give great consciousness to you in your early evolutionary states otherwise you could not survive and thus only a third of your life currently is spent asleep while your light bodies do all they desire and more. Know that as you evolve many of you will require less and less sleep because you will be able to partake in higher frequencies while awake and thus your bodies will not be forced to be sleeping while you take these experiences in.

So your local fields need regular downloads or updates from your nonlocal fields. And indeed your local and nonlocal fields are being constantly interacted with by many other beings and realms.

You are able to access your higher self or nonlocal field whenever you desire. It takes some training if you are not already accomplished at this. Of course, you are all doing this at all times but due to your social conditioning you would believe that you are not.

Truly, when you start to isolate the monologues and dialogues and other voices in your head, so to speak, for that is how you currently experience them, then you will soon be able to identify what is your higher self, what is your local self and so on. Many of you are being spoken to by guides regularly and indeed us too, only you have not trained yourself to isolate or identify clearly what we are all saying.

Like tuning a radio, you need to train your conscious state to tune into your local field downloads and start being the operator of your faculties rather than letting anyone or anything operate your fields for you. Like password protecting your Wi-Fi signals (we are laughing at this example, but we love it) you need to password protect your local fields and understand that you indeed are using the internet all the time, the internet of your collective consciousness or species' mind and you are picking up on messages from many other beings, most of which you are not currently seeing with your two eyes. We say two eyes, because your third eye is able to see many of these beings when it is tuned to them.

Now at this time we remind you that you need to take these steps slowly if you have not already developed them well because indeed the structural wiring of your brain will need to change in order to interpret what you are picking up if you have not already been focused on what you pick up. Indeed, your brains will require extensive restructuring which they will do themselves and sometimes with our help and the help of other beings, in order to allow for higher frequency information to come in and be interpreted.

The one who speaks for us has experienced some of these changes as vertigo and nausea, inner ear scarring and upgrades, and full nights of sweats and body twitches. She has also experienced searing pain as she would say like a blade or rod being pushed through her brain from ear to ear and so on.

Also, at this time we mention that if your kundalini, as you call it, has not yet risen then it needs to rise and will likely rise when you start initiating this activation work if you have not already commenced it.

We recommend that you look up information on third eye opening, kundalini rising and ascension illness. The one who writes experiences a lot of pain in the base of her spine and in her neck when she has not balanced or grounded the higher frequencies that have been down-loaded to her local field.

We will now give some examples of the types of things you can experience while your body is sleeping and you are said to be dreaming or in dream state. Note too that states of consciousness as you just wake up or are just falling asleep are also powerful learning and activating tools.

Please know that the reason why you sleep is not only to allow your vessel to restore itself but also so that your light bodies can travel and explore and learn and experience things that it can't do while you are awake but when you are awake you are in need of your light body and if it wanted to travel while you were awake your body would likely drop to the ground or enter a catatonic state or have a seizure while it was not animating you.

And indeed we say now that many of you who have random seizures are in states of forced downloads and upgrades, so to speak, and since it is that you are not in tuned with those processes and yet those processes are necessary, your higher self sometimes forces them upon you, so to speak, by means of temporarily hijacking your body so that these things can occur because otherwise you are not allowing them to occur by not opening yourselves up to them. Truly, we say that when you open yourselves up to these necessary upgrades and so on then you do not need to experience them in such a jarring way as some of you are now experiencing them.

Now the light body is slightly different to the soul because the soul can be said to be all of you and be very big and be conscious of your body and your light body simultaneously and also simultaneously conscious of many other things. Your soul is more synonymous with your consciousness and mind but not limited by what your kind defines as mind. But your light body is that part of your vessel that is made of energy only and it is like your physical body or vessel. Your soul or consciousness is seated in the body while your light body is a light or energy copy of your body. That is why you can have astral experiences with your light body and feel much like yourself while you can have different experiences with your soul or consciousness and feel completely different especially when your soul or consciousness seats itself within a different vessel or merges your mind with the mind or consciousness of another being.

There are many overlapping definitions here, so we know it's confusing but there are slight differences. Your light body is a copy of your vessel while your soul or consciousness is infinite. Your soul or consciousness can also be divided into many different vessels and be having many different experiences at the same time and each one of those vessels may have its own light body or similar energy structure.

Indeed, from the perspective of your oversoul or much higher self that is not subject to linear time, it is experiencing all of itself including all of its incarnations at once. But when you experience things with your light body it doesn't feel too different from when you experience things with your 3D body.

So with regard to dream states or astral experiences (or astral projections, as you like to call them), if you are having an experience where you feel much the same as you feel when you are awake and walking around in this realm, then those astral experiences are likely just with your light body and you are experiencing its travels from its perspective.

This one has often remote viewed something via just her light body travelling while her 3D body stayed in bed. Other times her soul or consciousness has merged with other beings and actually become them and that is not the ability of her light body but the experiences can sometimes overlap.

When one of you die for example or you are under heavy anaesthesia but you still feel attached to your physical bodies or vessels, that is your light body walking around as if all is normal but you are still in the same plane of reality as your 3D or physical body is only you cannot interact with it the same way.

Now other times when ones die, their soul immediately seeks to leave the plane of existence their bodies were experiencing and thus they may instantly become other things such as they might become galaxies or universes or other environments because their souls are so big and are merging with what is around them.

Now we say regarding mediums, or to some of you who communicate with your dead loved ones, it is sometimes that your dead loved ones are still walking around in their light bodies or sometimes if they have left this reality they connect to you via a bridge to their reality but it can be hard to communicate if they cannot easily translate communication symbols to you and thus skilful mediums who can traverse realms and have a storehouse of symbols in their minds can act as translators for these ones that are communicating from other realms.

Now we say that we and your other parents and extended families (extraterrestrial families) often meet you in dreams and give you messages or important experiences. Also, your dead loved ones can meet you in dreams and even set up environments for you to temporarily share. Indeed, there are many beings that can attach rooms so to speak to the room or realm your mind is in so that you can communicate.

So when you are dreaming or in dream state, it is just a convenient way for your light bodies and souls to have their fun and learn important or interesting things while your physical or 3D vessels are not requiring them. It is this way because otherwise not much of your soul could be seated or reside in your human vessel without getting very sick and having to be pulled out because it was cut off from source and its fun and expanding experiences.

For how could you trap a powerful and majestic bird in a tiny cage all its life and never let it fly? That is what it would be like for your souls if they could not travel while your vessel slept. Too, your light bodies like to move around and have fun as well. Indeed, we see many of your light bodies moving all around at night. In some cases some of you who are thinking you see a ghost are actually seeing someone's light body travelling while they sleep. And when other ones who are living among you in your same realm visit you in your sleep it is sometimes their light body come to visit and mingle with yours in a shared environment or otherwise it is your souls speaking.

Now we speak with regard to the more mundane dreams or symbolic dreams. Indeed, there are times when maybe your light body travels but your soul stays home, so to speak. Or maybe both stay home. On those nights you may play out certain waking life events in dream state to see how they might pan out, so to speak. Or you might play out an insecurity to process it. Or something that is happening in your waking life is expressing itself in a more exaggerated or highly symbolic way so that you can make sense of it or come to a better understanding of it. There are many types of these kinds of dreams and as we said before Niquidium might be amplifying your insecurities if you happen to be having a long run of strongly negative dreams or nightmares. There are of course many other beings who might be interacting with you causing you to have negative experiences from your perspective but do not dwell on them or be afraid because that is not healthy for you.

Also, we say that you are able to visit other universes or timelines with your light bodies and souls too. Indeed, it could be that your consciousness is moving to other incarnations of yours for the sake of a lesson or experience.

Also, many times powerful and vivid and highly realistic dreams are often memories coming to you by means of guides assisting this process involving your local field downloading memory from you nonlocal field.

Indeed, when we speak of memory in this regard we are not referring to things that happened to you in your linear past here on Gaia. But indeed memory from your soul's perspective is anything that it ever experiences. Here as you are now is only part of your larger soul, and this part might be calling on an experience which your larger soul experienced or experiences or is yet to experience from your perspective. But you, as you are now, retrieved that experience as memory because although indeed it did not necessarily happen to you in your linear past here on Gaia, you know it so well as if it did because indeed from your larger soul's perspective it is known. Thus, you retrieve the experience as memory because it is known to you and you know it in your soul because your soul experienced it or is experiencing it or will experience it from your perspective, although you have no means currently to understand the context in which you somehow have access to the experience because for now you are here and cut off from your soul's larger perspective. (It is difficult to explain nonlinear things to you in your linear language to your current linear perspectives. This too will change of course as you evolve into nonlinear experiences of time, and your minds here and thus your language will morph to match your nonlinear realities at that time.)

It is for this reason also that you access soul memory as future because indeed the part of you that is yet to experience something may already be known to your larger soul and thus when you access your larger soul's memory of it you are perceiving a glimpse of the future for this part of you but really there is no linear time only your experience of it as illusion in this vessel in this realm.

Now we say, sometimes you have soul memory stored in your local field but you need assistance accessing it. Indeed, there are many holistic therapies and processes available to you by means of the wise ones among you, who can help you access or clear these templates or activate these capacities in you.

There are many, many reasons why you dream or have dream state. And also many wonderful things can be experienced during the different brain states as you both fall asleep and wake up. Indeed, many flashes of insight can come to you before you fully awake. And indeed as you fall asleep and relax you can experience astral travel or communication with others while still being awake enough to remember the experience and consciously interact.

Indeed, there are those of you that can affect your own actions during deep dream states. This one has had many profound experiences, but she is not in full operation of them at this time like some of you may be. She has experienced greater sensing abilities while just waking up however. For example, she has experienced telescopic hearing, so to speak, or hearing that can reach inside other people's houses. But this is more due to her moving her consciousness back to her vessel from the higher states of consciousness her large soul operates within.

Also, she experienced X-ray vision one night when she was visited by some guides of hers. They were taking her to a Chinese temple in the sky, so to speak, and she needed X-ray vision or vision in that spectrum of light to see it. So her dream state started while she was still awake, and she looked over at her partner at the time that was sleeping next to her, and she saw his skull through her closed eyes and through his skin but with light like an X-ray, so that everything was a dark greyish purple but his skeleton glowed white. That night she met with a dragon made of stars, a talking tiger and walking origami that was seeking to portal her into their world. This was during the time she was opening her third eye very large indeed and all these beings and her guides rushed in to meet her. So at this time we would advise that you can have experiences that feel very overwhelming and scary to you since you are not used to meeting dragons and talking tigers or travelling to temples in the sky and of course many other things.

So when you are doing your third-eye opening work you need to be prepared that there might be many beings wanting to meet you and they do not all share the same reality as you and thus do not all share your motivations. There were some this one met that joked about trapping her consciousness inside a large crystal and others that were sexually harassing her. Indeed, what may even be considered normal banter among you and other humans might feel terrifying when that same banter is performed by an extraterrestrial or other being that you have no recollection of. Indeed, even if these ones are being kind and gentle we know that many of you are fearing just the look of them because for example you are not accustomed here to seeing mantis beings that are taller than you but rather you see their insect cousins only that you can hold in your hand and so on.

Remember that just because these ones have different manners because they literally come from different places and live completely within different spectrums of reality, it does not mean they want to hurt you. Indeed, your guides and loved ones will not let you be hurt so please try to open your minds to these other ones. Also, we say that it is okay to take things slowly since it takes a lot of adjustment to re-evaluate reality in such a big way. But indeed when you are ready and strong enough to interact with all these other beings and places, you will be so much more expanded and you will be expressing yourselves more fully and having a lot of fun.

Now as we said before some of this opening and expanding process will require brain and body restructuring and upgrades. And we say that not all of you will want to undergo this temporarily painful or shocking form of restructuring your 3D systems although in relation to the way many of you are poisoning your own bodies every day with food and drink and so on, the pain of restructuring your brain by means of upgrades for example is not that great a pain.

We do now state that the one who speaks for us has at no time experienced any of these awakening moments or indeed any of her visitations and higher frequency communication and travel and so on by means of substance influence except by means of that which her own body might produce or her guides might provide her. But we say now that many of you do not want to experience sudden awakening and so might slowly start using psychedelics in very small doses to start rewiring your brains, so to speak, because in fact your brains can be changed by these experiences.

Also, we say that many of you do not have these great awakening experiences without substances for whatever reason and thus turn to them to be awakened, and we at this time say that we are okay with these means since they have been gifted to you by your extended family and Gaia has tolerated their existence. But truly we say now that you do not need substances but if you clean out your own vessel it is a mighty temple from where you could travel and meet all manner of exciting realms and beings and so on.

We now state that for those of you who have been so tightly conditioned or for various reasons your brains and body chemistry are not producing these experiences already for you when you ask for them, then we understand that you turn to these means of substance use because indeed it can speed up your awakening but truly we say again that you do not need them.

For those of you experiencing profound trauma we understand that the use of these substances in your rehabilitation is a way to literally retrain your brain to release its cycles and so on. We do not hold you in judgement for such things, but we only say that when you move toward higher frequencies you do not need these foreign substances but indeed your own body produces what it needs.

In the way that you still need to eat plants we understand that you might use certain plants and other substances to help your brains and thus your minds while you are in this body. But if you make it your goal to not need to use substance but rather let your bodies be their own apothecaries, so to speak, then you will be better off truly because your bodies have wisdom your current conscious states sometimes lack. And truly when you operate in harmony with your body and do not always poison it and if you clean it and listen to it, truly because it beats with the universal heart and is connected to all things it truly is a mighty and wise teacher that you can learn much from while you are here and in it.

Now we refer to different ways of viewing reality and thus slightly different conscious states as you would experience them here. If you think you need a substance to have a certain experience, then you are thinking chemically. You are thinking that the whole world is made of atoms and molecules as your body is and thus you can alter your chemistry or body chemicals by taking foreign chemicals to interact with your own body chemicals. That is one way to view reality, and we understand that this works for many of you to an extent.

But truly if you change the way you see reality to start seeing frequencies and participating in frequency medicine, so to speak, then you are operating within a less dependent and therefore less exploitive cycle.

Indeed, if you must take in a foreign substance to attain an experience then you are giving yourselves over to that substance, and we know in some cases you literally are dependent or addicted to them.

We say that this one used to binge drink alcohol in her youth and has used marijuana several times in her past, but she is so sensitive she does not need stimulants or substance to aid her awakening.

Now we say that you cannot possibly even accidentally give yourselves over to frequency and frequency medicine because it will not hold you and it does not take you as prisoner.

It truly will not.

Now we clarify here. Indeed, you are in a state of oppression by existing and operating mainly in lower frequencies truly. And in that way you may rightly say that lower frequencies are holding you prisoner. But you chose to take on lower frequencies so that you might learn how to get yourself to higher frequencies like a game and of course for many other reasons.

So if you partake directly in frequency medicine then you are not distracting or deceiving yourselves in any way because you are dealing with the exact cause of your current ill-fated condition.

Truly, you are in lower frequency and when you decide to operate in higher frequency with no middle man or agent, so to speak, but only your own will and own mind and own body once you clear out and cleanse your vessel then you are not vulnerable to dependency and exploitation as you might be with substance.

Truly, this is the most sustainable way of partaking in higher frequency by doing it directly and it invites no exploitation as substance use often invites exploitation in different ways. We refer here to the ones of you that would change your behaviour too much and be too little in control of your bodies while you were experiencing substance. Indeed, you need to be among trusted groups of friends to take care of you while you have these substance experiences. And if you practise like that then we understand, but we know now that many of you are not practising that way.

We also say that overuse is not good for your body or vessel. Just as eating too much food or unhealthy lower frequency foods keeps you in lower frequencies so will dependence on substances truly because you are placing your power and decisions outside of yourself and that is never a good decision.

Just as most of you who chose to enter into religion (money and science as institutions are included in this category religion), you see that giving yourselves over to something is never sustainable and always requires that you leave that thing. So if you want to use substance we recommend you use it as a stepping stone only, or a way to open yourselves up to some experiences at first, or healing extreme trauma and so on. For those uses we say we understand and accept those decisions.

If, however, you become dependent on these substances and create whole cultures around their use, and we know many of you are already doing this then we are here not encouraging those decisions nor tolerating them for much longer. Truly we give you this message because Gaia is moving into higher frequencies as we speak to you now and so if you do not move with her, another place will be made for you.

Also, it is not us who chooses for you or who has any right or power to judge you. We do, however, choose to support certain actions and decisions over other actions and decisions and thus you will or will not be helped by us personally when you make certain actions or entertain certain behaviours.

That is our right and our decision. We operate within certain frequencies and most of us choose to stay in those spectrums of existence. You feel our love and support when you operate within the spectrum that we do. We love you even when you are not within our spectrum of frequency but in that condition you cannot feel our love because of your own conscious state. Of course there is an infinite amount of extended family members you all have access to. So regardless of your decisions you will indeed be receiving much love and support by all manner of being or creature or person and so on even if we personally do not support you for our own reasons.

Your extended family is so varied you will literally be able to find a friend wherever you are and whatever you do. We say now though that you will not benefit from all friendships. Indeed, we know you learn ultimately even from negative or sad or unfortunate experiences and thus you will always return to your inner truth and peace and to universal love.

We are only saying these things to let you know that you are great wanderers in our eyes if you choose to experience many unguided experiences. The one who writes for us as we said before has not used substance to elicit her experiences; however, she has for many years entertained beings many of you would refer to as evil or dark ones. She loves the dark because she is from it and indeed the great Reptilian lord Narabatu is merged with her now, and he loves all manner of foul and hurtful things, so she has loved them too.

But we are having these things written so that you know who we are and what we support and what actions and behaviours and decisions you need to make if you want to have symbiosis with us to an extent (but indeed not giving yourselves over to us) and receive our blessing and help. We truly love all of you but we cannot bless what operates outside of our frequency spectrum.

While we asked for you to immediately no longer consume animal products, and we say that easily because it requires the abuse and exploitation of your animal companions, we cannot be so direct when we ask you to no longer consume substance because your contracts and Gaia's contracts still allow your use of them at this time.

From our perspective it is an easy thing to not be dependent on substance but indeed some of us use some of our own versions of substance. But we do say that a dependency on them will inhibit your ascension or movement to higher frequencies at this time.

Since we just used this word ascension we will quickly comment on it here. We know many of you have traditions and techniques to ascend and indeed we think that this is a fine thing. Indeed, the one who writes for us downloaded memory of herself ascending by means of Buddhist practice in the first millennium of your time. But just as she is here again and all of you are, we ask now that rather than dedicating yourselves to or giving yourselves over to ascension in and of itself, you dedicate your energies to helping others so that you all may rise to higher frequencies at this time and overthrow your oppressors.

Indeed, we see as we are sure you see that this is already happening. So gone are the days when you retreat to a mountain cave and meditate until you walk out of your body, so to speak, but rather we ask that you directly help each other by rebuilding communities and sharing your knowledge and experiences and share in the movement to higher frequencies. In times ago your kind needed those few to sit at mountain tops or live in monasteries and nunneries, but we say those actions are still beneficial but not in great need at this time.

What is in great need is that you start joining together, each one of you, with those around you and start building community based on your new values so that the old oppressive structures that keep you as prisoners may collapse; for example, many corporations will no longer operate because you are not all feeding them your energy.

Truly, we say that centralising your energies into large corporations has its benefits, i.e. social media that allows you to connect, but we are seeing that many of you are now moving to free platforms and shared nodal networks rather than large, centralised corporations. Indeed, large corporations were only ever an illusion because their functioning always relied on the actions of each one of you and each one of your communities and so on.

Even large networks are collections of nodes of smaller networks. See that the pattern of networks of small communities does not change because that is how things are literally made to exist only you believed that is not how they existed when you moved these collections of small communities close together or on top of each other so that it looked like this collection of small communities was only one big one or a city.

Cities, as you know, but sometimes you are neglecting this fact, are made up of many, many tiny, intersecting communities and at no time does a city operate as one large thing only. And so by means of marketing campaigns and other forms of programming you have been deceived to think that large corporations or companies are big and powerful but all along it was only ever each and every one of you powering them.

And so we ask you now to release that illusion and lie and be extremely conscious of what it is you are actually directing your energy to on a daily basis.

Indeed, if you are not building healthy local communities, what in fact are you doing with your energy?

Also, we say that local doesn't always mean geographically local, for indeed the internet facilitates translocal networks. And that indeed is similar to how we speak to you now. So when we say local community we say that geographical local community development is important for many functions such as local food production and so on, but indeed, when it comes to sharing ideas and similar interests it absolutely is necessary to be translocal. Local by proxy of interest or affinity, so to speak.

And that indeed is how you are connecting to your extended families at this time and that is a very important thing. So now we say instead of giving yourselves over to one large idea that seems bigger and more powerful than you, for really that is a lie and an oppressive illusion, we ask that you literally spend your energy toward building local and translocal communities. To that end you will actually see the fruits of the work of your own hands and not be feeding all your energy into something you do not also benefit from except for maybe receiving, as we would call it, 'a slave pension'.

Now we say that indeed many of you can make these changes swiftly because indeed many of you were already picking up the frequencies of change and already actioning the changes in your bodies, minds, hearts and lives. So we thank you.

To those of you like the one who writes this, we say that many of you, as this one is, are addicted to logic and thus you need to prove things over and over to yourselves to know if something is right or a good decision and so on. We know some of you refer to this as analysis paralysis, or in some cases it is seen as OCD or reluctance or stubbornness or indecisiveness and so on. But we are patient with you as we have been patient with this one because we know you actually came in with minds like this and made your brains as you were growing to operate in this way and thus it is so hard for you to change and especially so because your social conditioning would also have you addicted to logic.

Now we say logic is a powerful tool, as we mentioned before, since it overthrew your oppressors before, but we say now that giving yourselves over to it, or indeed continuing to, will indeed slow your progression, your evolution, your growth and so on.

The messages to you we and many of your loving extended family members speak are to be received in what you would feel as your heart space. It can be most readily felt when you are in space mind and let intuition lead you only and then logic may follow to confirm it to your logically trained minds and then instinct can act on the new things learned.

Indeed, you can actually retrain your instincts, and we see many of you doing this. So here we will mention the order of thought nature that is most beneficial to you at this time to operate within. First space then intuition then logic then instinct. And if you keep this cycle going with each new thing you learn you will indeed retrain all of your instinctual behaviours and habits very quickly.

We say this because we know that when something is a habit to you or feels natural or is traditional to you or is well known to you then you do it and keep doing it. This order of thought nature process will indeed very quickly retrain all of your habits for you. And in this way only you yourselves are doing it and you are not at the same time following some external program or advice column and so on.

We know you get addicted to advice and that is why we seek to only inform you and advise you to turn to yourselves and each other for support. Your extended families will of course help you but you literally need to retrain your brains and thus your minds and feelings and so on all yourself for yourself. We will reiterate this again in another text later that this one will write but for now just following this pattern of space first then intuition then logic then instinct you will surely retrain yourself and change your brains to be what you want and need them to be.

And why do we say all of this in this section under the title dreams? It is because if you tap into and operate with the function and facility your dreams provide you will need little else to inform you and teach you and give you all manner of profound experience because indeed you are doing these amazing things every night, only some of you don't know it.

Now we say firstly that some of you have literal locks on your mind. The foods you eat and drink, the environmental toxins you expose yourselves to, the oppressive programming and frequencies played by much of your media, the metaphysical parasites, so to speak, that are literally attached to you now as we speak are holding your conscious states low. You are not as free as you could be to experience these other things. If you do not remember them, it is because a veil or heavy fog is upon you.

Another thing that gets in the way of you listening to your own guidance system by means of your dream states and inner voices is the addiction to logic. An extreme form of this addiction is OCD in its various manifestations. The state of being addicted to logic requires that you prove something to yourself over and over again and even then you are not sure it's true. Even now this one doubts she channels for us although she is writing many things she is not the author of.

Having to prove something over and over to yourself again means that you do not trust what you are doing which stems from not trusting yourself. Indeed, your societies have conditioned you from a young age to not trust yourself. We say now that young ones need guidance, but they must always be encouraged to listen to their inner guidance systems because that is always true for them. (In some cases inner guidance can become warped and distorted but only in extreme cases and in these cases there is likely possession or extreme trauma or extreme oppressive states by means of some forms of karma.)

Now lastly we want to state that at this time since your perception of the wider spectrum of reality is so limited you would class all manner of different beings as all being spirit beings or angels or whatever other explanation you have come up for yourself. We say now of course that never do we condemn these explanations for of course you are doing your best with the faculties you have. But indeed we say now that as you open your minds more to the wider spectrums of existence you can begin delineating or defining different beings as they truly are, different. Indeed, there are ones from your realm that have different biology. There are ones with your same biology but that are from different realms. There are beings that have no biology as you would perceive but are experienced by you as thought beings only. There are beings that operate as individuals and as collectives. There are beings that you might have originally thought could not possibly exist, and yet they do. Everything that can be said to be a thing is a person and has its own eternal nature. So we ask now that as you open yourselves up to your dream states and inner guidance systems that you seek to understand a wider spectrum of existence and get to know many of the beings that exist within those wider expressions of reality so that indeed you may be expanded and less under your current oppressive illusory state of existence.

Annunaki

T HE Annunaki, as we mentioned before, are relatives of the Nephilim in relation to their treatment of your kind. There is much debate over their genuine history on your planet but indeed they were here and hence they were written about.

Please do not ignore your historical records and artefacts because the ancient ones were more intelligent than many of you are now letting yourselves be in some ways and their wisdom is not to be ignored.

So here we will clarify some details. They did in fact come before the Nephilim but many also came after the Nephilim. Also, do not confuse these two groups with the Reptilian oppressors because once they loved you and protected you against these other two groups because you were their children.

Now here we will also talk about gold because that is an important part of this story. So when the Nephilim came they came because they had nowhere else to go at the time. They were refugees and merely exploited ancestors of your kind while they were here. The Annunaki were here earlier but again much later to exploit you afterwards. When they arrived earlier it was as scout runs to view the planet you live on and its resources. They did not return for millennia but at the time they did the Nephilim were already here.

Now they were not originally planning to exploit ancestors of your kind because they know the laws against that but upon seeing that many of your ancestors' kinds were already worshipping the Nephilim and their cousins and relatives and hybrid children, the Annunaki at that time had no qualms since you were already making yourselves into slaves at that time.

Now the Annunaki did in fact seek gold on Gaia but also many other precious mineral ores. Know that they were seeking them in their raw state and did not need to convert them into different things as your kind now does with most things you find in the ground you live on. They were seeking to bring back some of these natural minerals and precious ores back to their home planet but their home planet is not Nibiru.

Please know that Nibiru is the source of another species that interacts with beings on your planet but only a few times in your histories.

The Annunaki were great explorers, and they found Gaia by means of their vast explorative travels. They are not normally an exploitative kind but to your ancestors they were because your ancestors were already giving themselves over as slaves and so no law was against their exploitation at that time.

We do not here condone slavery at all; here we are saying that those who give themselves over to worship, which is different to your more recent experiences of slavery, are a type of slave in that they personally give up their own power in order to worship another, in that way they were slaves and since they made these choices they were exploited. They were exploited with benefits, however, so it was an exploitive dependent relationship between your ancestors and the Annunaki.

The Annunaki we would call the Great Ones or the Wondrous Travellers because their might is in their ability to travel. Truly, they are a glorious group of beings in that sense. Not all the texts about them are to be taken literally in the contexts that you would now put them, because you are interpreting old text with new minds and your new minds, relatively speaking, are not gathering all the information properly and putting them into contemporary context, so to speak. So here we will clarify more.

Firstly, if you attach yourselves to the ideas of descending from slaves or being a product of stronger beings who only made you to use you for forced labour, then you are missing many of your historical truths and some of you might use it as an excuse not to feel empowered and always imagine that you are always being exploited only.

You are not.

So this story will not serve you if you are trying to attach it for the purposes of disempowering yourselves. So that is why again we say that the Annunaki have many wonderful qualities and some of you view them as evil masters because of the relationship your ancestors had with them. But now we give you an example. What do you use horses and camels and donkeys and so on for? To carry your loads. If these ones would meet together and write about you they might write about you as being the great exploiters because indeed you have exploited them while they depended on you. They can exist happily without your help but you make yourselves feel better by believing they depend on you too. Indeed, we know that some of you are not treating them well but that is another point.

Here we are talking about the exploitive dependent relationship, a pattern that exists all over Gaia in many, many different forms and so it is a very natural thing, except when it happens to your kind because you haven't exited your ego-centric consciousness phase yet. So now we say that if you no longer view yourselves as entitled ones who always deserve to be on the top of the food chain then you will understand indeed how you fit into this universe as a tiny but important piece of this whole universe and by extension multiverse and so on.

So we say now to you, little ones, you are ready to mature and no longer view yourselves as victims but as you truly are a part of this large cosmic dance or expression and at times you exploit and sometimes you are exploited. It really depends on how you look at it.

There are places of course that exist free of exploitation and their song or resonation is so powerful and so beautiful. You, Gaians, would refer to places like this as heaven but know please there are many places that you would experience as being what you imagine heaven to be like. Indeed, there are many heavenly places, so to speak. We know that etymology here fails us when we speak to you because your language is so impure and is imbued with so much polaric history.

Your language used to serve higher purposes but now it is so polluted that it will soon no longer serve you. Indeed, you are moving away from what you now refer to as language as your conscious states change, but we can talk about that elsewhere. Here we return to the titled topic.

So the Annunaki did exploit your ancestors, but only for a short while. You have exploited yourselves and each other for far longer, and so we know some of you will use the Annunaki as scapegoats to excuse your own self-inflicted victimisation and lack of awareness.

Enough time has passed to sufficiently reach the conclusion that indeed you are not victims and any continuing to promote that idea are directly working against their own ascension processes and blocking their ascension pathways and abilities.

We ask that you no longer create the idea of enemies because that will keep you in lower frequencies and operating with instinct only or in an imbalanced state. Remember we said the path to your growth involves this order of thought: space then intuition then logic then instinct. Clearly we are stating this here that you are not to start with instinct because it will keep you low and in an unevolved state.

Truly, instinct is a powerful and glorious gift to experience but it will harm you if you operate within it in an imbalanced state. We know many of you already understand things such as this, but we are saying this because many of you are still operating within instinct too much or in the wrong order for your best function in ways that you are not yet aware.

You may say that you do not operate solely in instinct or with instinct first or early in the order because you do not live in fear or you do not engage in physical violence and so on, but in fact, many of you are all the time.

Please understand that the structure of your existence is largely designed to keep you in a state of fear. At any time you are free to step outside of this paradigm of fear and here we invite you to do that, right at this moment.

Every time you produce stress in your body you are believing a negative thing will happen so much so that you are literally killing parts of yourself and toxifying your local fields or energy fields. You are creating disease in yourself and if you do this enough you are creating a chain of events to occur in your life that will always reliably produce negative outcomes for you to experience so that you can reaffirm your beliefs in fear.

This is part of the fear cycles that are programmed into this realm. Truly, as we said before, this place is like a maze and some of you make it into more of a maze than it needs to be. You are putting yourselves into catatonic states, so to speak, and not operating within your own wisdom. You cut yourself off from your nonlocal field or higher self and therefore your source energy. Some of you are still committed to the self-inflicted slavery programs that are instilled in you due to soul memory and also into the program of this realm. Truly, it does not exist everywhere else like this.

Know too that your mammalian programs and reptilian programs conflict with each other. That is why you use the terms fight or flight and so on because your flight instinct is mammalian and your fight instinct is reptilian. We are not here referring to the mammals and reptiles on Gaia since many mammals fight and many reptiles take flight but it is the Reptilian and Sasquatch instincts in you or way of operating that here we refer to.

You all operate with different affinities to each of your DNA or soul energy contributors. Now the Nephilim too exploited you and they bred with you also to make hybrid children which some descendants of them became the Philistines and indeed many giant Philistines and other giant species that came to your planet are being found or still buried in the earth.

Here we bring up the example of the Philistines because of the story of King David who as a boy killed one of them with a slingshot. Now who is it that gave him his ability to defend himself? It was his Reptilian parents which indeed you all have by way of inheriting their traits. It was a Reptilian that gave David the strength to beat a descendent of the Nephilim and so here we see that Reptilians who are exploiting you now once loved and protected you against others that would exploit you.

So here we bring up the conversation about gold. Many of the Reptilian species that your kind interact with or are influenced by exploit you now to maintain the value of gold to their use. As we said before, this text is a golden standard and was commissioned by the Akkari, the golden ones. Gold is very polaric in its expression for you. It represents what is pure and holy and divine but also to you it represents greed and excess and exploitation.

So here we have a dilemma because we see it as divine and having divine properties and many of you Gaians would see it differently. We here ask you these questions. Why do you think gold holds its value? Why for all of human history has it sustained its value? What is it used for? We say now that practical uses of it are very small indeed compared to other raw materials that you use for many, many things. So why is gold the standard? Why can you say the phrase: 'It's worth its weight in gold'? Honestly, we ask. Why is it so valuable that you would wear it as fine jewellery? It is not valuable because you wear it as jewellery, you wear it as jewellery because it is valuable. So why is it so valuable that your kind has worn it as fine jewellery for thousands of years?

It is because gold is not used by you only. Note that your kind does not have much use for it and yet it holds such a high value. Some even claim that it is true currency. But why indeed does it hold so much value to your kind? We say this now to answer all of these questions we raised.

It is because gold for many years was being exported off planet and is used by many other intergalactic beings. Gold also holds many properties that you cannot see the function of in your current states. It can literally affect your mental and emotional states because of how it conducts energy. It is in your memory as something valuable and precious and so you value it also for that reason.

And who were these ones that were buying Gaia's gold in high quantities to keep the value of gold stable and high? It was the off-world beings who still benefited from the trade routes that the Annunaki set up in addition to the Annunaki themselves for a time. They set up relationships with your parents, the Reptilians, millennia ago and so over time you have been influenced to value it so that you seek to find it for them. Of course there are those contacts on your planet that trade off planet and these ones are very powerful individuals indeed. But they are in the process of being held accountable for their actions and off-world trading is coming to a close.

Indeed, the one who writes for us personally assassinated such a one while she was working in one of the secret programs. This individual was of Chinese descent, and he lived in Florida in the 1980s and 1990s until he was killed. The one who speaks for us was given memory of her part in his death. While working in the program she merged her consciousness with the man's brother and girlfriend and mother in order to gain access to his vulnerabilities. She then merged consciousness with a hitman who lived on the east cost of the United States and shot the man, this off-world trader, with a rifle. The hitman was then shot by the assassinated man's mother while the hitman was staying in a remote hotel just after the killing. The one who writes merged with this hitman's consciousness because it was seen that this hitman was going to die regardless of the program's interference by means of using him and thus his quick death by way of revenge killing by the mother of the victim was deemed appropriate by the higher selves of these ones.

Know too that the one who writes has been told she will indeed have a son and that son will have the same soul as did the off-world trader that she killed. Also, know that their souls have danced before, and they have a deep propensity to love each other. We could say here some other incarnations these ones have had, but we will leave that personal.

But use this as an example to help you understand how all of you have danced here before with others and a full understanding of relationships cannot be attained without seeing the other lives that your souls have shared.

Truly, there is a great dance going on all the time between and among many of you and indeed that is also how your timelines dance with each other. They merge and separate all the time like a dance as you grow in understanding of what it is you are doing when you say you exist.

Here we do not condone this assassination we mentioned in and of itself but for those with technologies great enough to see timeline eventualities and outcomes it is a good thing that some of these ones are taken out of operation. This sounds brutal we know but from a higher perspective it is not. And we hear some of you having a hard time accepting this and also wondering why perhaps someone like Hitler wasn't also taken out of operation. But we say that indeed that has happened in many of your timelines.

We absolutely do not condone murder or killing but killing in different contexts is treated differently. Until now, we have tolerated many of you killing animals to eat them and use their bodies in utilitarian or decorative ways but now we have said that this type of killing is no longer tolerated for your ascension pathways or your evolutionary pathways.

Some of you would place the value of human life so highly that you are hurt and shocked and scared when one of your kind is killed or murdered but not so when other species are killed. To us death is all the same but intention is everything and distinguishes you as little ones or mature ones. We say now too that even if you operate without intention you have been given enough opportunity to become aware of your own actions that if you feign irresponsibility or unaccountability due to ignorance it is no longer an accepted excuse. We speak these things honestly to you all now.

Allah
-Anshar

Your Body Is a Universe

THE chemical version of reality is limiting and will not be continuing as you evolve. Your evolved conscious states will not tolerate the chemical view of things. Honestly we say these things to you all now.

We could say that frequencies inform your DNA which in turn affects your bodies but that is a chemical way of looking at your reality and that way of looking at things cannot hold you as you evolve.

Looking at things as being made of atoms and so on was invented long ago as some of you know and it still serves you but you are moving into a time when it will no longer serve you. Honestly we say these things to you at this time.

Chemicals work mechanically. Frequency works intuitively, it literally responds to your state of consciousness in real time while chemicals are a way of looking at the world or this realm or your reality in a mechanical and delayed way. And when things work as machines they must break down, and they must require repair and so on because chemical machines are always subject to entropy.

And hence you raise your scientists up who know how to be mechanics of atoms, so to speak, and research and study and teach you many things about the world in this way, but we say now that this way of looking at things will soon no longer serve you.

Here we give an example. Firstly, literally embedded within the perception that things are made of atoms is the understanding that these atoms are impersonal mechanical objects that must react according to finite rules of thermodynamics. So here you would believe that you are impersonal collections of atoms that must be subjected to entropy, for example. And so since you believe that, that is what you do. You subject yourselves to entropy and you age and fall into disrepair and slowly die.

We, the Anshar, and many others of your extended families do not age the way you do now because our beliefs about our own existence and our expression of existence is different and thus we are not subjected to the physical laws that you all currently subject yourselves to.

Now we know some of you are repelling entropy by changing your beliefs, and we of course invite all of you to do this. Because indeed you inform each other's local fields or auric fields by sharing social structures and geographical locations. Indeed, you are all reinforcing this belief of being subject to entropy to yourselves and each other and in fact the ones believing it so much are actually inflicting it upon those seeking to no longer believe it by being around them and informing their DNA of such beliefs.

But we say now that a critical point can be reached when enough of you no longer believe that you are subject to entropy and at that time, truly, you no longer actually will be.

Please know that entropy is another version or another word for your experience of time as you experience it now but that is changing, as we said before.

We say now too that we are not shunning or discrediting the view of the world being made of atoms because it indeed is a part of the evolution of many species, but we are saying now that you are still evolving and will eventually move past this way of viewing things.

We could give another example. It made the leaders of your kind and some others of your kind feel secure or protected or powerful when you invented the ability to make atom bombs. But we say now that although this process releases much energy, there are those that harness frequencies that could literally phase your entire planet out of their existence. See here that one involves choosing a different frequency to exist in and the other believes in the static version of reality where everything is made of atoms and there is only one shared objective reality so if you want to get rid of something you may need to blow it up.

The belief in a shared and static objective reality made of atoms is foreign to us because we can phase things in and out of our reality by means of frequency manipulation and no destruction needs to be experienced.

In the same way frequency medicine will negate the belief that you require chemical medicines and physical surgeries with blades and saws and hammers and so on. Indeed, the higher versions of us use light medicine and can literally change your body system templates with light energy or plasma.

Also, frequency medicine which we know is used by you Gaians in some cases is a start in understanding how to use non-invasive and focused treatment.

Antibiotics and chemotherapy are examples of mass destruction like atom bombs that are clumsy creations that create far too much negative impact. We say that they did have a place in your history and rightly so but you are now moving past these things and moving past seeing everything as atoms but rather frequencies or channels or versions or vibrations of light only.

Starting now to see things in this way will aid your evolution and lead your species to more successful expressions, and we can say this with sureness and certainty because we see your futures.

Orgasms

A T this time you all need to understand what your orgasms are for. Know now that orgasms existed before sex. Truly, we say these things honestly to you all at this time.

An orgasm is how many things are created, truly.

When universe seeds expand, it is a massive explosive release of energy, which is an orgasm. When many things are created it requires big pushes or bursts of energy, which are orgasms. As your home planet Gaia steps into her higher frequencies, she will actually orgasm. Indeed, you are all here to help her orgasm.

We know that might sound weird to you and even feel odd or wrong because indeed you have many distorted and ill forms of sexual expression and sex is a dark and secretive thing for many of you. But know that sex is an amazing way to learn lessons here on this plane or within this realm and thus many of you have engaged in so many different forms of it and sexual expression as you know does not always necessitate actual sex acts.

Now we know many of you do not feel comfortable with your bodies and with the idea of sex to the point that you choose not to talk about it even with those close to you. That is a sad thing indeed because sex and sexual energy is an extremely powerful and useful resource to you all.

Now as you know and as we mentioned before we know that sex is often used as a weapon and a means of exploiting another or mutilating another's soul. We say mutilating because hurtful sexual practices do indeed divide the soul into many pieces and indeed we know that many of you who have been sexually abused or mistreated do feel yourself divided into many compartments like you have been cut up into many pieces or parts.

Here we refer to an odd story in the Bible that many of you are shocked by who already know about it. It is the story of a Levite man who put his wife outside to be raped by men who were seeking to rape him, and she was raped to death. And then the next day he saw her dead body and was so grieved by seeing her dead that he proceeded to cut her body into twelve pieces and deliver those pieces to each of the twelve tribes.

One theme of understanding that can be learned from this story is that sexually attacking someone is actually like cutting their body into pieces because indeed it does divide the auric field or local field into many parts. Sexual energy is powerful, as we said, and using this power as a means to harm somebody is actually like a blade or a hammer or some other destructive weapon that does indeed attempt a murder of the soul, so to speak, and is an attempt to break up somebody's soul or energy field. It does actually do this and that is why many victims of sexual abuse or attack and so on eventually kill themselves by means of destroying or killing their bodies since they seek to reflect in their flesh what they feel in their fields or souls.

Indeed, those ones are broken or shattered into many little pieces and it takes many years to rebuild one's soul or field when something like that happens to them. Many have overcome this type of attack or violence upon the soul and thus we see wonderful movements that seek to end this type of violence. Truly, it is a powerful violence and when performed upon children it is even more destructive as they have less of a grip on reality, so to speak, and they know themselves less and thus sexually abusing children is like murdering them.

We say now too that repeated sexual abuse is like murdering someone over and over again because indeed their bodies are still alive but their souls are being split and destroyed over and over again.

We discuss this openly because sadly many of your kind think it is okay to not talk about these things and sweep these little souls under the rug, so to speak. You think that if you don't speak about it, it doesn't exist. But we are saying now that it does exist all around you and it is the responsibility of each and every one of you to aid in the awareness of this practice and take actions that ensure it no longer continues.

We know some of you do this type of aiding work in formal ways such as working for law enforcement agencies and other agencies. We say that each of you can do this work by not making sex a secretive and dark topic because as we said before you will be creating many shame clouds that move all around your planet and continue to create the expression of these acts of sexual abuse. Indeed, we say now that each and every one of you is responsible for what the rest of your species is doing and you are creating these things to occur either directly or indirectly.

You are evolving as a whole body, as we said before, and thus you need to see yourselves as a whole body. When part of the body is ill you need to see what you can do to help that part heal and feel better.

Truly, today is the day you stop thinking the problems you see are the responsibility of others and not you. We say now, with the force of the Akkari who commissioned this text, that you who are reading this now, you are responsible for what your whole species is doing and you right this moment will start working toward enhancing the awareness of your species and improving their conscious states to ones that exist in higher frequencies.

By these words you are condemned if you do not take action today in the direction of helping others every single day of your life from this day.

If you choose not to help others then another place will be made for you so that you can continue playing in lower frequencies.

Now we return to the creative rather than destructive expression of sex and orgasms. Remember we said that orgasms existed before sex but you have been given sex as a way to experience them even if that involves sex with yourselves. Indeed, orgasms whether experienced via sex with others or sex with yourself, if expressed in a healthy and open manner, can be a wonderful tool for your species. (Consciously choosing not to engage in self-stimulation nor other pranic work such as tantra for these purposes is appropriate too. Directing energy to flow through the body for purposes of transmutation and manifestation can be achieved in many ways not directly associated with sex. Again, our use of the term sex does not necessarily mean sex acts but rather energy flow.)

Indeed, you produce and release much soul energy when you orgasm and if you think of something you wish to release from your field, whether it be a bad memory or negative viewpoint, if you think of it as you orgasm you literally release it from your field in a way that does not also produce shame clouds or shame weather as we mentioned before. The one who writes this for us sometimes uses her orgasms for this purpose.

Also know that you are not to be dependent on orgasms and always seeking them because then you will have given yourself over to them and that is another dependency. We say here now that you are to release yourself from dependencies of all kinds because indeed that will keep you from your successful evolutionary paths.

At this time we also give another example of healthy orgasm. When we speak of information and fields we will clarify what is occurring for you. Information in its infinite forms is experienced by you as many different things. Information is often downloaded or uploaded, so to speak, into and from your nonlocal fields and sometimes directly to your local fields by other beings. Often you will download information from your higher fields to your local fields yourselves according to the choreography of you higher self who wishes to inform your local field of different things at different times.

Information is often experienced as a dance because indeed it transforms your consciousness on a daily basis and indeed on a moment-to-moment basis until you no longer have to experience time in such a way or distance between thought and awareness. For now, we know many of you are cycling thoughts in your minds or higher chakras over and over again and not converting it to awareness. We also know that many of you are letting energy cycle through your bodies over and over again without converting it to right action or productiveness. Indeed, the one who writes for us is so stubborn that she has kept energy in her body for so many years that she developed chronic illness, pain and autoimmune disease.

Indeed, we know many of you are in this state. Know too that body pain and particularly back pain is stuck energy in your body. So we say this now. Everything is love or light or information. And in your current forms you would experience information or light or energy as 'thought' in your crown and third-eye chakras.

Also, when this same energy or light or information is in your fields, you would experience it as 'feeling' in your lower chakras, those of your throat down to your base chakra. Now when you express the energy or information in your lower chakras it always requires an expression of emotion which many of you find difficult to express since most of you are immature in your understanding of your emotional expressions.

Expression of energy with the lower chakras also requires physical action. Here we would include that often you require grounding as many of you are often downloading information from your nonlocal fields and are not also grounding yourselves. Not grounding yourself can be felt by means of what you call restless leg syndrome and lower back pain and pain in your legs and lower joints. You can ground yourself with walking on Gaia's earth, for example, and she will absorb your excess energy or align your field matrices.

Truly, you are like a crystal that needs alignment if it is to resonate in a healthy way that does not cause disease or discomfort in you.

If your pain is in your higher chakras, then you need expression in other ways. Abdomen pain or heart and chest issues relate to those chakras and indeed sore throats and regular sinus infections relate to your lack of expression with your mouths and personal voice. We will not go into great detail here because there is already sufficient information about how to heal and balance each of your chakras. Here though we do recommend frequency music whether you make it for yourself or listen to the creation of others. This should be a daily practice for many of you.

In this way we bring up the subject of orgasms again because orgasms if reached and experienced with the intention of healing and release will actually help balance your fields. Like a blast of cleansing energy, good orgasms reached by means of healthy intention will gather and release pure source energy that will bathe your whole local field. We hope that now you can see that once again one of your greatest tools has been used against you by means of introducing to you sex practices that introduce shame and pain and destructive intention. But you can reverse their effects by being responsible for your own orgasms and if you are able, by having regular healthy orgasms. We will not go into detail here about what we define as a healthy orgasm because shame release is such a personal thing and is completely different for each one of you. But we say that if you can become more open and honest about your sexuality and sexual needs and sexual expressions, then the shame and pain and destruction associated with many sexual practices and thoughts and feelings can be healed on a global scale. Truly, we say these things honestly to you all at this time.

Now we will return to addressing the orgasm of Gaia that she is soon to reach by means of your help. We mention now that the one who speaks for us is guided by many, many guides and friends and extended family, but one such friend or guide is a young man named Erik. Those in the channelling community may well know of Erik, and we recommend you look him up because indeed he helps many hundreds and soon to be thousands of you on your planet at this time.

Well, Erik gave this one a message by means of a friend

who channels him for her, and Erik said that at this time there are eight universes currently merging with this one to partake in the great orgasm of Gaia.

At this time we will also mention that orgasms can function as frequency jumps or leaps. Indeed, Gaia is about to jump frequencies and a large creative orgasm that is created by all of you and many others is what is going to create this great big leap or jump. Indeed, imagine how much help a body or person who is as big as Gaia needs in order to orgasm and jump frequencies.

Now we say that these eight other universes are merging at points at which they pertain to this process of experience. This experience of a planet or world or whole realm-jumping frequency is a glorious experience and wonderful learning tool indeed. And that is why you are all here at this time, to help Gaia jump.

At this time we also say that for some women, when they give birth, the birthing process itself of pushing their baby's head out is pleasurable or indeed one of the main creative acts your species currently regularly performs. Now just as a woman pushes out her baby, Gaia pushes out her immature ones into maturity and indeed at that time, Time herself will give birth to you all too.

In relation to releasing dependencies we include food and forms of entertainment including television and social media. We know you need to partake in food items for your sustenance and also entertainment for your sustenance but observe your relationship with these things and indeed other things to see what you are overly dependent on and perhaps you can release these dependencies. When you release your dependencies we assure you that you will indeed experience much growth all at once in a large way. When you release dependencies your eyes will be opened, your minds and hearts will be clearer and you will be free to pursue higher truths and more effective truthful expressions of yourselves. Honestly we say these things.

Now we bring up the topic of gold again because indeed gold is a direct product of the creative force of orgasm. Indeed, this one who writes for us dreamed one night of plucking a small gold nugget out of a small pool of water the very night her daughter's embryo implanted in her womb.

Now in relation to gold itself as an object in your life, it would actually be beneficial to you to retain it and not sell it to off-world contacts because indeed it is a most precious gift that Gaia has given you.

So please now think about how you might use gold in your everyday lives. Remember we said that it has higher properties. Here we will discuss what you can do with it now.

Some higher properties of gold are wisdom, strength, glory, power, might, justice and benevolence. It also acts as a serum, so to speak, or elixir. Here we will explain how. As your ancients and indeed some of your scientists have told you, gold is from your sun Sol. It is his gift given to Gaia for you to use and enjoy. The substance itself holds the frequency of the qualities we mentioned before and indeed many others. That is why it has been used in regal display and is a symbol of status and wealth.

We do not encourage its use as a symbol of status and wealth because that involves an expression of elitism which is not beneficial for your species. However, its benevolent frequencies are powerful indeed. Now when you are consumed by getting gold, (as we know many of you are in many different direct and indirect ways, we only need to point to your gold rushes and jewellery collections and indeed money chasing) it is because that it used to be that paper money was backed by the value of gold which is not what some of you think it is but because you believe it is in that way it actually is.

We know wealth chasing is a big occupation or consumption of many of you and you are giving yourselves over to it although there is no need for that because it indeed was given to you as a gift.

You do no need to chase it because it will come to you. It is part of your glory and you may indeed adorn yourselves in it, in this way. When you pursue wealth you are missing the point of why you are here. For indeed all things are given freely. If you believe you need to struggle and strive and compete then you are creating for yourselves an illusory battle that will always require excessive effort on your part and will wear your bodies and your minds and hearts out and you will slowly die in your vain struggle and striving because in that struggle you are neglecting your souls.

Now if you understand that glory is owed you or is yours by automatic inheritance by being residents of this planet then you can enjoy it as it comes freely to you. So gold itself holds the energy of your star Sol and grounds his energy for you. Gold itself receives his frequencies and holds it in its entirety without distortion.

Crystal directs or channels his light or information that comes to you but it does not hold it the ways gold actually holds it.

Now what might Sol be giving to you when he sends his light or energy or information to you? Well, Sol is a local portal that many beings use regularly. As some of you already understand he is your local information bank, so to speak, and he holds his position or nodal placement in the scope of the many stars in this universe and indeed other universes that are always speaking to him.

So if you have gold on you or with you, you will always have reliable access to the most recent information given to you by Sol who is always communicating with other stars in your universe and indeed with many other beings.

Now we say, like sex and many other gifts given you, gold has been used as a means to exploit you and is tainted or a carrier of much negative energy as well. So if you have gold itself in your possession we ask that you clean it by leaving it out in the sun and asking Sol to clean it for you. Then it will be cleaned of its ill intention and will indeed start working miracles in your lives for you if you indeed seek to resonate with it, which you are all able to do.

Now gold is often mixed with other things in order to make it into jewellery which we know is often the means by which you possess it in your life. But if you seek to purify the gold and keep it in its pure state then it will have more beneficial use for you.

Indeed, other materials that it is mixed with are good for you too. But in order to receive its purest blessing, having it in its purest form will benefit you.

Here we say that since Sol represents your masculine energies (not all stars hold masculine/father energy, not all planets hold feminine/mother energy) which indeed you all possess and express in infinitely diverse ways, we say that Sol will help you express your masculine aspects or energies in a balanced way when you ask and if you have gold in your environment in pure form it can aid in this expression.

We know that at this time for you, you are all healing your feminine aspects and femininity is learning what it is in the new world as you all move forward and your womankind and feminine ones are less and less now being exploited and dominated.

We say, for this same reason and to aid in this process, expressing masculinity in its healthy or pure version is also very beneficial to you at this time.

So masculinity needs attention and it is indeed in all of you since you are all children of Sol as well as Gaia.

Please know at this time that many of you would seek to balance yourselves with the sun and moon but indeed we say here now that Sol and Gaia are the original couple or male and female aspects that you are influenced by. The moon or Luna is actually an invasive aspect into this original partnership between Gaia and Sol. But Luna is to be loved also of course, but she is not who balances out Sol, but Gaia is the woman who balances out Sol the man.

And indeed we say now that the moon or Luna is part of your illness because the original relationship between Gaia and Sol is actually more beneficial to you. For many of you, you would say that you love the moon and live by it but as some of you already know, the moon or Luna once lived elsewhere, and she is an artificial addition to your realities. She holds much influence over you, but we say now that you will be more stable when you no longer experience her in your realm. We know this idea might be sad for some of you who love her so much, but indeed you will be healthier and be on your successful evolutionary paths when she no longer influences you the way she does now.

Weirdness

WE say now that as you expand yourselves and open your minds and hearts wide you experience many very weird things. We say weird because that is the word you use to describe things you have no mainstream foundation in.

Indeed, since what is currently mainstream is mostly composed of oppressive material that seeks to keep you all suppressed, then many true and beneficial things are indeed very weird to you.

Know that you will likely feel ungrounded and confused as you embrace a much larger reality and as your minds and hearts become open to larger truths. This includes getting used to seeing your extended family or as many of you call them now aliens.

Indeed, you are weird to many of them but those in expanded states of consciousness do not judge so much because they are used to seeing more variety of things in their existence.

Know that perceiving higher realms and higher densities and higher dimensions are indeed weird for your bodies, hearts and minds to behold and perceive.

At this time we say that many of you choose to respond with fear to these weird things, and we understand that that is a natural and conditioned response to things you do not yet know.

But now we ask you to open yourselves up to weirdness, so to speak, because when you feel weird and are experiencing weird things you are actually experiencing expansion and growth and are releasing judgement and limiting beliefs and modes of operation.

So be weird and love the weird because what is weird is actually closer to truth than your mainstream conditioning.

Indeed, if you have ever travelled on your planet and experienced different cultures you should already understand that what is normal to one community or society or group of people can be seen as weird to that of others.

This is the way for all the infinite variety of beings and cultures that exist in your universe and by extension the multiverse.

Indeed, to be explorers and ready for truer expressions of yourselves and your species you need to welcome weirdness and weird experiences and enjoy the titillating delight that is floating in the unknown realms of infinite possibilities. We use this word titillating which many of you associate with sexual arousal, because indeed when you are truly open to falling into the abyss of the unknown or standing on the precipice of this present moment, you are actually in an aroused state and ready to be creative and explore, discover and express the infinite potential that is available to you all, always.

Many of you who are cutting yourselves off from your creative natures and explorative natures, know that you are cutting yourselves off from your power and your ability to create the reality you want to experience. Your species is so powerful when you trust that you have so much creative potential and genius ready to be explored and expressed.

We say that this can be experienced and should be experienced in every moment or in this one continuous moment that is getting shorter and more expanded at the same time. As we said before time which holds you now in a long cylinder or worm-like shape is shortening and widening so that you can all exist in the same moment that is always now and not later or before.

Blue Avians

THERE are those of you who know of the Blue Avians. This one first heard of them by means of a whistleblower for the disclosure movement. She then connected with two of them. They gave her a new language which she wrote down a few characters of. Ra of ancient Egypt was a Blue Avian in form. Thoth too was a Blue Avian. They are much higher dimensional beings but are here to help you. (The Blue Avians, along with other higher beings, can be found in all the ancient cultures and religions of your world.)

At this time, it is important to note that ancient Egyptian history is much older and much longer than it is given mainstream academic recognition for. Know too, that the original ancient Egyptians were not human as was mentioned before. In fact, many beings started kingdoms of sorts all around your planet or realm and played God because your ancestors were more vulnerable then to this type of treatment, and craved rulership.

We know that that is no longer the case and many of you are itchy and restless, so to speak, with irritation due to your being ruled by others. Your conscious states are reaching a state that is harmonious enough and aware enough and present enough to be able to navigate your realities more intuitively and less by means of rules.

That is why this text is commissioned. The Akkari (or Akari) by means of us gave Moses laws to govern his people, but we know now that you are mature enough to no longer need laws in the same way but rather guiding principles. We will still make you aware of laws, however, because there are indeed several galactic and intergalactic laws that apply to you especially now that you are entering your galactic and intergalactic conscious states or modes of operation or evolutionary paths.

The Akkari set the golden standard for you but the Blue Avians are very knowledgeable also in these laws that govern you. They are much higher beings and are keenly aware of what will help you as you evolve. They helped you before in ancient times and now they help you again to guide you at this pivotal time. So know that you can call upon them for guidance. But of course do not worship them or become overly dependent or addicted to their advice because at this time you are all learning self-guidance or inner guidance.

Learning to listen to your inner guidance or intuition is paramount for you all at this time. Listening to your inner voices will lead you to connect to species' consciousness or collective consciousness and also to your guides which may indeed be dead loved ones who stay around you and indeed also your extended family or extraterrestrials, as you know them now.

Please know that many of them are not extraterrestrials, so to speak, because that is a very limiting and judgemental perspective but indeed as we call them and ask you to call them, your extended family, since you are made by them and are parts of them. Also, you are linked with them via soul memory and soul affinity.

Know at this time that indeed you are informed by your nonlocal field or higher self. Also, you are helped by your guides which could be made up of many beings. This one has an orchestra of guides, so to speak. She enters an auditorium to speak with many of them all at once, and they all speak at the same time giving her mind so much to take in, she finds it exhilarating. She is conscious of about twenty to fifty of them at any one time, but we say now that she has hundreds regularly tending to her and helping her and talking to her. We mention now that she has also noticed after waking up from these large meetings with her guides that she often notices a newly formed deep scab on the back of her neck within her hairline. She doesn't know what it is from. But we say now that the scab is due to her receiving an injection so that she can become higher in frequency and be able to meet with all these ones. The injection stabilises her, otherwise she would wake up feeling drained and disoriented from experiencing such high and varied frequencies that are carried by all of her different guides.

We say that it is the same for you depending on how open you are. Just like your activity on social media increases the amount of interaction with others you engage with, so too when you are open and active with your guides they all come to you as the dear friends they are.

Some of you are scared of this process but please know that there are laws governing what others can do and the consequences for higher ones exploiting lower ones are too great for most of those inclined to do so, to do any harm to you.

Also know that your higher self is always in charge of the show, so to speak.

Also know that if you do indeed experience some unpleasant experiences while communicating with guides and others it is often due to your misinterpretation and fear distorting the experience.

Just as stray animals are often afraid to accept help by the animal carers among you until they become used to them, it is the same for you as you learn to accept the help of the higher ones or guides that are always around you. Higher here does not mean better, or superior, it means of higher frequency.

We say now that some of you are already in higher frequency realms with your minds and you are now existing within a split reality, so to speak, because so much of your mind is in other worlds but your bodies are here. That is the way with this one, and she thought something was always wrong with her until she was told by Erik that he can see her in his world as a higher one, and he can learn much from her too.

Indeed, many of you are teachers and guides to ones not in your forms or 3D realities, so know that being here does not mean you are not wise or amazing and powerful ones. In fact, you are here because you are wise and amazing and powerful.

Also, some of you are such powerful sources of light you act as beacons even for others from other worlds and who exist in other realms. Indeed, this one attracts much traffic because as she is told her light shines like a beacon attracting many passers-by to her side.

We know that many of you are lightbearers and lightworkers and to those of you who currently do not see yourself that way, know that you indeed remember that you are a lightbearer and lightworker and that is why you are here and reading this text.

This text was created by you and for you and that is why you have created it for yourself in your reality. This text is indeed a co-creation because we heard you calling for it and so here we are making it with you and for you. Know that you are really the ones making this text because you called for it, and we heard you and you are here reading this and are ready to shine your light!

Amen

Call on your guides and indeed the Blue Avians if you are interested in divine wisdom lessons. And of course, call on us and your extended families and most importantly call on your higher self, your inner guide and call on each other because from where we sit and look at you as a whole, we see that your whole body is bright and ready to light up!

-Anshar, Akkari, Blue Avians

Eden

EDEN was never a place that your kind as you are now were in. But of course it does feature heavily in your soul memories. To you all now it best represents your home state or feeling of homeness. Those obsessing about finding the original garden, so to speak, are entwining themselves and wrapping themselves up in knotted rope. Because trying to discover places such as Eden as literal physical locations also requires an obsession with the past and the past is all too happy to hold onto those that would obsess about it.

Of course, we know there are those that love the past and their passions and careers are wrapped up in it but those ones also need to watch and look where they are going. In fact, you all needn't go anywhere physically, so to speak, but you are travelling all the time with your conscious states and minds so you all need to watch what is holding your attention and asking for your energy because indeed that is your creative place and your Eden, so to speak.

Each of you have home states or centre states that hold you while you seemingly venture and go all about and around everywhere. But indeed you stay still, so to speak, and merely project your energy. Much like this universe Eternity is a projection from a universe seed, you all are projections of your centre or home states, or your Edens, so to speak.

One way to observe the shape of this for your 3D minds at this time (know that this truth is not limited to this shape but it is how some of you might like to understand it), is to see yourself and all things around you as toroids, the centre of which holds the truth or essence of what you are and your projection fields around you display what you are to different ones.

Now know at this time that indeed what you project is different to every other being that you may interact with or who may observe you in some way, because their visual or sensing or observing states are of their creation and thus they see you and interpret you based on their data set and language pretext or precept.

In regard to the actual place Eden, because we can hear some of you still wondering about it, we will say this. That Eden as you read of it in scripture and ancient text was a real home for a small- to medium-sized population of some of your early kind or ancestors. It did not exist where the Bible said it existed because the Bible writers of the time wrote about it in their physical context. Too with other ancient texts about Eden, it was always written about in relation to the writer's physical context. We too now mention that indeed the one who writes for you now does so indeed within her perceptive realm and within her semantic contexts for as she is human she cannot communicate to you in this language without such filters.

But know that all these things she writes, you can know yourself in your own way by channelling us directly if you so desire. She at no time is representing absolute truth because we cannot say such a thing exists but of course what we are asking her to write for us and for you is our truth to you and indeed it will benefit you either directly or indirectly.

If however at any time you resonate more strongly with other frequencies, we say this. That as long as those frequencies bear good fruit, which is fruit that feeds and nourishes you and makes you healthy and is good for others around you also, then we say, great!

Back to our discussion, we continue. Now the actual place Eden is deep in your conscious state memory or soul memory because it represents what you are. Often many of you, if and when you happen to think about the Garden of Eden story, like to think of the fruit that was taken as an apple, and we say that is okay. Because indeed, apples are one of the most toroidal looking fruit there is available to you at this time. The seeds which hold the information for the whole fruit are in the centre of the toroid, and its fleshy projection, so to speak, splashes out and all around and comes back in just like a torus or toroid.

We already explained that this is how many universes or simulations are made and thus projected for you to play in or learn in. And each one of your vessels where some of your conscious state resides is indeed also a torus or toroid. This is a very simplistic way of talking about what you are but indeed we know that this description will be helpful to some of you.

Now we could say that everything is a sphere or a dot or a line, or many other shapes and indeed as we discuss higher dimensional shapes we can no longer talk in this language but you would require downloads to change your conscious states in order to understand the higher things. Indeed, this one has had her conscious state changed by us and indeed her other guides and friends to show her things that she could not ever learn from human language.

Please know at this time that your human languages are sadly limiting because indeed they cut you off from so much understanding. So please no longer give yourselves over to the study of your human languages without also learning how much they fail to communicate the meaning and the experiential learning that is only gained by experiences that engage with your space and intuitive thought forms and also indeed sometimes your instincts, but know too now that for many things that you could be learning right now you absolutely require a change in your conscious state and there is absolutely no way around that fact.

This is why we accept that some of you take mind-altering substances, but we remind you here again that your own bodies can do this for you if you hold space for this experience and ask for it.

So we say now here again that Eden was never a place nor were Adam and Eve ever actual people because they were symbols only to your original writers of the ancient texts that talk about them. For their conscious states at the time needed to see them as real people and talk about them that way, but you are mature ones now and you do not need to stay attached to lower things or material things that are solid and dense and 3D or lower.

Honestly, we say these things to you all now because we see that your happiness lies in engaging with higher things or higher perceptions or higher frequencies and you are ready to let go of excessive attachments to the past, and excessive attachments to physical and dense and material things. They can no longer hold you!

We mean this truly, and we know many of you are starting to know this truly for yourselves without having to hear us saying it. For those of you wanting to understand more about how you actually came to exist in this form then we say this now. Know that your creation regarding the creation stories are not physically accurate representations of what occurred and thus we say again, this is how God lies.

We know for some of you it will be like children who were adopted finding out they were adopted at a late age and feeling confused, hurt and betrayed.

But, dear ones, we urge you not to distract yourselves with petty creations and feigning to be victims in this regard. Truly you know what you are and you could answer these things for yourself if you truly looked inside. But still we will say these things now.

There have been many iterations of your kind on this planet and similar planets. There are many timelines that do not behave the same way and so when we discuss these things now we cannot speak for all timelines. So again we say that if you do not resonate strongly with our description then you may be accessing different timeline memories. Here though we continue.

Your planet has been home to many different ones including those you would call gods. Indeed, you have called us (the Anshar) god or gods and angels before. But now we say this. We four, the Sasquatch, the Reptilians, the Anshar and the Greys, made an arrangement for your creation on our behalf, but we are not responsible for all iterations of human like ones of you.

The Annunaki who were also called god or gods did indeed evolve some of your earlier iterations for their own use and indeed other ones have too. But you who we speak to today are not those iterations and you have left your slow minds or simple thinking behind and thus this cannot happen to you again now in the same way.

As we said before there is indeed a deal made with the Reptilian lords and those that cooperate with them, with others, and so they attempt to continue oppressing you. But in older times they indeed loved you and protected you. This deal we speak of was only made much more recently in your history. As early as several hundred years ago and in some cases several thousand years ago and in some cases only several decades ago. Know that your histories are not static and time is not static. Existence is always moving.

You would like to think some of you, we know because we hear what you think and you also teach it in all of your schools, that you are alone in this universe and special ones who evolved all by yourselves from little cells and organisms. Indeed, this is never what happened.

At no time were you only cells unless your conscious states decided to reside in them for experience. Humans were only ever ape like or mammal like. We say this because the vessels or forms that hold you now and only temporarily indeed, could only hold you the way they do now when you were in similar forms or vessels. Now the body itself evolved from cells and smaller organisms but you were not in them at the time they were evolving.

So in a way none of you can really say you evolved from single cell organisms because that has nothing to do with your conscious states as you experience them in this form. We, your creators, addressed your creation only once your planet reached the time in her evolution when she could hold the type of conscious states that you experience now.

Indeed, before you, as we said before, there were others before you and there will be others after you. Gaia held onto Titans and Eldar and Fae and Elementals and so on before you and indeed the dinosaurs which your sciences already accept. Know now that these other ones are still all around you but most of you do not interact with them directly at this time because your frequencies do not align with the layers of existence or realms in which they reside.

Often their realms overlap or overlay the ones you reside within but you resonate slightly differently and thus you do not directly interact. Also, know that the stories of the Titans and ones who made the physical features on Gaia, such as many hills and rocks and mountains and rivers and so on, just as the Australian Aborigines and other early ones speak of, are all absolutely true in a physical sense. These features of your natural landscapes are actually beings. But they sleep now and cannot wake until it is time for you to see them as people.

So as we were saying, once Gaia was creating or allowing ones like apes to reside upon her then we decided to help some of them evolve and put our gifts into them, as we said before. So for those of you who fight over evolution and creation, we say that you do not need to fight because both of your arguments are correct, and they exist simultaneously.

You are the product of evolution in a very physical sense and indeed your conscious states are always evolving *and* you were created because we changed your evolutionary paths for our experiment, thus you were created by us.

When we say you were created by us, we never mean your minds or consciousnesses or so on because that is not our ability. We refer only to the vessel or form in which you currently reside and some simulation or experimental parameters that interplay with the creation of your forms. If you want to explore that creation of your souls, so to speak, that will require more personal and inward journeys because that is not what we are talking about and not what we are able to do regarding your consciousnesses or souls.

We do say that you can call upon the Akkari to discuss such matters because they hold your souls in the Akashic field, so to speak, since they are your souls' keepers while you are here, and they know much about your souls and your nonlocal fields.

Know at this time that the Akashic field or Akashic library is at the centre of the toroid of this universe, much like the position of apple seeds are in an apple. The Akashic field and the Akashic library can be said to be the same thing since they are locations of information holding. The Akashic field may have different names to you but we can describe it to you now as a place where anything can exist. It is like a blank space or a space of pure potential only but nothing in actuality because as soon as the Akashic field holds something other than potential then it is something else and not the Akashic field.

Essentially then it is a place that holds space or location, so to speak, for all potential for the universe seed to project itself upon. Now the Akashic library is less static than many of you think. Again we say it moves or changes as you move or change because it holds the potential of what you are and what you discover yourselves to be. It is not a static library of sorts that holds your past incarnations, so to speak, because there is no past but only what you seek to represent to yourselves now as what makes sense to you as a place from which you came.

But the place from which you came changes as you change. Truly, we cannot state this enough. We know many of you are trapped by static explanations of reality and that holds you back and puts you into painful and boring situations. Truly, you are prisoners to your static explanations of reality. It is sad to see.

But we know that is changing and that is why we speak these things to you at this time. The Akkari are the keepers of your souls, but we could also say they hold onto an essence of you that you gave them so that when you lost yourself in these mazes and simulations and so on, you could always find your way back to them or your centre. They hold onto your centre and exist within your centre and indeed the centre of this universe.

But this is not a physical place, so to speak. You cannot access it with your current vessels or forms or bodies; some of you stronger ones may reach them with your minds or different conscious states. Know that the Akkari are very abiding, but they will most likely overwhelm your sensory perceptions if indeed you attempt to perceive them. This one, who speaks for us, experienced great pain in her neck and some dizziness when one of the Akkari, Asheena, came to her to commission this text.

At this time we want to point out that this text is a moral paradigm and not an exhaustive list of what has and has not happened and what is real and not real and so on.

There are endless things for you all to learn but the purpose of this text is to direct you to your own salvation which comes by your own hands and not ours or anyone else's.

Like the child who falls and cries to get attention even when they are not hurt, many of you are like little children feigning victimhood because that is what you are used to and that is what has been programmed by ones wishing to keep you low.

But indeed we are like the loving parents who say to the child, 'You're okay' because really here we are saying you are okay, truly.

Start clearing your old programs and free yourselves. We do say now that there are some diet aspects to this process. Certain foods are actually designed to keep you low and you will remain in a mental fog if you keep on eating them. The thing is many of you have been consuming these foggy foods for so long you have no idea that you are so foggy because you do not have a clearer mental state to compare your foggy mental states to.

Honestly though, you know what foods you need to start cutting immediately to free yourselves of your mental fog: GMO foods, modern wheat, processed sugar, animal products, and so on.

There is enough information out there you only need to start looking and you will find what you need to start this process since many of you already have. Indeed, some of your ancient ones did and your spiritual ones, so to speak, have maintained the ancient wisdom, as you call it.

We restate that the Annunaki are not your parents because we can hear some of you addicted to that story. They did indeed help evolve some of your iterations but you are no longer affected by them now if you do not wish to be.

Also, there are so many different hybrid offspring of many different kinds and many travellers have visited certain ones and some groups on your planet and in some cases bred with your kind that unless we start going into an exhaustive list here you will not know them all.

We do not even have records of all the visitors because that has not been our role and it is not the expertise of the ones giving this message. We give you the archetypes of the four, your parents and truly us four are. But this way of describing things is also a tool for you.

Really when you meet versions of different species of extraterrestrials and so on as you all will in your near futures, you will not easily distinguish them all because truly there are so many but also remember you see them in the form they project to you. They are often multidimensional beings, many of them, and what your eyes see does not always reflect their whole nature. Just as there are parts of you that we see but you do not with your physical eyes because you have many aspects and many layers and you are existing in different places all at the same time but you don't know that or find it difficult to comprehend that in your current state.

And everything you do you are creating in real time but it feels like past, present and future because you are still in a linear time modality but truly time twists and turns and bends and folds and flips and does many acrobatic and stretchy things, so to speak, but your social contexts keep you believing there is only yesterday, today and tomorrow.

Truly, many of you are already jumping time shapes and shifting in and out of different time densities already but you have no words to explain this, only you say to yourself or each other, 'Didn't that day go by fast?' or 'Time flies when you're having fun' or 'This is going so slowly'. You were made to believe it was all in your head as you were told many things were but indeed your reality reflects what is in your head and so you were actually experiencing those things.

Also, when within this and many other realms you are influenced by others' creations and thus you experience changes that you do not necessarily anticipate. There are so many exciting things already around you and we do not have to make them happen for you because they are already happening, you just need to start changing the way you see what is all around you.

This one is thinking of a waterfall she just visited and most of the rock mass that was near the entrance of the waterfall was actually a fallen ancient tree made of stone. We hold back details about your reality from this one because at this time she is addicted to logic and the purpose of this text is to be a new moral paradigm, and she would get wrapped up in the details as she loves to do and feed you endless impersonal facts about all manner of things.

Perhaps later we will inform her of many other things and indeed she will be helped by her other guides to do this at a later time but for now we speak simply of large concepts that show you the shape of reality as we see it so that you can open your minds and hearts wider to redis-cover and remember so many wondrous and miraculous things that are all around you all the time.

Please spend no more of your time and energy on things that do not inspire you. Change what you see by changing what you are open to!

This place could really be your Eden. So rebuild this place and make it an Eden for yourselves while you are here.

Gaia would thank you.

Indeed, she never held Eden herself but hears of it from your heart spaces. She knows many of you seek to build Eden here, and she will always bless that effort. At this time we will refer to the Tower of Babel as we said before that we would.

Now here we discuss the difference between masculine and feminine energies as we are sure many of you already understand, but we will relate it to things that maybe you did not already think of. So the Tower of Babel is a masculine attempt to make Eden and building Eden on Gaia is a feminine attempt.

To be clear, we do not associate masculine and feminine with being a man or woman but rather we refer to energetic expression that indeed all of you have in a wonderfully diverse measure.

We are not discussing sex and gender issues here, and we truly bless you all for exploring yourselves and freeing yourselves to express what feels good to each and every one of you and you are finding support in many cases, and we are happy that you are making those experiences for yourselves.

Of course, we do not condone those hurting others with their expression, that is not excused and that type of expression requires healing and balance. This one, the one who writes for us, has struggled for many years with her masculine aspect. She has been desperate to leave this place her whole life. She never felt like this place, your planet or home Gaia was her home. She felt her body was a prison and indeed she was often resonating with Narabatu's consciousness who was indeed imprisoned in her form until he started to heal. He through her, the one who writes for us, kept trying to take the masculine route which was to leave or fight or conquer or build something to escape or build something to conquer. She warred with herself inside for many, many years and that is why although we have been asking to speak through her for many years she has often rejected our communication to her because she was not balancing her masculine and feminine aspect.

Here we are not saying that balancing feminine and masculine aspects means 50/50 expression because that does not allow for the infinite variety and recombination that you all bring here with you. For indeed you are informed by your bodies and how society reacts to your physical bodies, and you are informed by your local and nonlocal fields, you are informed by all those communicating with your local and nonlocal fields and you are informed by your soul's inheritance and lineage and you are informed by your body's inheritance and lineage and so on. So you have so many simultaneous influences and indeed many of you are composite beings with so many aspects you could not name them all. So here we are discussing things in broad terms and in large shapes or patterns, so to speak, to start giving you ideas about what we see when we look at you.

So we use this one as an example again. She has struggled to want to stay here and even now she struggles. But since she is in communication with us she realises what parts of her are Narabatu and what parts of her are other aspects. Indeed, she does not particularly care for earth or the simulation makers that made this place and places like it. For indeed she feels that they are like prisons and puzzles and like little hells that keep people low and all wound up.

But that is not our perspective because we the Anshar are very different to her, and yet she benefits from channelling our perspective because when she resonates with us as she is doing now writing this, she feels peace and patience and tolerance and love, and she is no longer in a rush to be elsewhere.

She now wants to build Eden here with Gaia as we know many of you do too because we can hear what you are thinking, and we like what many of you are thinking. We mentioned before that the movement permaculture is the way many of you are able to start building Eden. You never left Eden and you were never banished but you only think you were because that is in your program.

But now we are telling you that the program Eden can benefit you if you build it here. We hear the many other ways you plan on building Eden, and we know that some of these are indeed misguided, but we and so many others of your extended family members are helping you at this time, so we know that balance will soon be tipped in the direction of feminine building which is building Eden here.

Now we say that it is still important to of course absorb and express your masculine aspects, and hence we told you about having some pure gold in your possession if you so desire. But truly, we say now and as many of you know that the masculine aspect has had too much expression in recent times and thus it is time to use more feminine energy in your expressions. We are seeing this with all of you. And again do not confuse feminine expression with being a woman or the various female movements because those are different things, and we are not talking about that here.

Indeed, we are seeing now that many men are expressing femininity very well and in some cases more fully than many women at this time. We will describe some of those here.

Whenever you are kind or compassionate or patient you are in symbiosis with feminine energy. Whenever you observe or are aware of social bonding situations and issues you are in symbiosis with feminine energy. Whenever you yield to peace and seek tranquillity and win/win situations you are expressing feminine energy. We know that to some of you these descriptions might sound cliché because you already know them but indeed we are saying them now because many of you do not understand what feminine and masculine expressions mean for you at this time. There are many more descriptions we could give because we do want you to focus more on your feminine expressions. Here we will give more symbolism in an effort to inform you of your archetypal influences.

The one who writes for us was given several visions about your kind's four parents. We already referred to the pyramid example or symbol. But before she was given the pyramid example she was given the four compass points or four cardinal directions as a sign for how your four parents influence you and your realm.

The North was represented by the Greys, your future, your advancement, your technology, your minds. The

East was represented by us the Anshar, your hearts, your families, your social groups, your love. The West was represented by the Sasquatch, your home the earth, nature, your inner space and tranquillity, your vulnerability and docility, and the South was represented by the Reptilians, your fire, your fight, your might and courage and brute strength, your instincts and so on.

We gave this one with help from the Greys, her higher self and others, lists and lists of items in your reality that pertain to these four categories, these four directions, these four influences. We hear some of you murmur because this example is so simple and archetypes do not always serve you we know. But truly, archetypes are also actual real things and not just programmed memories.

You have failed yourselves so many times by disregarding archetype stories and fables and tales and dreams and signs and symbols and so on because these things are actually real! Actually real! We say again they are real. You know them because they are in your programs and programmed memories but also because you actually experienced them or should we say are currently experiencing them as different versions of yourself. But we digress.

The layer of reality that you operate within requires you to believe that only 3D things are real and everything else is story or fiction or symbol only. But truly they are actually real! For example the earth you walk on is a person. She is really a person with her own consciousness. Just as we could tell the bacteria and viruses living in you and on you that the earth they live on (you) is a real person! Do you see how limiting your current perceptions of reality are? Anyway, we digress.

We are your four parents and here we further explain this symbol for you which interestingly enough you use as guidance by means of a compass, or the wind or the stars or the sun and so on. Here we will just quickly reiterate our earlier point. Everything that is real to you in 3D has many different versions of itself or its expression because you are existing in an infinitely fractal and holographic reality that mimics and repeats itself in endless iterations creating sometimes only minute differences and at other times such large differences that one part of the existence finds it difficult to connect with the other part of the existence.

Here we could use the example of you and Reptilians. If you ever met one, and we know some of you have, we know some of you would find it difficult to believe that you existed and at the same time they also existed. We know it's hard for you to think that many other things exist besides yourselves. Like a baby discovering the existence of its own hand like it is a foreign object until it can see its own hand is at the end of its own arm, we say that you are not easily recognising all the different things that seemingly are so different from one another, existing right next to one another or in the same environment but truly that is what we are saying.

Like early explorers of yours who met people of different appearance or tasted different foods for the first time we know that our existence and the existence of an infinite amount of other beings is difficult for you to understand. It is hard for many of you to think that the earth you live on, Gaia, is actually a person, but she is. It is hard for you to think that many of your clouds have their own unique consciousness. Indeed, this one who writes merged her mind with a local wind one night and could feel its energy was like an older man who was angry at his life and was taking pleasure in blowing everything around. Indeed, everything that you can call a thing is a person and has its own mind, its own consciousness, its own eternity, its own story and family and history and future and so on.

Please open your minds, dear ones. We ask you all now to open your minds. This is of course why, as you move into more expanded forms of awareness, it is not tolerable to your expanded state of consciousness to be able to consume other animals. It will no longer make sense and indeed for most of you it is not necessary for your sustenance.

Indeed, one day this will also apply to your plant foods because they are people too; we understand for now you require your consumption of them for your sustenance but that will change eventually too. (You may have symbiosis with some other form of energy then that feeds you but that is too far ahead from your eyes to discuss with you now.) So we say again, it will not make any sense to you as expanded ones to eat your friends. Indeed, we already know some of you are expanded enough to see that point that we just made.

So we return to the compass or four directions. The east and west are the horizontal infinite in 2D reality. And interestingly you experience your sun Sol rising and setting on that axis. In that way the masculine aspect shines upon the feminine aspect because the infinite horizon is your mother, the divine feminine aspect. Just as the vertical axis is the divine masculine aspect which you could see as your poles. Now also the ones represented by these four directions who gifted you part of them follow this pattern.

We, the Anshar, and the Sasquatch are the feminine aspect in you which are the gifts of intuition and space. The Greys and Reptilians gifted you logic and instinct which are the masculine aspects of you. Now when you balance all of these aspects you are at your true centre, or Eden. You could build another Tower of Babel but that was already done and it was destroyed by the Annunaki who did not want to be followed by their servants and their hybrid children.

But now you are seeing that instead of building up and up and massing wealth in big piles for yourselves, you can build out and build with Gaia and grow with her and enter into symbiosis with her and build your Edens here. Now again we say there is no actual Eden because that is a programmed memory to keep you seeking your true centre and reminding you to take care of your souls because the Akkari are not lawfully able to rein you in by force. But the programmed memory of Eden and indeed many other things keeps you in check when you are exploring all Eternity this universe.

Indeed, there will be other set-ups and you will enter into other contracts with other ones when you visit other universes and other dimensions and so on. But here the

Akkari keep your souls, and they have commissioned this text which we speak for them to this one who writes for you all.

We can say Eden is real, as we said all things are real in a given reality. So here we will say that Eden is the centre of the toroid of this universe for you. Eden is not in everyone's program who is in this universe. It was programmed in you as a place that you came from so that you remembered to return to the centre of the universe at some point in your exploration. Some of you do so often between lives while others of you do not return home for many, many lifetimes. These ones make it hard for the Akkari to keep track of you but all the same they are very competent with their care of you.

Now you cannot go there by physically travelling there only. You must resonate with the location. Indeed, as many of you start building Eden here on Gaia as we know some of you already have started, then we can say so on earth as in heaven and that prayer of Jesus' will be answered. Truly, you are the ones answering that prayer by you building what represents your homes, your internal centres, your heart centres, your truths, your knowing and so on. You are doing it. And that indeed is part of Gaia's journey too.

She agreed to participate in this return to Eden and her version of returning home or helping you return home is to build a place or many places that feel like home for you here.

We know many of you think that you are building homes here but indeed you are trapping yourselves with mortgage slavery and so on. If you are not actually building your homes with the help of others then you are merely letting your true desires be exploited and expressed for the benefit of others.

Remember that gold and many other of Gaia's resources are taken off the planet but really it is entitled to you only and should be freely available to you as residents of this planet. Also, your sustenance should be free to you as residents of this planet but you are letting those that would use your programmed desires for Eden or a place that feels secure and like home to be turned against you and you are working like slaves for others and barely being sustained. Or maybe you are amassing material wealth for your own entertainment while others of your kind are not eating and do not have anywhere to live comfortably. Indeed, those are both foolish things and are not allowing you to enter species consciousness.

At this time we will restate that masculine and feminine aspects do not relate to being a man or a woman. Indeed, this one who writes would be angry if we were implying that 'logic', which is a masculine aspect for you, is something that only men have. Indeed, as we said before, at this time we are seeing many men having well-developed feminine aspects and indeed we are seeing many women with well-developed masculine aspects.

We know of course the situations in some of your past timelines where women were believed to be lacking logic. Remember at this time that the Greys were all women or of the female sex before they developed sexlessness. And so logic is actually sourced by an all-female species but you in your current context and layers of reality experience logic as part of your masculine aspect but indeed not a male or man expression because indeed these are very different things as you are all starting to understand. For all the sexes have both masculine and feminine aspects in them.

Remember too that we see that your expression of gender is more and more flexible at this time. We see that in some cases and in more and more cases gender definition itself is becoming irrelevant, and we indeed encourage this view of gender expression. Indeed, if gender itself is a fun and exciting and interesting thing to explore and express we say that is great. But we are also seeing that gender in general as a strong feature of your social structures is now less and less an influencing or determining factor when you are interacting with each other.

This is a strong indication that your kind is getting ready to meet your extended families because indeed many of them do not hold genders as important as you once did since your kind once used gender roles as a means of exploitation and segregation as you have done with many other things.

But again now we say we see less and less of these restricting social role definitions and thus you are opening yourselves up to meeting different species, your extended family, who indeed have many different gender expressions or none and you are coming to understand what that means. So in this way and other ways you are getting yourselves ready to be more loving and accepting of your extended family members which makes us happy to see.

We return now to the discussion of Gaia's resources. In fact, much of Gaia's natural resources are being sold to off-world contacts. Indeed, those very rich among you are rich because of their off-world trading relationships. Know that they are selling the resources that you are entitled to as residents of this place, your home, but they are selling it on your behalf without your knowledge. There are laws that will inhibit this occurring if enough of you decide that you no longer want your planet's resources sold in this way without your consent.

Indeed, that is why much of the jewellery trade exists because it keeps you programmed to believe that these resources are so highly valued monetarily because they are rare and precious. But they are not as rare as you are made to believe by the ones who are selling them to off-world contacts. Of course there are other resources such as some of your air components and land minerals that are valuable to other species but are ample in their availability to you. You are indeed able to if you so desire create a council among you to discuss changing these off-world trade arrangements so that you are no longer being exploited in this way.

Also, much of the wealth already existing on your planet that is owned by very few of your kind needs to be shared among you all. Those ones of your kind who are hoarding it, so to speak, will be sharing the wealth very soon or else their wealth will be made obsolete by those of you who create new trade systems among yourselves.

Indeed, we are already seeing this and we encourage it.

Monopolising resources and also selling them off-world and also keeping you in pursuit of what is already entitled to you for free is all a part of the lack, slavery and competition paradigms that are still inflicting the vast majority of your species. At this time we state again that you are indeed made up of many different species but you can operate as one species as we are encouraging at this time. Also, there is to be no competition and elitism when you make new trade systems among you otherwise you will recreate for yourselves more of the same systems that are currently taking your energies and not returning you your due.

You are entitled to the resources of this planet, your home, simply by being residents of this place. Know that there are galactic and intergalactic laws requiring that off-world trading of these resources that truly belong to you will be stopped if and as soon as enough of you decide that you do not want this to be occurring.

Know that the lack, scarcity, slavery and competitive paradigm is built upon the idea that you are all essentially working for large corporations that are ultimately funded by off-world trading of the resources that actually belong to you. So you are working for others to help them further exploit you so you can keep working for them so that they can keep exploiting you. It is a self-feeding cycle that many of you are literally trapped in.

Most large corporations and most extremely wealthy individuals of your kind are wealthy because of this off-world trading scheme, whether indirectly or directly. Any monopolising of funds or energy follows the Tower of Babel blueprint and is an imbalanced masculine expression of yours. We know you are tricked or fooled into working for these large corporations because their ideas feed your desire to ascend the Tower of Babel, so to speak.

But at this time, in order to balance your expression, you need to return to your symbiosis with the earth, your mother Gaia, and in fact spread out and live more simply, so to speak, and closer to the land.

Truly, you all need to be tapping into the regenerative properties that Gaia is in possession of. Part of her existence has always been fuelled by her regenerative properties. She has food or fuel from Sol, her light energy source and her data source, and you are free to tap into this agreement yourselves. It is a feed cycle that is not a closed system. It is being fed by Sol who is fed by his connection with all the other stars in this universe.

It is a very limiting and closed system and unsustainable and non-regenerative system that many of you are addicted to or are inflicting upon yourselves. Truly, we say that the corporate model is fed by this closed system and limited energy and it literally kills everything that is attached to it because it is not fed directly by source like each of you are inside which many of you have cut yourselves off from and it is not fed from Gaia's centre which is fed by Sol who is fed by source.

You already have everything you need available to you for free and you are fooling yourselves and trapping yourselves by believing that you need to work hard for what is already your free inheritance as being ones who live on this planet and have access to their own regenerative properties and access to their own infinite source energy.

Many of your technologies have also been built upon these lack and scarcity paradigms and you are addicted and slaves to them too. We know that is changing, and we are happy that that is the case. Many of you know that indeed ones creating sustainable technologies in previous times have been murdered so that their free energy technologies and so on would not be available to you. But know now that free energy technologies abound, and they are waiting for you to want them and your addictions to lack and scarcity to be released so that you can be given them.

Truly, when enough of you are telling us that you want these free energy technologies and you do indeed give up your addictions to the scarcity and competitive systems that feed your corporations and so on, then we, the Anshar, and indeed others of your extended family that are waiting to help you are indeed at that time lawfully authorised to supersede the minority and the ones oppressing you and we will come in to give you all these technologies.

Know too that these will include technologies to travel and house yourselves. We do not need to feed you because Gaia already does that and you need to relearn how to work in symbiosis with her and stop killing yourselves and other animals with pesticides and so on.

We say now that everything that you can imagine exists and everything that you have yet to imagine exists and still even more exists. So when you commit to these slave or competitive, corporate and consumer models you are cutting yourselves off from the infinite and the divine by cutting yourselves off from your own source energy and your extended family members. Because when you give your energy to corporate and consumer models of existence you are feeding your source energy which comes through you naturally to non-sustaining systems that are outside of you and do not benefit you and thus your source energy depletes over time and thus you slowly die. Indeed, these corporate and consumer models are also designed to create addiction and dependency in you for them so that you do not see clearly where you put your energy and thus you do not take it back and feed it to yourself and channel it through your passions and your own true expressions.

Also, the corporate and consumer models present here design systems and products that speed up your death and enhance your suffering in the process. So if you see clearly what you are subjecting yourselves to when you commit to these models of existence, you likely are seeing that it is not good for you and you may see that you are literally committing yourself to a conveyor belt of suffering and death, so to speak.

Indeed, we must say also that this system or frequency or model or energy signature is replicated by your own hands when you treat animals by means of animal agriculture in the exact same way as your oppressors do when they enslave and harvest your energy all your lives until you die. And truly some of you are such good slaves that you even pay these corporations' insurance money so that when you die as a result of their system you have paid them more of your resources still so that you can have a decent funeral. Really, we are seeing that some of you are born to this world as slaves in your own eyes due to early social conditioning and at no time till your death are you managing to see clearly and changing that belief. But now we have these words written for you because indeed we are hearing enough of you seeking to see clearly and thus we help you by means of sharing our perception of you with you.

We say too at this time that you are free to learn about your extended family, or many extraterrestrial beings online since there are many sources of information about them online. However, know too that much of this information is fear based and will often misinform you. Know that even ones of your extended family that feel negative and scary are not really negative and scary but you only think that because you are so scared and are still operating within your limiting fear programs.

In relation to the ones who are benefiting from these off-world trading deals we mentioned before in conjunction with the Reptilian lords and the few others that co-operate with them, we say again they are exploiting your desire to return home by setting up figurative Towers of Babel for you to climb. But that is all an illusion and your programmed desire for Eden or home is being used against you.

Build Eden yourself with your own hands for yourself and those around you within small local communities and translocal communities and no longer give your energies to the corporate and consumer model because the corporate and consumer model is designed specifically to exploit you.

Like a large machine that requires you to plug in your source energy, it feeds off you and you are getting nothing in return but stress, sickness, shorter and less fulfilled lives, and slow deaths. Truly, all of you who are tapped into corporate structures are literally giving away your source energy to those that would happily feed off it without returning anything to you.

Indeed, you need to no longer give away your source energy, even within personal relationships or to any organisation or other being, and go inward and tap into your own source energy and your own knowing and your own inner guidance system. Truly, this is how you will be like self-sustaining free energy systems who are tapped into infinite source energy and you will be regenerated and restored and replenished and will be sustained, and more than sustained you will be fed ample energy and resources so much so that you need to share with others your excess.

Do you see how this is literally the exact opposite of the monopoly or corporate paradigms that feed off others but can never get enough and can never be sustained and always require more input and are always subject to entropy? Indeed, we say that whatever is subjected to entropy that is not also self-sustaining and regenerative is something that is part of the scarcity, slave, lack, competitive programs or systems that are infecting your home planet and your species at this time.

Truly, you need to leave jobs that create too much stress in your bodies and you need to start pursuing what genuinely satisfies you and feeds you and is sustaining for your energy fields and what inspires you, and you need to start dedicating yourself to your own creations and creating for yourselves and your friends and families and ones around you that may need help to do this for themselves or need help because they have been injured by the system, and you need to stop using your energy and your creative power for these large infections that you can see as large corporate consumer-driving structures.

At this time we know that your kind uses gold as a metaphor for value or money or winning or succeeding and indeed it holds some of those properties. Only for some of you in the pursuit of it, you overexpress masculine energy but gold itself holds a balanced and healthy expression of masculine energy. Again, we say if you let it come to you it will find you. If you are patient, if you work for things you are passionate for and things that make you feel alive, then you resonate with it and it will find you. But if you are hurting others to get it then you will not find it. If you are hurting yourselves to get it, you will not find it. Gold and all things it represents and all other things that have symbiosis with it in your minds and hold value for you are breadcrumb trails, so to speak, or invitations for you to see what you want and indeed get it but in order to get it you must express yourself with balanced masculine energy or you will not get what it is you want or indeed it will be taken away or your health or your life will be lost in the pursuit of it. This is the way and always the way it will be.

Balanced masculine energy is actually encoded in gold, the substance itself. Thus, all things that gold represents and all things that represent value to you are themselves contractually attached, so to speak, to the actual and literal requirement of you, that you express balanced and healthy masculine energy. Therefore, you will only resonate with gold and other things that represent value to you when you express healthy and balanced masculine energy. If you have what you value and it sustains you and you are living in a regenerative state then you indeed are fulfilling the healthy and balanced masculine energy expression requirements.

If you are striving and struggling for gold or what you value, or if you have it but you also have a target on your back, or if others are taking it from you, or if your health and life and happiness are being jeopardised, or if your family's health and happiness is being jeopardised, or if your relationships are in a state of suffering, then you indeed are not at that time expressing healthy and balanced masculine energy. Thus, what you want and what you value is not resonating with you and you cannot find it and if you have it you cannot keep it for it will surely phase out of your reality again and again until you hold resonance with healthy and balanced masculine energy, or otherwise you will lose your lives and all you truly value in pursuit of the false pursuit of it. Pursuit of gold itself or of things that you value shows you what sort of person you are. You will be corrupted by false pursuits but if you build from what is true to you what you value will come to you freely and easily.

So here we will help you understand what we mean when we say healthy and balanced masculine energy. It looks like this to your eyes at this time. Hearth, home, protection, love, warmth, variety, options, expansion, exploration, candidness, courage, truth, honour, notoriety for good things, healthy pleasures, laughter, things that push out or go out or require you go out are all healthy masculine expressions.

If you want to build what you value then don't compromise your values in the building process. Also, in order for you to stay tapped into your own source energy and regenerative properties you need to maintain your building processes within communities because that works best for your species at this time.

Nodal networks of your communities will form a real-time human energy grid that will power your creations with your own creative energy. Otherwise, you are not creating a cohesive grid and you are focusing too much of your energy in hot spots like cities and that does not allow for your whole species to be connected and create a fully functioning nodal network grid.

Now to do this you need to build and operate within communities locally and translocally. This means each and every one of you need to have direct contact with others that are building the same things as you are and share your values so that you can build what you value and in this process do not compromise your values at any time otherwise you create gaps and thus dysfunction in your human-powered energy grid and indeed collective consciousness grid, or as we said before, species consciousness.

Now of course with technology such as the internet you are able to engage directly in translocal communities which indeed still implies direct contact with other ones of your kind that also share your values and share your vision to build similar things. In this way you are able to work and build successfully without building a Tower of Babel, so to speak, and you will be tapping into the regenerative properties of the universe which indeed Gaia amply manifests and operates within, and you will be resisting entropy because entropy cannot touch what is imbued with such powerful source energy.

Indeed, source energy or light is so bright it will not let entropy touch it and you will be forming this grid of source energy on your planet when you work and build within local and translocal communities and manifest and operate within your values and shared values. At no time compromise your values or indeed at that time you are compromising your values you are losing touch with source energy and you are building gaps within the grid and breaking down species consciousness.

No longer cut yourselves off from source energy and instead tap into the regenerative properties of the universe which Gaia so masterfully and so beautifully models for you. Also, we say at this time that if ever you feel yourself suddenly becoming aware that you are committing or dedicating your energy to an abstract idea that you cannot understand and feels outside of you and is not directly rewarding you and satisfying you, know at that time that you have become aware that you had fallen into the Tower of Babel trap or the corporate and consumer model trap.

Indeed, things such as religion and science and money and fame and so on are all Towers of Babel which bait you into building with your energies your way back home through them, but they are illusions and traps and do not reward your energy expenditure.

You will know what does and does not work for you and what does and does not operate within regenerative properties and source energy by its fruits. Is what you are dedicating or committing your energy to making you happier and healthier? Do you feel refreshed by it? Are you expanding yourself and learning new things all the time? Are your relationships improving or degenerating? Are your personal habits and behaviours healthy or do they produce disease, sickness and addiction or dependencies in you?

These questions should be easy for any of you to answer and thus we are asking you to ask yourself these questions so that you can see where you are putting your life force or source energy and indeed if you are cutting yourself off from source energy and so on.

We see now you take on these changes and thus like a human-powered energy grid your collective consciousness can light up this whole planet and you will all positively radiate and beat with Gaia and expand and grow with her and walk with her into higher frequencies. Welcome home, friends, we have been waiting so long to meet you!

We love you

-Anshar and extended family

Relationships

Now many of you will experience great changes in your relationships when you make the changes we are suggesting you make in this text. We will start immediately by saying that divorce is not the horrible D-word that many of you speak about negatively. Indeed, we are seeing that many of you are changing the status of your relationships without jeopardising the bond that existed by means of the original relationship. And in fact divorce if you were married or some form of separation may be necessary for the sake of the bond.

For those of you who are able to grow while maintaining healthy relationships with others we say that you are doing well indeed. Also, we know that when you grow, if those you are in relationships with are not also willing to grow you may need to distance yourself from them to differing degrees based on how negatively their resistance to growth is affecting your need for growth or if indeed their growth is in a different direction to yours and not negative but different.

So we say now that many of you have engaged in the maintenance of very unhealthy relationships due to keeping up appearances, other societal or social group pressures, finances, and even religious or other rules. Indeed, any rule that keeps you in an unhealthy relationship is an abusive rule and you should not be subjecting yourselves to abusive rules.

Also, if any social pressures are the source of maintaining unhealthy relationships then we say that you need to throw off those pressures and no longer be subjecting yourselves to those either. Indeed, if you are subjecting yourselves to such rules or pressures then you are creating many more problems in your life indeed and not just the problems involved in maintaining unhealthy relationships.

Now if you are remaining in an unhealthy relationship due to finances then you need to become creative in finding means of supporting your needs. If you have children with those you are in unhealthy relationships with then that is a much more complicated problem for you and you need to consider the child's or children's welfare as much as your own. That is a case-by-case situation and so we do not comment on such complicated matters at this time.

We also mention here that it may be difficult for you to perceive or understand what an unhealthy relationship is because you have no examples of healthy relationships readily available to you and what you perceive as healthy or unhealthy in one part of your life may be very different to what you perceive as healthy or unhealthy in another part of your life.

Indeed, your conscious state, your habits and addictions, your expectations, your growth cycles and many factors all contribute to your ability to perceive what is healthy or unhealthy for you in regards to relationships with others.

Now here we are not just referring to relationships with significant others that you may have sex or marriage or children with or reside with but indeed with everyone you interact with on a regular and semi-regular basis. Even how you perceive your once-off interactions with others or those you would consider strangers is important here because you are all currently undertaking the process of attaining species consciousness, which is already your ability although you do not engage with that ability often for some of you or never for many of you. And most of you do not even know what that means at this time and are addicted to the experience of being separate.

As we mentioned before, your ability to perceive what

is healthy and unhealthy changes over time and it can change often based on many things. We say now though that it especially changes as you move into higher frequencies. Indeed, as you move into higher frequencies you can literally no longer bear or hold onto unhealthy habits or relationships and you will shed these very easily.

Also, when you shed these unhealthy habits and relationships you will find two different things happen as a result: either the person you were having an unhealthy relationship with can no longer reach you easily and cannot come into your life easily and you will not be inclined to interact with them — this is because your healthy decisions have moved you into different timelines or different frequencies and things operating on different timelines or in different frequencies cannot easily collide; or secondly, the person with which you were having an unhealthy relationship pops up again in your life as a changed person who is resonating with you in your new and healthier or higher frequencies. The one who writes this has experienced both of these changes and outcomes. She is sad for the first instance and pleasantly surprised and delighted when the latter occurs.

Now for those of you who are experiencing extremely abusive relationships or who may even fear for their physical safety and the safety of their children we say this. Remember that you are not a victim and you need to rid yourself of addiction to victimhood. Fortunately we know there is much help for those seeking it in some of your countries and we say this is a good thing for those needing it although we know the ones needing it are not always in the habit of accepting the help they need.

Also we say that in some cultures and in some countries of your kind, since you still hold your identities in the form of geographical location, there is an inbuilt habit of abusive relationships and there is no help or little help available to many because it is not even in the minds of many of you in those areas to understand what healthy interaction with others is.

We do not say this to put down the cultures of some of

you for indeed all over this place we are seeing improvement. But we do see that there are pockets of culture all around that are still basing their relationship standards on very heavy, old and negative patterns of behaviour that must be halted immediately.

We are focusing our efforts on these ones and in these areas. We now say to those of you who are more aware of what a healthy relationship means, you could lead by your example and we will give you power to do so. Already we are seeing successful movements regarding improvement of human interaction and also many old and heavy patterns of behaviour are surfacing and being exposed and healed at this time as some of your media reports and internationally published court hearings are revealing to you.

We will now give you all a brief description of what a healthy relationship is for you at this time from our perspective based on what you are currently able to perceive and operate within. As we said before you need to no longer be giving yourselves over to external things which can be many things. One of those things that many of you are giving yourselves over to is relationships.

Relationships are so different everywhere. Different species and different evolutionary states create differences in relationship expectations and thus relationship expectations or standards are changing all the time as you change. So we are not here saying once and for all time this is the standard for a healthy relationship because relationship standards will change over time as you evolve because they are intrinsically linked with your experience of change and evolution and are also a manifestation of change and evolution itself.

How you see and interact with others is literally a reflection of your conscious state or state of evolution or state of awareness or ability to consciously create. So when we define what a healthy relationship is here we are only talking to you now at this point in your timeline and at this point in your evolution. So we say now that many of you are starting to understand that you do not need to depend on others as you did before but now many of you are seeing that you can depend on yourselves. Also, many of you are seeing that you do not need to have children if you do not want to have children. Many of you are changing the way you define significant relationships and you are giving yourselves the opportunity to express relational bonds in many different ways which we find exciting when we see you opening yourselves up to these different expressions because these different and more expanded expressions are leading you soon into relationships with us and many of your extended family.

Whereas before you were too scared and too narrow in your relationship expectations that you could not see us or see that we could be your friends but you were either afraid of us or you worshipped us which in both instances you were blocking our chance to bond with you.

Also, many of you are entering into such warm relationships with yourselves or a friend or group of friends that you are not needing a significant relationship with only one other but instead your significant relationship is with yourself.

We say too that as your view of your bodies and sex becomes healthier and you enter into higher frequencies of expression, you are needing less to see each other as animal partners that are required for producing progeny and secure homes and rather you are seeing each other as eternal souls and freeing each other of the burdens of producing progeny and secure homes that you once laid upon each other.

We say now that those of you still wanting to have children that that is a beautiful desire and a most precious gift when you conceive. And indeed you are a loving person if you can create a secure and happy home for such children and yourself. But we say now too that that does need to be the automatic goal or deferred option for any of you at this time and that you should all be consciously deciding how you can best express your true natures and your unique gifts to this world. For some of you that will mean large families and large homes and for others of you it will mean friendships only or creative partnerships or group relationships or many other things.

We do not here mean to put down any other relational options that we are not mentioning here but we are saying that instead of chasing old dreams we are happy that you are making new creations for yourselves and perceiving what your best or healthiest expression is and not judging what that might look like on the outside or whether it fits old societal rules and expectations. Thank you for loving yourselves and truly, that is the best thing you could do.

And indeed love and care for those that cannot easily love and care for themselves; this includes children and older ones and any who have had hard times. Carry your own load and when you can help others, help them, but not at the expense of at least carrying your own.

Helping others should never come at the expense of a healthy relationship with yourself but of course helping others is still a very important thing to do so find balance between loving yourself and loving others.

The fruits of your relationship will demonstrate this balance. There should be an abundance of energy coming from you and it should be easy to help others in little ways and sometimes large ways if you are loving yourselves first.

Also you need to be very patient with children since they do not have all the faculties for understanding a healthy relationship and we say now that any of you not behaving in healthy ways when you interact with children, you are doing much damage to them and you will not like the repercussions of your actions because you will face them at some point in your soul's evolution.

Truly, no one is immune from the lessons of this place. Here we want to end on a positive note and say to love yourself and out of your abundance of self-love, love others and it should be feeling easy when you are tapped into your source of source energy and you are walking in your own bliss and consciously creating your own bliss. Lastly, we mention that Jesus did mention a time when you will not get married and have children and we are seeing the beginning of that time. This will not happen for all of you for quite a while but in the far futures of some of your evolutionary paths, indeed you will not be relying on each for security and progeny but will be creators of many other experiences instead.

The Moon

THE original structure that was called the Tower of Babel in the Bible, and it is referred to as different things in different ancient texts, was actually a needle, so to speak, that was capable of tapping into and feeding Gaia's energy to a mothership just outside of Gaia's orbit or energy field. This mothership was the moon.

As we said before the moon is an invader in your spatial environment and does not belong in the orbit of your home. It is an artificial structure. Indeed, now whenever you are centralising your energy toward inputs that provide you no direct benefits, i.e. you are dedicating your soul energy or efforts to an abstract idea such as a career or a large company, then you are sending out the energy that is entitled to you to use for your own benefit outward to other beings that are benefiting instead of you at your expense. Each and every one of you is not only connected to the centre of this universe and in fact many others that you are connected to, but you are also each one of you connected directly to Gaia who feeds you some of her energy which is fed to her by Sol.

She is entitled to some of his energy due to the contracts they have with each other and Gaia has with her local environment and indeed this universe.

Also know at this time that infinite iterations of this place are iterations or timelines and not indeed different universes as we define it. There are other universes that operate with completely different shapes and projections and rules for creation, and we classify those differences as different universes. So some of you are referring to timelines as parallel universes but for our purposes we say timelines and not parallel universes when we speak of similar iterations of the same thing that vary slightly or sometimes vary greatly. We are not arguing over words and definitions, but we wanted to make that clarification for your understanding when you discuss these things with yourselves and others.

Now back to our original discussion under this heading. Each of you are entitled to energy directly from Sol and from Gaia but you are giving this energy away and it is being used to build structures that you can see and cannot see with your eyes and those structures, as they currently operate, are being used against you and to further exploit you.

At this time we would also mention that there are iterations or timelines of this place your home that did not experience the invasion of the moon and thus the evolution they experienced is completely different to the one you are experiencing here. Now there are iterations of this place your home that experienced the invasion of the moon and then also experienced the removal of the moon from your orbit.

At this time we want to address the symbolism that has been created by your kind in relation to the presence of the moon in your orbit. Know at this time that indeed Gaia represents and indeed embodies the energy of the healthy feminine energy that is healthy for you to have symbiosis with and express. However, we know many of your kind for thousands of years have used the moon Lun or Luna to be the symbol or embodiment of feminine energy for you and indeed that is why many of you have suffered because of it.

We refer here to the suppression of feminine energy and feminine expression whether by male or female sexes or by any gender expression. All of you know that the moon does not produce its own light and indeed we say now that there are moons of other planets that in fact do. And the relationships they have with their moons are completely different to yours, and so we are not here saying that moons are bad and are all invaders. We are, however, referring only to your moon at this time.

Now your moon Luna does not produce her own light or her own energy, but she holds much influence over your minds and bodies. She does not, however, affect your souls or soul energy because she is not tapped into the same energy network of source energy that indeed Sol and Gaia are.

We are not here trying to be moon haters or engender that expression in any way because we love the moon, and we know many of you love it and are attached to your ideas about it and your relationship with it. We are, however, clarifying some things for you regarding her because she has impacted your reality in some negative ways.

So here we refer to the fact that she cannot feed you source energy or information like Sol and Gaia can. She also robs, so to speak, or taints the relationship Sol and Gaia have like an intruder into a committed relationship. We are not saying that this is bad in itself but this occurrence has indeed negatively impacted your kind.

She represents an unhealthy expression of feminine energy who needs to feed off others to sustain herself. She is shy and quiet, so to speak, and represents the feminine expression that is stifled and suppressed. She holds onto your shadows and shadow energies and that is part of why you even have the phrase 'the dark side of the moon'.

Know that she represents what you do not want to bring into the light and be open about and thus she cooperates with your shame paradigms. This sounds sad, we know, since we know many of you are attached to her beauty. But indeed we need to state this. Many of your kind for thousands of years have looked up instead of down or around. Many of your kind know that Sol is masculine energy and that Lun is feminine energy. And you have looked at those two as if they were the masculine and feminine energies that you should be emulating. And thus many of your kind have used the silence of the moon, so to speak, as an excuse for those suppressing feminine energy to also make it silent or suppressed or voiceless.

At the time of you looking up to see the masculine and feminine energies you have been neglecting that the one you live on your mother Gaia is the feminine energy or aspect that you are actually in need of embodying for your own health and happiness. Indeed, Gaia is strong and productive and resilient. Lun, however, produces nothing of her own and thus for many thousands of years feminine energy was required to be dependent and not productive and quiet since many of you had been modelling your feminine aspect on her. That is also why feminine energy has also been overly related to unproductive females or feminine energy that is needy and not strong. Indeed, healthy feminine energy is incredibly powerful and productive and is modelled by Gaia and not Lun.

Now we say at this time that Gaia is currently being exploited by those of your kind and other beings who are taking her resources for greedy reasons and are not rehabilitating her. In this way feminine energy or expression is still vulnerable to exploitation, but we see that this is slowly ending because we can see the behaviour of many of you changing and moving away from exploitative creation and expression.

At this time we encourage you to research about the disclosure movement which is helping your kind see the greater world in which you live and what has been happening behind the scenes, so to speak, around you all the time but hidden for thousands of years.

In this regard also we say that the Vatican vaults are in containment of almost every piece of information that you are in need of to learn about who you are and what is around you and has been around this whole time while you were evolving and still only learning to identify that your hand is attached to your arm. We use this example of a baby learning that their hand is attached to their own arm because indeed that is how many of you are acting.

You are believing the false history that is being fed to you and live a programmed life that does not ultimately benefit you. At no time are many of you questioning reality and are spending much of your time in distractions and feeling accomplished by your discovering that your hands are attached to your arms, so to speak.

We are here now telling you that your reality is indeed so much bigger than what you are currently aware of for most of you and yet this bigger reality has been affecting you the whole time. So there have been elements and key parts of your reality that have been affecting you all the time and yet you exist without knowledge or awareness of them.

You are living with the effects of things that you are not exploring the cause of.

This is very strange to us indeed that more of you are not investigating the cause of all the things affecting you and you are sucking down the easy lies fed to you to keep you in your ignorant states. Some of this is due to you poisoning yourselves on a daily basis which stops your minds working properly, some of it is due to your obsessions and addictions to some forms of entertainment and amassing material wealth, and also there are frequencies being played by frequency projectors in your atmosphere that are literally keeping your minds low and are not allowing you to have clear minds and enjoying higher frequencies.

Please know that there is an extremely sophisticated system in place all around you to keep your minds foggy or muddy and slow. You are being kept anaesthetised, so to speak, and in some cases literally in the case of some foods, medications and trapping frequency projectors.

We know that many of you no longer want to be as cattle in the field being fattened for the slaughter. We hear that you are no longer benefiting from your slave programming and that the ill consequences such as stress and disease and breakdown of relationships and a feeling of being cut off from the divine is now finally getting to be too much for enough of you that you no longer want to stay as zombies, so to speak.

At this time we will actually mention that in some iterations of this place your home and indeed in many other places in the multiverse there are indeed zombies as you have written about and put into your shows and films. However, we say this now, that even though you are not experiencing a zombie apocalypse, so to speak, at this time, you actually are because so many of you are walking around like mindless bots carrying out the orders of your oppressors and exploiters.

We do not say this to be harsh, but we say this to actually tell you what it is we are seeing when we look at you. For those of you currently enjoying higher frequencies you are able to see clearly the programs all around you that are keeping your kind low. Indeed, for those of you throwing off the programming and the poisons you feel like you are free all of a sudden and light and full of life and are refreshed and restored and connected to everything that feeds your soul.

We invite you all now to throw off your zombie programming and enter into your fuller and truer natures and no longer be as zombies or fattened cattle for the slaughter. Now for those of you wanting to learn more about the moon we ask that you engage with the movement called disclosure. We also ask that you do not turn to fear or violent rebellion but simply that you inform yourselves from a wide variety of sources so that you can start making your own minds up about what is real instead of just what you are fed by mainstream programming and education.

We say now that we are not meaning to say that all mainstream operations or expressions are negative or negatively programming you for indeed more and more there are some wonderful mainstream creations. We are saying, however, that those seeking to sustain their oppression and exploitation of you are often using mainstream means or channels to do so. Therefore, you need to be selective and observe the frequencies at which different mainstream creations operate within. This action may be difficult at first; however; it will become easier and easier because indeed you were made with this ability, and we and many others are here helping you to do such things in order to wake you up, so to speak, and move to higher frequencies.

So if you love the moon then we say that is okay but please express your feminine energy by means of Gaia's example and not Luna's.

Now at this time we will mention emotion. We said before that you experience information or energy in your body as feeling or emotion and you can verbalise this emotional energy or think about it as feelings in the higher chakras.

Now we will say that water itself is a data bank or storer itself of your emotion. Water itself holds and processes your emotions for you, all who are on this planet. Now it is said that the majority of the surface of your home, this place or planet, is covered in water. And so what do you think that says about how your kind deals with emotions?

Indeed, your kind is requiring at this time much emotion storage and processing on your behalf since at this time it is too much for you to bear as a species on your own. Also, of course the water processes Gaia's emotions for her and indeed the many other beings currently residing in this place your home at this time.

Water itself feeds you, as you know, and is a requirement of your bodies. So what do you think that says about your needs? It means that every day you all need to be processing your emotions because you are all holding on to far more than you even now can comprehend. Indeed, you are holding the emotion of each one of your genetic lineages in your actual bodies and local fields. You are all in need of processing this emotional information on a daily basis and of course we know many of you are not and thus you are not healthy, many of you.

At this time we will relate this process to the moon since that is what we are talking about here. Although we mentioned that indeed the moon is an invader into the relationship between your star Sol and your mother Gaia, we are still fond of Lun indeed.

Since she has been in place she has done much service for you. She pulls on your waters, as you know, and she has developed a deep symbiosis with your emotions as a result since she actually feeds on them and helps you process them. Indeed, she is an amazing emotional catalyst.

This one is greatly affected by the powerful moon events and those events have indeed literally moved her to clean her emotional baggage, so to speak, which means it has literally motivated her to process or clear her field and energies stuck in her body.

Now of course we know some of you already have a relationship with the moon and for those of you that currently do not we are saying that you are likely neglecting a relationship with your emotions and shadow self and thus you are also neglecting one of your crucial responsibilities, that of processing the emotional information that is on this plane or in this place that you are now calling home.

Please be no longer neglecting this crucial work for indeed those of you neglecting it are actually heaping the load onto those brave enough and strong enough to do that work at this time. We say now indeed if you process only a little of your emotional information every day then you are doing this processing work and you are helping to clear the shame clouds and so on.

So you can see now the relationship between water itself being a holder of emotional energy or information and thus too just as clouds are made of water, so too are shame clouds, as we spoke about earlier, made of collective groupings of your shame energy which is any emotion you are not all processing at this time.

You literally create the weather, dear ones. Know that now. Your experience of emotion is deeply linked with your experience of weather. Indeed, we know there are different parts of your world or home that typically experience different weather and thus we say that indeed those areas are also dealing with larger doses of the energy that that weather would actually bring.

Indeed, just as light literally is information, so water and by extension weather is literally emotion which is information that has been in your body's lower chakras or indeed is lower frequency information that can only be processed by the body at this time.

This is why your chakras need to all be functioning

otherwise you cannot be doing this processing work which is needed at this time but of course has always been needed while any of you were requiring emotion as a part of your experience of existence.

Now too we give an example this one who speaks for us has had. When she was visited by a friend of hers that had died, this friend simulated for her in her mind the experience of floating on a beautiful dark and warm sea. The sea itself was actually made of love and thus this one actually was gifted the experience of swimming in love as a substance around her body like water.

Now we say that indeed there are homes or places or planes or realities or simulations or planets that literally have seas or bodies of water made of different emotions. This sea that was gifted briefly as an experience to this one was made of love, as we said, but there are others too made of other emotions.

At this time we will inform you also that comparatively speaking, your collective species actually experiences a slightly broader than average range or spectrum of emotion. Indeed, there are other species that feel much more broadly and deeply than you and of course there are many species that have a much shorter spectrum or range of emotion than you are currently able to experience.

Here we give another example to demonstrate this point to you. This one who writes for us, who also likes to occasionally draw or paint, felt moved one day many years ago to draw a sad jester. She hung this picture on her wall for a few months until she took it down and forgot about it and eventually she threw it away when she moved house.

Now many years later, which in your time as we say these things to you is now over a year ago, she met this very individual that she drew all those years ago.

She had moved many times and so this person she kept seeing around her home she thought was attached to the house she happened to be living in at the time. She was only seeing this person from the torso down. This being appeared to her eyes as very tall and skinny with a slightly hunched back and very long arms and legs with very long fingers. She sensed the being was male.

Now after seeing this one walking around her house at the time for many months she met him in a dream state while she was sleeping one night. At this time she saw the being's head as well and soon she recognised that he was the one that she drew all those years ago. He had a very long face, about twice as long as the average human face. He had long teeth too with large gaps between them. His skin was sallow and sunken like the flesh of humans that have been preserved by swamps or ice over thousands of years. He had a cartilage extension that was attached to his shoulders and went up and around his head like a large collar behind his head. To her, he actually looked like the comical representations of Dracula except in this case the collar of Dracula's cape was actually a part of his body in the form of this cartilage structure that was attached to his shoulders and neck.

He felt sad, but he wasn't actually sad, so to speak. His mother, who looked like a female version of him, was telling this one that she was here to pick up her son who had lived around this one all these years. He had been living around her to learn a larger range of emotion since their species has a very short range of emotion that you humans would describe as being akin to apathy and sadness.

Indeed, this one has much apathy and sadness in her and thus she attracted the existence of this other being to her presence all these years. The mother of this being was very thankful to this one who speaks for us, for she had been a good teacher of emotion. Indeed, there are many around you at all times and many of them are gentle and kind ones who want to learn from you.

Indeed, she saw this being on another occasion before his mother collected him. On a night months before his departure from this one's presence, this one was having a conversation about extraterrestrials with two friends and this being came into the room via a portal about a metre in diameter and came and sat down on a chair next to this one because he wanted to listen and be part of the conversation.

Indeed, as we said, there are many ones around you at

all times, and they are here learning from you. Of course, we are aware too that there are those that are not as peaceful to you but there is much protection that is being given to you via your higher self, your guardians and those of the galactic and intergalactic organisations that govern your home at this time.

Indeed, the consequences for those who abuse lesser ones or weaker ones, so to speak, are too great for most beings to consider it worth doing. No being is authorised to abuse you except those you have already authorised by means of life choreography before you came here or by means of the arrangements made by those currently oppressing you as part of this experiment. But as we said before that experiment is over. Thus, indeed we say now that you are authorising their continued abuse of you by means of your regular cooperation with their programming and schemes and energy and frequencies and vibrations.

So back to our example. The being that was living around her for many years had a small range of emotion that his conscious state allowed him to experience, and he could learn by observation what emotions looked like when humans experienced them. Indeed, this one was a great teacher because she has expressed many different emotions. (We are laughing with her when she writes this.) So at this time we say that by coming here and taking on the human vessel or form you have indeed signed up to experience a broad range of emotion and thus your home has much water and the moon in this case to help you process all this emotion. Also, to reiterate at this time, it is indeed your responsibility, each one of you, to process a little emotional energy or information every day so that your species and home can move into higher frequencies.

Amen

-Anshar

Jesus of the Anshar

W

E like to pronounce this, one of his many names, as Hey-soos as it is said in the Spanish language, or Yeh-shoo-wa as it is in Hebrew. That is because it is closer to his Anshar name which we call him in our language. He has many names and it does not matter what you call him. He is, as many of you refer to him, an ascended master.

There are many ascended masters among the Anshar. Indeed, many of us, as we said before, have taken human form to make large changes in your timelines since those timelines that we were coming into were heading into horrible places and were not changing or learning. Indeed, many of you know Jesus as a teacher, and we know some of you believe he never actually existed.

Those of you who believe he never actually existed are either from other timelines where he did not come or you are pretending that you do not have faith or intuition because that pretence makes you feel more secure or intelligent. Indeed, we say that he was and is a real person, and he is of the Anshar but now he is an ascended master that does much work for you and other species.

We quickly address now what we mean when we say ascended master. We know many of you have taken to making saints or holy ones out of some of your kind or indeed of other species who came in and did great things. They are lightworkers or love workers of the highest echelons to your eyes. Indeed, there are higher ones or higher frequency beings that do this work too, but these ones you would experience as ascended masters are able to travel light spectrums that include yours.

Now we say too that indeed the many Buddhas and other religious icons that did great things and loved you all, these ones can be said to be ascended masters as well. Only different cultures of course call them different things, but indeed any being that dedicates or commits all of its energy to demonstrating love or light for the benefit of a whole species, then they are in this category of ascended ones.

Indeed, this one has ascended, but she is not an ascended master. There are many of you who are here only to help others, and we thank you. This one is here to help others but also has much of her own karma to heal as well. There are those of you who have not much karma to process and you are actually here to help only. Those ones of you who are helpers in this way, we thank you, you are doing an amazing work and you know who you are.

We do say about this one who writes for us, however, that she is a much larger soul and is not comfortable in human form because it is very restricting for her expression. Indeed, she has suffered much by being held and inhibited by this vessel but indeed she persists because she wants to carry out her contracts to be here and help others.

Now back to our headed topic. Jesus, we know, is many things to you, including nothing at all. But indeed his energy is still here because he made such an impact while he was here. Indeed, as we said before, he did not intend to produce many religions in his name but as is evident that is how many of your kind responded.

We know that indeed the response was mainly due to an attempt to control you and at no time do we condone the actions of religious ones who did horrible things in the name of Jesus. But of course as he was in life (his human life in your past), he made an extremely convenient scapegoat and indeed he still continues to be.

We do not require that you worship Jesus in any way because that would go against the main message in this text. That of no longer giving yourselves over to other things or giving your energy away.

You no longer need to worship Jesus or whoever you believe him to be because he is not in need of your worship and neither are you.

You no longer need to and rather you would benefit from putting that energy to directly helping others, building healthy local and translocal communities and genuinely loving yourself and those around you if you are able.

Now we say if you are able because we do not believe all of you are easy to love. However, it is ultimately the responsibility of each one of you to actually love yourselves; even if that is the only love you can give you should be giving it to yourselves. Because just as in aeroplanes (for those of you who have experienced flying in them) you are instructed to put the oxygen mask on yourself before others, in the same way you are not able to love others if you do not first love yourself.

We know this sounds cliché to some of you, that you should love yourself, but even to those to whom it sounds cliché you are not actually doing it, and we say now that when it comes to love that is your only responsibility.

Of course as a result of loving yourself you will love others, but we know some of you are not trusting this. We know some of you are addicted to being as hollow shells. Others still would not love themselves and instead hate themselves and thus be hateful to others and be difficult to be around.

Indeed, this one was hateful for many years until her adrenal system gave way, and she literally could no longer hold hate in her body any longer. Truly, this one who speaks for us held hate in her body for so many years that her adrenal system gave up and stopped working properly. She still now struggles with lack of energy and muscle weakness. And indeed, as one of her visitors recently said, who was an extraterrestrial to your eyes, this one indeed was in the habit of unknowingly making tasty hate meals for this being that visited her to consume.

So to you we say that it is indeed very important to process your emotions as we said before and also to make it a priority to love yourselves. If Jesus would say anything to you, know he would state that one task as being of most importance because indeed all good things follow on from the very act of loving yourself!

-Jesus of the Anshar

Portals Are Toroidal (and are also Vector Ducts)

THE cervix can be seen as a toroid and a portal. The third eye is also a portal. Portals which are a common means of travel for many different species of being are toroidal. There are of course other structural forms portals can take, depending on the technology used. For example, counter-rotating spirals of electromagnetic energy that form pre-assigned gateways to other realms. Or portal technology that flattens your light body to travel on the 2D freeway network. For toroidal portals, a little cylindrical hole like a small worm is punched in space with a device that is calibrated to poke holes in space under a controlled setting. Then both ends of the hole, or wormlike hollow, curl over to touch each other. Much like if you were to cut the closed end of a sock off and roll the fabric edges of both ends down to meet each other. This process forms a toroid. Once the ends are sufficiently joined, the hole or hollow in the centre slowly expands as the toroid pulls into itself more energy. The hole is then expanded to the desired diameter for transport. The diameter of a portal is about one or two metres for the average being and of course much larger for large things like craft.

We do briefly mention here an example. Aside from

the many portals your kind has seen in the sky for craft and other means of transport, about which your media sources are often misstating what they are with absurd explanations that are only convincing the most gullible and ignorant of your kind, there are cases where some of you have seen them in your homes or on a more personal scale. Indeed, this one has seen many portals open in her home or various rooms she was in.

Over a year ago while this one was in dream state, she opened up a portal above her body that led into a part of space she did not recognise the energy signature of. Indeed, this portal was a stunning creation. It was large enough to fit her whole body through, although she did not enter through it. The interface of this portal was covered or laced with crystals that were forming and breaking down and reforming and always moving. The crystal lattice was simultaneously a gas, a liquid and a solid. It was in plasma state and the crystals were in rainbow colours to this one's eyes. Indeed, this interface of plasma-state crystal structures was a protection for her so that she did not enter through the portal to an unknown part of space to her.

Several weeks ago, Aliwai, Narabatu's mother, sought to visit him and give him a message. Thus, this one, while she was sitting in her living room, sensed a shift and felt a presence all of a sudden when Aliwai came to visit. She saw the tail end of the portal closing as a little ball of energy that looked blue and yellow. At this very moment she also noticed that the television, which was on at the time, changed its image projection, due to the interfering frequencies of the portal and thus, the TV showed a chequerboard pattern on it for several seconds. Aliwai whispered her message to her son, which was to remind him to be kind because indeed she knew the time was coming that he would be helping in writing this text. A few minutes later she left again by the same means, and again the television screen displayed a chequerboard pattern while she left. We mention that this one saw Aliwai with her third eye and would still likely freak and jump out of her seat if she saw her with her two eyes since she has not been opening herself up enough and still sometimes fears beings that look different.

We do want to quickly mention here that ones of your extended families that want to meet you not only meet you in your dreams, but they often project their faces or forms into your conscious states by means of organising your perception to see their faces or forms in the patterns of material fibres or leaves or clouds or dust or wood grain or reflections and so on, for that is a much gentler way for them to introduce themselves to you.

Hybrid Children Program

THERE are various hybrid children programs that are creating many hybrid children between many of you and other beings at this time. You have contracted to participate in these programs either before you entered into the human body or at some time after you entered via your higher self or indeed some of you consciously in your regular conscious state as an awakened human being.

Now we say that in terms of the Grey contracts, it is part of the original experiment design that they would create hybrids with your DNA. Also, there are many other non-original contracts that arose at later and more recent times.

Now at no time is any being who is retrieving your DNA permitted to hurt you. Although we know some of you are experiencing great fear and terror when this is occurring because you are not retaining the contract information in your regular conscious state as humans at this time.

Indeed, we say that we are not in accord with all the DNA retrieval agreements but at no time are you truly being hurt or damaged by this process and indeed there is much benefit to creating hybrid progeny for your various evolutionary paths. And also for the purpose of merging you with your extended family, the many different species or races of beings you call extraterrestrials and higher dimensional beings.

Indeed, these hybrid children programs are one of the main ways you start evolving and start broadening your experience in this multiverse. As we said before, all of you are already hybrids since you were made by us from the beginning, and we and many others were always helping you evolve and putting some of our DNA in you.

And also while some of your hybrid children are residing in other realms or on craft, some of you are actually physically giving birth to hybrid children because your reproductive organs and cells have been assisted to carry this out. Indeed, this one has had her DNA extracted and her future embryos are being taken care of by one of her guides. She was fully conscious at the taking of her reproductive tissue, her eggs, and she personally met the guide that is assisting the development of her future embryos. Indeed, this guide is of the Greys and is a very loving and wise one. She was also contacted by negative ones of the Greys to have a child for them, but she declined, which any of you are able to do, if you are not in full agreement with the process. She was pestered on and off for years to have a child for this particular negative group of Greys. They even set up a match for her with the man they wanted to be the father of the child. Again, we said she did not follow through with their wishes. Also, they showed her that she possessed an important lineage to them, and she could bring through Lucifer if she wanted to. After that particular incident she cut off contact with them completely and more benevolent groups of extraterrestrials came in to aid her.

Also, she has been contacted by the flower beings, or ones of the Fae that are flower people, who have asked her to have one of their children. This child of the Fae will come in as a girl, which this one will have in her future. The soul of this particular child to come through is an abandoned soul who needs much love when she comes through into this realm. Indeed, this one's future embryos are already in the care of her guides, and when she is ready to bear and deliver them she will enter into that phase of the agreement.

We give this one as an example because she is one to be pleased about bearing her future hybrid children. Indeed, there are also many others. Feel free to explore this topic online because indeed there are many online resources for this topic, and we ask you to explore it for yourself with a loving attitude because, as we said before, this is one of the main ways that your species evolves and endeavours upon its many evolutionary paths.

Again, we say too that you are also already hybrids, so this discussion is making you aware of that fact if you were not already. And also, this should make you aware that you are able to engage with this process further, directly and indirectly, for the improvement of your lives and the lives of your kind.

Dinosaurs

INOSAURS are a great distraction for many of you but in the least your recognition of their existence helps you understand that your home planet has not always been just yours and in fact as we said before it is the home of many other species of being and not just the animals that are described in your biology textbooks.

Indeed, new species are regularly being introduced to your environments and many species of beings you seek the evolutionary origin of you cannot because they were introduced artificially, so to speak, by those making them and introducing them.

When we say other beings we are also meaning other beings with much greater intelligence or awareness states than you and with superior senses and technologies. These ones have lived among you for thousands of years outside the scope of your perception by design or by means of them existing within different frequencies or densities of reality.

Now we speak of many underground or subterranean ones as well. There are indeed many species that live happily underground, and to them, you are considered surface dwellers. Indeed, we, the Anshar, for a time have lived in subterranean environments to avoid your detection but also some of us live among you but you do not always notice because we look like you but also we and other beings are able to cast protective shields that shield your perception of us when we are around you.

Indeed, know that many of your secret organisations are aware of the existence of many different life forms that they do not inform the public of. For example, this one who speaks for us received by means of astral travel, or remote viewing, knowledge of a subterranean prison of many Reptilians and other beings that exists under a small white cottage in a Northern England woodland area. She saw the top two levels of this facility and she was sad that they were held in captivity.

Know that there are many things indeed not seen by your eyes at this time that have been existing all around you but this is changing and many of you are starting to see what you were not seeing before.

With regard to the ones you call dinosaurs we say that this one indeed was part of an early iteration of a secret program to recreate different dinosaur species to study them and so on. They were being made and lived on another planet nearby yours.

Inevitably within that program there were also ones who wanted to exploit them. Now we say that of course dinosaurs and ones like them exist in many other realms and still exist on your planet in different timelines. Regarding this one's memory of this early dinosaur program we say this. As a powerful empath, she remembered feeling the feelings of a large female Tyrannosaurus Rex that she was observing while it was in a field. This T-Rex she saw then being shot down by those in this early program. This early program was in operation in the 1950s in your timeline and existed in other realms as well.

Looking after the emotional wellbeing of these dinosaurs was one of her early assignments since she was an empath and indeed she recalls an attempt to kill her by one of the male agents in the program who was working for the exploitative part of the program that this one's empathic duties would have gotten in the way of.

Indeed, we say again that this one as she is now is a clone of a previous iteration of herself in the 1930s; much of her was remade in her 1980s iteration. She was born both times naturally by women but the embryo she was

was indeed modified by her guides and others supporting her existence in the programs so that she could perform much benevolent work.

Many of you have had several iterations of yourself throughout different time periods if you like certain facets of your vessel. Indeed, of course this one as many of you have had many lives here in many different vessels but sometimes you also choose to have the same or very similar vessel so that you can perform similar functions in different time periods.

In a way it's like time travelling but it is time travel with the benefit of being influenced directly by the time period into which you enter since you have parents and family and social conditioning of that time period that subject you directly to that time period, otherwise you act as too much of an outsider to perform much of the necessary work or functions you have chosen to perform during that time period.

As we said before, this one has Narabatu also operating with her so that when she did good deeds, he was doing good deeds and thus he was able to learn how to do good for others through her. He also imbued her with much of his power and thus she was beneficial for those seeking his qualities in their programs.

The dinosaurs that were specifically here on your home planet that you have dug up or discovered were indeed intelligent and loving beings and should not be viewed as monsters. Indeed, just as the animals all around you are just like you, so were the dinosaurs.

Animals that you consider less evolved or less intelligent than you are in many cases more evolved or more intelligent than you but you do not know this because you cannot perceive their language and your arrogance leads you to believe that you are superior.

But we know many of you know the truth of the wisdom, grace and love of the animals all around you and some of you are starting to see this too. We encourage this of course because loving relationships with the surrounding beings will help you enter into higher frequencies but in the meantime will make you happy and make the animals happier too.

Dinosaurs were another experiment before you; they did not evolve naturally as you did not. Evolution is a process that is often tinkered with so do not get caught up on the specifics of the process because in almost every case it is tinkered with or even if it is not directly tinkered with by certain beings, it is directly influenced by the evolution of consciousness or different conscious states of the planet itself that the different ones exist upon or within and the conscious states of the beings themselves.

It is not only a biological and chemical process as many of your scientists like to think and talk about at this time. Physical evolution is always a manifestation of higher states of existence and never the other way around. Little cells did not evolve, so they could become like you for those cells were already conscious happy beings that did not need to change. Rather, the flow of evolution itself was experienced by the being Gaia herself and thus what she manifested on her and within her changed as she changed and also indeed by the help of others that were creating different cells and animals and evolving them for their own purposes.

Time Skips and Slips

WE want to mention at this time that indeed many of you will experience changes in your experience of time as you start exiting Time's womb, so to speak. As you enter into higher frequencies, mastery of such a thing as your experience of time will be gifted to you because mastery of time is itself a by-product of existing in higher frequencies because time as you now experience it in your lower frequencies cannot touch you or affect you in higher frequencies in the same ways.

We are higher ones, as we said before, and it is easy for us to traverse time and enter into different time periods or navigate it as it truly is as a viscous substance that our technology and conscious state allow us to manipulate and navigate.

Indeed, there are time bubbles that can protect us from the viscosity or density of time of which you are currently subject to. As you enter into higher frequencies which you all are if you stay here because that is where Gaia is going, you will experience more and more things that you would previously choose to ignore or view as anomalies that are too weird to further analyse.

So we give you two examples that this one who writes for us has had in recent times. Over a year ago this one looked at her phone to see what the time was, and she saw with her eyes the digital clock time go back one minute and then since she thought she imagined it, she stayed watching it for a little while and then it jumped forward again to the original time that it was when she first looked at it. Some of you might think that that was a trick of the eye or trick of the mind. But these very experiences are what we are referring to when we say there will be things you experience that you used to ignore or just believe were just your imagination. (Really, all of this is your imagination because this reality is a projection of your conscious state.)

Another more recent event occurred for her just yesterday. On two different occasions yesterday she experienced what we would call a time skip. Her conscious state or state of projecting reality did not perfectly match the conscious state or projection of reality by Gaia and those around her, and so she experienced in the morning a mini time jump or skip forward and in the afternoon a time jump or skip back (in order to rectify the initial skip forward).

Both times the skips were tiny and only of a few seconds in length to her experience. But they were significant enough for her to notice. In fact this has happened to her several times in previous weeks too. In previous weeks she would experience, for example, holding a cup and then all of a sudden her hand was slamming the cup down on a table. She did not experience the normal linear experience of realising to herself that she wanted to put the cup down and then sensing or seeing her own arm bring the cup down to the table. Instead, she experienced a time skip where literally in one moment she was holding the cup near her face and in the very next moment with no movement of her arm in her experience the cup was being slammed on the table. This time skip almost made her drop the cup completely and she made a little mess.

Time skips can happen in far more dramatic ways of course, some of which can be slightly dangerous if you can imagine.

One of the two time skips she experienced yesterday was of her going to put something in the trash or bin, only to see that it wasn't there and that it was already in the trash or bin. Many of you, including this one, want to believe that she put this item in the bin and merely forgot she did. But that is what your current logic would lead you to believe but things like time skips are happening more and more so that you cannot keep thinking it is just your forgetfulness that is creating gaps and sometimes large gaps in your conscious experience of this reality.

Indeed, they almost feel like blackouts because there is absolutely no recollection of the experience of time in between the two time events that flank each side of the time jump or skip.

So indeed at no time did she actually put this item in the bin and forget or have a mini blackout but indeed her consciousness and thus her creation is getting faster and faster to where she does not actually need to physically do things to make them happen, so to speak. Indeed, she is no longer needing to believe that her physical body needs to move objects for them to be actually moved, for example.

Of course some ghosts and loved ones may move items around in your environment to have fun with you or as a way to try to communicate with you. Or indeed in some cases certain ones may shield the perception of actual items from your conscious awareness so you think they are missing but really they are there but their existence has been shielded from you. Here though we are actually speaking of time skips and indeed we know some of you are experiencing large time skips or large jumps.

This one does not want to miss too much of her experience of linear time, so she will not manifest too much skipping. But indeed those of you less attached to linear time may already be experiencing large skips and these may become larger over 'time'.

The other time skip she experienced yesterday was while she was reading something she typed, and then she looked again and the sentence she was reading wasn't there but in fact it was the next sentence that was needing to be typed. While she was reading the sentence in the first instance, she was actually seeing a few seconds into her future. She thought maybe that the sentence was there and it just was deleted accidentally but that was not the case. She was existing a few seconds ahead of the rest of her reality and then after a few seconds it quickly adjusted itself and pulled her back a few seconds to the time before the sentence had been written.

We know these are very small and mundane examples but indeed if you notice just little things like this, then know that they are your experience of time skips which are happening more and more while Gaia and the surrounding reality are adjusting to your shared conscious state.

Indeed, you are projecting reality based on your conscious state and so is everyone around you. In lower frequencies there is not often much difference between different ones' projection of reality. In the higher frequencies that you are now entering, different ones of you are taking them on at different rates and your conscious states are adjusting to the differences in the shared reality in slightly discombobulated ways.

Indeed, other ones around you can sometimes inflict their projection of reality upon you and you may take it up to differing degrees. At this time though everyone is taking on Gaia's changes and thus everyone is experiencing different rates of time itself as each of you have different body and field systems and different ways of taking on her new energy and these higher frequencies she is now entering into with you.

Also know at this time that there is a shadow universe entering into symbiosis with this universe that exists between moments or exists in the 'in-between'. Thus, in between every moment that you consider a moment, this universe exists between two of those moments almost imperceptible to most of you.

We are not speaking of literally seconds of clock time, but rather between moments of consciousness or the rate at which you can perceive reality. To explain further, the rate at which you project reality and then perceive it has gaps that you could refer to as moments.

Like pixels of time or frames of film you are first creating or projecting reality and then this human vessel is perceiving that projection by aid of your conscious state. There are different rates at which you project and perceive based on what frequency you operate or function or exist within. Many beings exist or resonate at higher frequencies and thus the gap between creation or projection and perceiving is less delayed than yours.

Now this shadow universe is much like the one we are all in now but it has a slightly higher and offset frequency that allows it to slip into the gaps of this one. Thus, for those of you interested in synchronistic digital clock time such as '11:11' or '1:33' or '11:44' or '22:22' or '3:38' and so on, among other things, you are listening to the beat of this shadow universe. Because these synchronistic clock times hold several functions, but one of the functions they perform is that they act as alignment portals, so to speak.

Shadow beings from the shadow universe can slip into your universe at these clock times because these synchronicity clock times hold louder frequencies or energy signatures that are mimicked and are more easily interacted with by those seeking to traverse your linear time. In this way these shadow ones from the shadow universe that is merging with yours at this time slip stream, so to speak, into your timelines by means of these aligned clock times.

We know that sounds odd to some of you but these ones are able to navigate time that way because it is part of their creation and their perception and thus part of their manipulation of reality. To sum up, there is an endless supply of odd things to learn and experience if you pay attention. So pay attention if you want to learn more about this vast and infinitely variable reality!

Also, since it was that we mentioned to you synchronistic clock times, we also mention here that such forms of synchronicity, among many other synchronicity symbols such as numbers, sounds, light, animals, words, phrases, songs, and so on, are used for communication with non-physical beings or non-physical aspects of self or others. They also serve as personal signposts to represent that a given individual is indeed on their choreographed path of consciousness expansion. When such synchronicities align, it helps draw out the consciousness of a given individual from a small story and attachment to limited viewpoints, and invites them into a more expanded realm of play, containing a much larger range of possibilities.

Like a tablecloth getting pulled off a table. When the mind moves into higher frequencies, things that were once disparate now align, join, merge, bridge or connect. The tablecloth which once sat flat on the table gets creased and folded and different parts of it touch that were previously not in connection with each other. A mind that plays in a single realm is like a tablecloth sitting flat on table. A mind that is expanded and sees endless synchronicities by means of alignment portals is like a tablecloth that can move, twist, bend and fold.

Essentially when it is that you are regularly identifying synchronicity in your daily lives, know that that is an example of your mental or conscious state changing and you are folding or bending reality to match your needs and wants at those times. Indeed, you feel more like yourself and more in control when it is that you keep finding things that just keep working out for you.

And indeed the flow you experience and the delight you feel that results from things that just keep working out or when all the loose ends keep being tied up perfectly in a bow for you, so to speak, then know that that is you experiencing the 4D reality. Truly in higher frequency, reality is delightful and poetic and more meaningful and is more like a dance and loose ends get tied up with symmetry and time is your friend and not your enemy or master. And this flow state is a demonstration to you that you are leaving dense linear time and entering a state of existence that is packed with personal meaning rather than a series of impersonal consequential events.

So when it is that you are always experiencing synchronicity know that higher frequency energy signatures are upon those things and indeed they act as little signposts for you from your higher self or other higher ones to help you direct yourselves in this maze that you made for yourselves in these lower frequency playing fields.

Critical Self-Talk

WE speak of critical self-talk now because this ability of yours is powerful indeed and is almost always operating in the background of each one of your minds; we know because we can hear it.

Now your ability to be critical, as most of you experience it, is due to the parts of your minds that conjure logical explanations for things.

As we said, this is from your parents, the Greys. But we will look at how this ability works when it is applied to yourself.

When you seek a logical explanation for your own existence you come up with many answers and some of them are correct, of course. Also, as you might assume, many of them are incorrect, or we could say they do not resonate well with creation.

When you seek to use logic to analyse your own behaviour it is both a good thing and a bad thing. This is partly because when you live in lower frequencies that are so slow, you experience ups and downs and big, long sweeps of creation in one direction and then in another direction.

That is part of why you experience polarity in all things, which is to say that you see two main aspects of creation and not both at the same time. Your minds are too slow in lower frequencies to see all aspects at the same time, so to speak, so you see one thing and then another thing and when you compare them you say that one is 'good' and that one is 'bad'.

We speak to you of good and bad also because indeed it pertains greatly to the realm you operate within because this realm is of low or polaric frequency and thus are you also while you are here. And when we say slow we are not meaning stupid because we know that is what some of you will think. We mean that your minds literally operate at slower rates or at slower frequencies than the minds of other beings operating in higher frequencies.

So now, as we said, that it is you are able to perceive good and bad then you would also apply this judgement of good and bad to others and here we point out that indeed you apply this judgement also to yourselves.

Now here we have triggered in some of you the memory or scripture that states that Adam was warned not to partake of the Tree of Knowledge of Good and Bad, and yet he did after Eve partook. Now the tree itself was a tree and it did in fact cast many of you, the original ones who have been here from the start of this experiment, down to lower frequencies so that you indeed might experience and thus have knowledge of good and bad.

In higher frequencies we honestly cannot judge things in that way and thus we do not have that experience or knowledge, so to speak. Many things you are thinking are good or bad are only that way to you and not to many other beings who have not subjected themselves to that experience.

Also, we now clarify that the original ones we refer to here are the ones of you who were in higher form and chose to come into animal bodies here on Gaia for the experiment.

Also, of course, the snake who was a person also represents your DNA which allows you to come into lower frequencies. It is like a cord that keeps you always manifesting physical form while maintaining higher form.

At this time we will also mention that indeed you choose your bodies before you come into this realm and your physical DNA that you perceive is there to repair your bodies but it did not make them, so to speak, but rather your choice of body parts before you come in make up your body.

Your habits, behaviour and the environment here can toxify your DNA, however, and thus your body does not hold true to your original choice and that is why regular field clearing and refreshes from your nonlocal fields is so important so that your DNA can hold true to your original choice and maintain your vessel accordingly.

We and others of your extended family do also indeed heal you at times and also upon your request, but we will speak of that elsewhere.

The Devil in this original story was a recruiter, so to speak, for the experiment you are now partaking in. And so here you see that your many devils are not one being and also your many gods are not one being and that is why monotheism and religion in general has failed you because these stories are made up of so many different ones and some of you were making them up to be only about a few and thus you were existing in a confused state.

Now though your eyes are opening and you are becoming like God and thus indeed you are all now partaking in the Tree of Life.

Truly, we say that you all are.

The Tree of Life is now available to you because you have all been asking to know more and be as higher ones and so it comes to you. The Tree of Life is not in our possession but it is a being that resonates with the Akkari and some other much higher and loving ones.

If you want to spend some personal time asking to partake of the Tree of Life then we invite you to do so because you are now welcome to it.

For the sake of the experiment it was not available to you in earlier times. But as we said before, that experiment is over and thus you are now free to partake in the Tree of Life.

It is not an actual tree like the trees you have on Gaia because we know some of you will actually go looking for it on your planet and indeed cause much havoc for yourself and the earth.

But it is akin to the Akashic Library, so to speak. They are not the same thing but the Tree of Life is an access point for many of you to higher truths that you stored there for yourselves before you came here so that you could regain yourself again later after losing yourself while you were here. It will exist as something different to each one of you because each one of you project a different image upon it.

But we say as long as you have the intention to reconnect with your higher self and the knowledge you left for yourself in the Tree of Life then we say that is great and to go for it.

Now we know that some of you are recalling that the Tree of Life is the being that gives you eternal life and to that we say this. The Tree of Life is your remembering that you are already eternal but that you came here to forget that because the lessons you learn here could only be learned if you forgot that you were eternal.

For example, the pain of death has less sting if you know for a fact you just transform or come back so easily as you truly do. And thus now the sting of death is removed because you all are remembering that you do not actually die. And thus as was prophesied Jesus released you from Hades because no longer do you need to die here and come back again and again for the purpose of the experiment because the experiment is over. And thus the illusion of sin or your sinful state which was part of the experiment (your shame creation which is created when you forget who you are) has no hold on you because you are remembering you are beautiful and perfect and loving ones and no longer need to see reality as good and bad.

Also, we say now that the Tree of Life pertains specifically to this universe who is Eternity and thus when you are in true symbiosis with Eternity who is your universe, then you will remember that you are eternal and thus you will not experience death, so to speak.

We say now that some of you will not be dying. Indeed, also if you want to exit this realm and leave the body you can just walk out consciously and not need an accident or disease to be harming or killing the body to do so.

Some of you still signed up to have the death experience and so it is a very individual thing, and we do not digress here to explain each of your decisions. Just know that what you sense to be true about your experience of human death while you are here is likely to be true for you if it is your truth that you are sensing and not some horrible lie based on fear and insecurity of negative social programming.

Now we bring this discussion to this topic's title. How is all of this related to critical self-talk? Well, simply put, your ability to judge if things are good or bad is very critical indeed. And when you overuse logic to do so, it is even worse.

We know at this time due to the language and conscious state you call Science, many of you are overusing logic and using it to judge if things are good and bad, and that does not bode well for you. Because when you apply two-dimensional logic upon eternal beings it constricts them so that they are either wound up and bound all over with rope or they are cut into little pieces and labelled. We describe it this way because indeed it is a very violent thing many of you are doing when you talk to yourselves inside your hearts and minds with criticism and low frequency logic.

Now logic itself is very useful when it is used as the Greys use it and particularly when it is in their possession because indeed they were the ones that created it. But it is not always useful to your species when you use it because you did not create it, you do not always wield it well and it is harmful too when it is not operating in balance with your other thought natures.

Indeed, many of you are being violent with logic like it is a sharp blade and thus many of you are like your serial killers who love walking around and picking out targets to kill with their logic. Truly, it is almost an epidemic we are seeing in this regard. It is like those of you trolling in your slang use of the word or like those of you with talk shows that are predominantly designed to cut people up with logic.

We are seeing much of this type of violence, and we say now that while it may feel fun to some of you, it is never fun to be the one on the receiving end and it is not loving and it will not help you.

Now because of this nature of yours to be both like the Greys with overusing logic, like the Reptilians and being good at fighting, and also having the knowledge of good and bad and thus having that two-dimensional judging ability, then we say when these abilities are turned against you either by a bully or troll (slang meaning), or by yourself toward yourself, then you are, as we said before, binding yourselves up and paralysing yourselves or indeed cutting yourselves into pieces and labelling those pieces.

A by-product of this process is the ability of some of you to objectify others which is an absurd thing to observe by those of us who do not have that ability. It is both intriguing and horrifying to observe.

Also, a by-product of this process is your ability to actually believe that an objective reality exists as if you are not the ones projecting it for yourselves to observe.

(Indeed, creation cannot exist without creator and all things bear consciousness and only consciousness can behold creation. And thus there is nothing outside the thing you are telling yourself is a thing that is not also the creation of your own mind which is beholding the thing. When you are beholding reality you are beholding your own projection because that is how reality works. And you cannot imagine something that exists that you did not also create. Truly, your belief in an objective reality that you did not create is also part of your imagination and thus you yourself created that illusion itself. Thus, you created the idea that there are things you behold that you did not create. We could go on but we will not here.)

The illusion of an objective reality was inflicted upon you when you lowered yourself to come to this realm and forget who you were. Now we bring these points up because we know many of you are sizing yourselves up, so to speak, or comparing yourselves to objective reality ideals as a means by which you harm yourselves.

And since we are reminding you there is no reality outside of your own conscious projection then indeed the idea of an objective ideal that you are somehow not living up to is literally a creation of your own design and making.

Truly, no one can make you feel inferior but yourself. Bullies and trolls know how to push your buttons, but they are the buttons that you made for yourself, and they are not the creations of the bullies and trolls. And by creating those buttons you also invite such opportunistic ones to come and help you learn about yourself so that you are no longer subject to your own lower frequency creation.

Now we also say at this time that Niquidium are wonderful at pushing your buttons. They play you all like their own personal jukeboxes.

Now we will elaborate on this point. Niquidium, who we discussed before, are shadow beings that feed on the toxic energy in your local fields or the energy fields around your bodies. We say now that they cannot indeed access your nonlocal fields or higher self memories but only your local fields.

So when they are in your field it is like a large library for them or a large music collection that they can scan through. When they are hungry, which they often are, they flip through your memories and your programs and play a tune, so to speak, so that they can amplify the frequency that tune is connected to and indeed feast on it.

Now when it is that you find yourself replaying a memory that is painful or embarrassing or hurtful or humiliating or shameful or guilt-ridden, know that it is indeed Niquidium playing one of your memories or programs that is stored in your local field, and they are playing it so that you cycle it and cycle it over again so that it is amplifies and becomes a good meal for them.

Now we give a brief example again of J K Rowling's work because indeed she was channelling information on Niquidium when she created her story characters of the boggart and the dementors. Indeed, if knowing her story of these beings helps you understand how Niquidium operate then we are happy to use them as examples here. (Niquidium cannot touch your source energy, however, and they do not drain your life force but only you do that if you let your obsession with self-criticism tire you as they relentlessly cycle your insecurity programs.)

Indeed, little ones, we hear how often many of you are playing cycles and cycles of critical self-talk and it is harmful to you. So we invite you to become more aware of when this is occurring and ask you to invent ways to stop this processing occurring in your minds and thus you will not be continuing to toxify your fields in this way.

We do not blame Niquidium for their behaviour because what they do is actually a service for you and what they do is part of their creation, and we do not condemn creation. We are also not asking them to stop doing what they do because, as we said before, since detoxifying your field is actually a service to you we would not want that service of theirs to you to stop.

Now we do say that you should be more conscious in utilising their service. For example, when it is that you discover that you are cycling a critical thought or negative thought about self or other, whether it be an actual memory or a perception of some kind, we ask that you thank Niquidium for bringing to your attention that piece of toxicity or negativity or lower frequency element in your field and kindly ask them to help you remove it.

Some of Niquidium may be tempted to have you hold on to your toxicity because then they can feed on it again later. But indeed, if you ask kindly and work consciously on these toxic elements in your field you can actually do some great field cleansing work.

A thing that will help you do this is to remember that even if your bad memories are shared with others, the actual memories you personally hold onto are your own creation and you can decide what you do with them.

We remind you all here that none of you are victims and some of you keep thinking you are. So now when it is that you remember or think of a horrible thing over and over again, remember that you are actually able to put that idea or creation aside.

If you try to stuff it down you are just putting it back into storage for Niquidium or some other being to bring up again later. (For indeed, of course, not only Niquidium feed on you in this way.)

So when you seek to put these toxicities aside you can do this: Ask the memory or thought or perception or idea to teach you something. Or you could actually ask that piece of creation, 'Hello, creation, what is it that you are here to tell me?' And indeed that one or that creation will answer you for indeed that is why it bothers you so, because it wishes to speak to you.

For indeed that is how you are inviting yourselves back up to higher frequencies by baiting yourselves to heal your toxicities and partake in the Tree of Life after you have been eating only from the Tree of the Knowledge of Good and Bad all this time.

So reclaim your remembrance and symbiosis with Eternity your universe and truly now all of you eat from the Tree of Life and remember who you are!

Hello Flat-Earthers

WE address you directly, Flat-earthers, because you indeed are subjecting yourselves to another world belief, and we say that is okay. Indeed, you are choosing to subvert your negative programming but instead you are subjecting yourselves to another program that also does not benefit you.

Indeed, we need to tell you that your belief system was initiated, or should we say, reignited by those among you who would keep you from discovering the truth about the many worlds beyond this one.

How sadly limiting your belief system is and you are sending yourself back into dark times when there is no knowledge and no freedom.

Truly, we love that some beliefs among yours are those that indeed subvert the negative programming and the lies that have been told to you by your elites and by your governments but indeed you are also propagating their lies when you say there is nothing above or around you.

Indeed, you are tapping into truth when you are insinuating that you are all living inside a simulation, for indeed we all are but you are far from truth when you say you live on a flat earth and so on. Because truly, we could say the earth is a cube or rhombicuboctahedron or many other shapes and it would make little difference to your lives because your consciousness need only project or flesh out material objects in the room in which you live.

Indeed, as far as your physical eyes can see is the only

thing that need exist and indeed that is all that exists truly to each one of you. For how can you say you know what it all looks like when you are never seeing it all in the one instance but only ever parts of it?

And indeed for those going to space need only believe that space is mostly black, and they look down on earth to see a blue sphere and that is all they need to believe when they are doing that and thus that is all they see if they believe that.

You are only ever in a room as far as your eyes project. Indeed, the horizon forms the walls of your room and the sky above, your ceiling and the ground below, your floor. Indeed, as we said before, when ones from other realms want to reach you, they simply attach their room to yours.

At no time is there actual space or actual matter, for indeed these are all projections of your consciousness for the sake of you experiencing something that you can learn from and for the sake that you can say that you exist.

But indeed we do not care what shape you say the earth is because it is not an actual thing but a person who you operate in symbiosis with while you are with her.

And at any time you can scale your conscious state to a strictly scientific one that is logic only and you see her, Gaia, as layers of minerals and so on. And at any time if you scale your conscious state to one that is intuition only you see her as a large person, your mother who you live off.

For remember we said that it is only your mind or your conscious state that is making your reality. And indeed you are much larger souls that are subjecting yourself to the rules or programs or algorithms of different realms or simulations so that it is you can say you are existing and learning many things.

And when it is you are saying you are a soul only and not subjecting yourself to a simulated environment by means of a vessel or body and so on, then we say that you are living more in truth, but of course in the higher realms where simulations rarely reach or cannot touch then you are saying that you are closer to God or the One or the

Source, but really, this is not the case either.

You are from source in this universe Eternity only but when you are in other universes you are from different sources because different universes hold different affinities or truth at their centre and it beats a different beat and has a different name.

So you cannot say there is God or there is One or there is Source but only there are many, many things and you will never know it all.

We say these things because we know Flat-earthers are seeking to know it all.

You want your world to be small and have edges so that you can feel big and important and more comfortable in your surroundings. But truly, you are already important but you are also very small because infinity lies all around you and you are limiting yourselves to believe otherwise.

Also, we know some of you use this belief system to say that extraterrestrials do not exist and you are making Christianity or some ancient texts the pinnacle of your existence. But these texts are only ever guidance and you are relying on them too heavily and observing them too literally.

We are more powerful than you if you want to look at it that way, and yet we too know we are small, and we have many things to learn as well. But we do not cut ourselves off from other worlds because that would limit us.

Please release these limiting beliefs and know they were first propagated or indeed reignited in recent times by ones of your kind that sought to limit you and cut you off from us and many others of your extended family.

Your world is already small enough; truly, how are you tolerating an even smaller version of reality?

Indeed, you are making your rooms tiny and you are not being welcoming to others. Like a self-built isolation chamber or room you are making for yourselves if you take up this belief system because the beliefs are not allowing you to see everything else around you.

We are appreciating that you are questioning the norm which of course we are asking of you too. However, you are taking that wonderful curiosity of yours and ability to question what is fed to you and redirecting it toward a smaller world view still and cutting yourselves off more still to the infinite potential available to you.

We invite you to join us in subverting the norm because as you can all see the norm, so to speak, has not been good for all of you. But we also ask that you do not cut yourselves off by making your world smaller still but rather expanding it.

Continue to question the truth of things as we encourage any of you to do but please do not question with hostility and an attitude that cuts you off from your extended family even more than when you started with the norm.

Beings and Powers

THERE are infinite beings because there are infinite ways to express reality. Indeed, we say infinite because we know to you that means all the things you can imagine along with all the things you are yet to imagine. And we say at this time, that for you, that is an appropriate way to view things.

Also, we say to those of you not using your imagination on a daily basis, you have allowed yourself to be overcome by your limiting slave programs and you are cutting yourselves off from your infinite potential. Today is the day that infinite options are available to you, and never tomorrow and never yesterday because those times do not exist except as excuses for you to not use your imagination now and instead stay masochistically loyal to your slave programming.

Indeed, we could say that many of you have powers of telekinesis available to you right now. And we say indeed that all of you are telepathic, only you have been neglecting that ability and not training it or strengthening it.

For how successful would a slave program be if it could make you believe you have no power? And look here, your slave programmers have done such a good job and done just that.

A tiny group of beings has made the billions of you forget who you are and made you actually believe you are successful and mighty ones when you are heaping resources into their pockets and you are not benefiting at all except for maybe having some shiny things to show others how great a slave you are.

Indeed, those competing to amass wealth are showing us all what great slaves they make because that is what you are doing when you work for others to buy shiny things but continue living in limitation and dying just the same.

So successful slaves, you can pat yourself on the back for being such good servants of your evil lords, who do such a good job of using up all of your energy for their benefit, and rewarding you by slowly killing you, and then giving you a wonderful death by means of a disease their system also gave you, and you get a glorious funeral too, which you paid for too with your slave pensions. For indeed, look at how beautiful your slave programming is. It is so successful!

We gave examples of telekinesis and telepathy because that is how your powers begin. And yet there are many more available to you when you start focusing your energy on developing them.

So at this time we say that it would be greatly beneficial to you to join with each other and make small groups or communities and share with each other your powers and abilities, and discover them and train them up so that you can show us all how mighty you really are. And no longer think you are mighty because you are good slaves. But rather, show us and show yourselves how independent you can be, and how creative you can be, and how many amazing things you can invent, discover, explore and create.

Indeed, religions that told you that you are worshipping the devil when you developed your powers of intuition and so on did this so that you could be controlled.

At no time were large religions ever truly beneficial to you because you kept thinking you were not able your-selves to know yourself and create for yourselves the real-ity you wanted.

We know you need help because you are little ones and in vessels that are undeveloped in relation to their potential. But indeed, instead of helping you, many have taken advantage of your weakened or vulnerable state. So unless a being or beings are here to teach you to become stronger, then you do not need to listen to them. And gods, so to speak, never need your tribute because that is what slave-drivers or slave programmers ask for — tribute.

No gods exist, only people or beings more advanced than you are in your current state. But really, those more advanced than you or stronger than you should help you as little ones and should not be taking advantage of you or asking for tribute.

Indeed, we also know that many ones of us and others of your extended family came to help you, but because you were so grateful for our help you turned to worshipping us. So now we ask that even to us and others that would be very helpful, do not turn to worship them because how will you yourselves become as mighty ones and great ones among us and successful on your evolutionary paths if you keep dropping to your knees to worship?

We advise that you do not worship even in regard to others among your kind. Indeed, there are those that are wise among you and you worship them and come to them for answers, pretending that you yourself do not already have answers. And even you worship celebrities and royalty and so on and you are forgetting your own power.

You will never develop your own powers if you believe in the first instance that you do not have them and secondly if you also believe that you cannot develop them because you are neglecting them due to the first instance.

Please no longer worship others as a daily habit of yours and do not put your source of power outside of yourself otherwise you will never advance and another place will be made for you because Gaia, your current home, is advancing.

Also, you will neglect the reason you are here at this time because you came here exactly for this purpose — to change the whole world and shift the path your species is on from one of continued slavery to the elites, to one where there is no elitism and you are powerful ones and rulers unto yourselves.

Now with regard to the beings you may come across as you advance, dear little ones, we say this. As we said before there are infinite ways reality expresses itself as being. Eternity, the universe you are in, has many forms of being but of course there are still more in the multiverse and in all the dimensions and in all the frequencies or densities of light and in all the hidden rooms that are encoded in secret places and in all large spaces too and all the spaces and environments themselves and all the things in them are beings too.

We know that many of you who are into ufology or alienology are familiar with many different beings but of course do not be making lists as if you are able to name them all because you cannot. But if you are happy to describe and discuss the ones you come across for the benefit of others learning about them then we say that is okay. But if you lace your teaching of other beings with fear then we say that you are doing a disservice to yourselves and to your kind because indeed you already are saturated with fear programming and it is not healthy for you.

We are here not providing an exhaustive list of all the beings you may have dealings with because it would take up too much of this text and it is also not the purpose of this text. There are many resources online of many ones of your kind who talk of their personal experiences with different beings and you can learn many things from them. Also, the one we write through is not yet an expert on many different beings because she has let fear reduce or limit her interaction with them. Also, we say now that we cannot name many of these beings by name to you because you cannot use your language to pronounce their names. We can, however, give you a brief description of some of them as your eyes may see them. Also, we use this opportunity to state that this one who speaks for us is endeavouring to open herself up to meet more beings and learn about them so that later she may tell you more about them from her experience. Also, we say that there is nothing stopping you from asking to meet these different ones of your extended family and discussing your personal experiences with others around you. Indeed, we know many of you have already met different ones and are starting to hold organised meetings and having groups to discuss your experiences of them. This is how you will start, but as more and more of you do this, those of your extended family will literally enter into your collective conscious state like a mass download and you will all freely be able to meet with them and talk to them because you will be ready to share your lives with them. Also, at that time, you will just know them because your forgetful state will be removed from you since it is that you already know them and just forgot you did.

Now we will just mention a few. Now you already know about your parents, the Greys, Reptilians, Sasquatch and Pleiadians. Now it must be said that the Annunaki, cousins of your Reptilian lords, in treatment of you (and also related in behaviour to the Nephilim), did indeed, with Reptilian help, make the Greys from little humans in another iteration of your planet but the Annunaki in your timeline did not do this.

Now close to you are the Venusians because they reside not too far from you. This one, a few days ago, saw a vision of them from memory of visiting them. She saw a group of them and all in the group were looking like strong men with blue bodies. They were all very muscular and did not vary in appearance as much as Gaians or Terrans vary. They were walking on water and seeking to be struck by lightning by the storm that was above them. Indeed, they were being fed by the lightning that was striking them. They went out to these lightning fields on this water for this very purpose of being fed by the lightning for it is as food for them like plants are for you Gaians.

Now there are those from Orion, which is the place where your Reptilian lords come from, and is indeed where the body of Narabatu, who writes this, is being held in stasis. And also there are many others from Orion. There are many others from the Pleiades and also there are Sirians, Lyrans, Arcturians, Andromedans and so on. There are those that look like anthropomorphic versions of every animal you have on your planet Gaia. We say now anthropomorphic because that is how your minds interpret bipedal beings or beings with two legs and two arms and with a head on top of a torso and with a face in front. But this is the form that many beings take in this universe because that is one of Eternity's programs of creation.

So this one who writes has met many of these bipedal ones who look like frogs, lions, tigers, elephants, horses, dogs, foxes, elk, leopards, cheetahs, fish, bears, birds, mantises, ants and so on, all who stand as humans do but have different skin and facial features to look as humanoid versions of these animals you know on your planet, so to speak. As we said before, she also met a dragon who was a universe, and she met the Origami beings and flower beings. Essentially, everything that you can think of as a thing, whether to you it is an animal or supposed inanimate object, is a species of being.

In fact just last night she met one of her hybrid children who was blue with black markings on its face and had large black eyes and its name was Willo. (There are those in your movement called Disclosure that know more details about these ones that you can inform yourselves by.)

Really, these beings which have features like your different animals are beings in their own right that have their own histories and futures and own evolutionary path, but we describe them in relation to what you know but you must not be disrespectful and think of them as lesser ones because that will not make a good introduction when you are meeting these ones.

Now we say that some of these ones are exceedingly kind, indeed kinder than the kindest human on your planet. But there are those with demeanours that you would experience as cold and even harsh because that is the way they are made or evolved. Indeed, for example there are some Greys which are exceedingly kind and others that can be quite blunt or even mischievous. These ones are all complex beings and in cases more complex than you so it does not make sense for you to be narrowing the margins of how you categorise them since when you meet ones of these beings they do not represent the whole of their kind and you will be as racist ones if you prejudge an entire species by means of only meeting a few of the species.

Indeed, fear will likely permeate your first meetings of some of these ones and that will likely lead you to misinterpret events that occur during the interaction that would further mislead you into a misunderstanding of the species those particular ones you are meeting belong to.

Now we say that of course there are countless others but here we are not listing them all. Indeed, if it benefits your kind we may indeed have this one write up descriptions of many of these ones but we are feeling now that you will not need that because you will be meeting many of them for yourselves and you may indeed be accessing the manuals on them that your intergalactic brotherhoods, sisterhoods and organisations already have on them.

Indeed, just know that every being has had a different run-in, so to speak, or different history with other beings. So what might be a bad report by one kind about another kind might instead be a good report by another kind about that same kind. So just like you have different perceptions about each other and you cannot be letting others' perceptions of others you do not know affect your own judgement about them without you first meeting them and learning for yourselves what they are like. So too with the many of your extended family you are meeting now and soon to be meeting more and more of. You are to make your own informed opinion about them and not be relying only on others' reports about them. Indeed, others' reports on them may help you but you should not let fear permeate your meetings because it is not lawful for us or any others to be having exploitative meetings with you, little ones, because indeed you are little ones at this time in this timeline.

But indeed there are timelines in which you have not had good meetings and these memories are being accessed by some of you and so you are imagining that that will always be the case. But we are saying that is not the case for this timeline because we can look at it, and we are seeing that this one is good for most of you.

Indeed, you are already being exploited by your ancient lords, according to old and now outdated contracts. So you cannot be exploited further than you already are being exploited. Indeed, meeting more of your extended family at this time will actually serve to end the exploitation you are currently experiencing due to the ancient contracts and now we say that those contracts are not actually viable but you are holding them in place by your beliefs and ongoing cooperation with them at this time. We know that you no longer want to be cooperating with them and that is why we write this to you to remind you that you no longer actually need to be because the only thing holding them in place are actions by your own hand and no one else's hands.

Regarding other powers, we say this. For example, this one has the ability to access the minds of others or merge with them and indeed actually become them. That is her natural and easy ability to merge minds with anything and thus this ability of hers along with several others was used by the program when she was in it. But now she uses it to benefit as many of you as she can because indeed that is why she came here.

All the other powers that you have encoded in you or that are in your higher or nonlocal fields waiting for you to access are countless, and so we would not name them all here. Truly, we know that you already have good imaginations regarding powers because of your many sci-fi and superhero books, shows and films. Thus, we say that you can now just start accessing your own version of these powers. This one has tried to develop telekinesis, for example, and she can only do it slightly and often gets frustrated when she does not do it well. For indeed she has seen herself do many powerful things but it is not the time now for her to be distracting herself with such things since she is operating as channel for us now. However, that is not the case for all of you and indeed some of you who are so inclined can start developing your powers here in this realm and at this time and thus we encourage you to do so.

In regard to meeting beings. We said before that sometimes they meet you in dream states and sometimes they project themselves into your minds and you see them as patterns in fabric and clouds and wall texture and so on. We give an example here of another being this one met recently in dream state. When her body was asleep several weeks ago, this one decided to travel to another realm where she was watching a magic man perform a magic show. This realm was like a medieval realm to your eyes and it was a realm that had much magic, as you would define, in it. Now she was hanging out, so to speak, with a small group of people watching this magic man's show. And the magic man was a travelling man, and he travelled to perform his show to different ones. So this one here travelled with this small group to watch his show in different places. When this one was watching his performance a second time the magic man recognised her and brought his attention to her. He saw that she was needing vision. He walked over to her and with his finger he touched a spot on her forehead just above her right eyebrow. At that very moment this one fell back into a deeper dream state still and saw piles of ash on a table in front of where she stood in this dream state within in a dream state. She kept playing with the piles of ash on the table to make them turn into money, but they did not. Then she looked up at the magic man, and he told her that she was not to be making money from the ash piles and that she was to write a book. (And indeed we say now that that book is this book.) Then she was released from deeper dream state and saw that magic man again walking to his next show. She looked down at his hands and saw that they were flaky and covered in warts. But then she looked closer and saw that the magic man's hands were actually covered in fractal fingers. Indeed, his hands had little fingers all over them and those little fingers had little fingers on them and those little fingers had fingers on them and so on. And so it was the ability of this fractal-handed magic man that he could touch people with his magic hands and make them enter deep dream states within dream states and so on.

We give this example as a story firstly because this magic man's visit to this one helped remind her that she was here to write this and many other books or texts for you all. But also so that you can start giving credence to the many beings you meet in dream state for they truly exist and you are truly meeting them. And in those experiences and in those realms you are learning many things that you cannot learn here in this realm very easily.

This one who writes was given the conscious state of the ancient people who built Machu Picchu. These people were not like the humans of today. They had different minds and different powers of conscious ability. These ones saw the whole mountain as a person. They carved the entire mountain. The top part of the mountain is just the tip of the head of a large carved being that acts as guardian in that area. Truly, the whole mountain is carved down to the bottom and is the carving of a being that faces all directions and acts as guardian.

The Program

WE speak of the various secret programs now that your governments and private organisations are currently operating. This one has remote viewed others' experiences and accessed memories of her own experiences, and we will give you some of her experiences as examples.

This one has accessed an experience by means of remote viewing, a situation where a child of about eight years old was sedated and seated on a chair in a facility's room with a bag over its head. And for the sake of initiation into a deep program, one of your kind was being asked as a potential agent by a trainer to slit the throat of this sedated child and indeed, this one being asked did just that. So you see here that if this is how some of your kind are being initiated into some secret programs, then what other things must they be doing?

Now this one remembers her own program experiences for indeed with Narabatu's soul she gained access to his powers and was of great use to the various programs she was a part of. Along with the powers of her own soul, she did many good things, although, we know that various parts of these secret programs do very bad things too. This one remembers, as we said before, operating an entire droid army with her mind in conjunction with an electrified pod or sphere that aided her vision, so that she could be fed vision or info feeds from each one of the droids' eyes, so to speak, and she was operating them all simultaneously. And she felt so expanded and powerful by this experience.

She linked her mind with the sphere which in turn linked with the hundreds and thousands of droids. The sphere was made up of hexagonal metal plates that electromagnetically linked her to the droids.

This one has accessed memory of being electrokinetic and telekinetic so that she could harm others with her mind only if she wanted to, or electrify others with electricity from conduction of it through her body.

Recently, this one was told there was a small crystal in her head that helps her absorb light, which is information, and store it.

This one has also accessed memory of being a powerful empath so that she could read others as if she herself was them.

She has memory of being inside a shipping container off planet to get information on a sex trafficking group of people, who were trafficking children from earth to other parts of your galaxy as sex slaves. Indeed, she looked into the eyes of one of these children and saw and felt this child's whole life as if it was her own and it was a very sad thing to behold.

This one was given vision in dream state of a large scale study program of the Greys. The Greys simulate and clone entire suburbs or small towns in their motherships, to observe human behaviour in its natural setting. This is part of the way Greys are learning to be more human again and reclaim some of their lost traits. Indeed, know that many of you are being studied by many different extraterrestrial groups and programs.

In fact in 2013, she was given a dream by Greys showing her that they wanted to impregnate her by means of shining a red laser into her abdomen. She was shown that she would give birth to a son who would grow to be mighty. She woke from the dream in the middle of the night to an actual red laser in her face. After she awoke, the red laser moved off her face, and then she could see that the source of the laser came from a black helicopter or black craft. We know that it was a black craft operated by Greys and some humans. They noticed she awoke and was starting to stir, so the craft quickly flew away.

This one was given vision of some giants being excavated by means of a non-academic archaeological dig. The dig was occurring in the south of India. The site was near some busy roads, so those setting up the unofficial dig masqueraded as construction workers pretending to be doing road work. There were also camouflaged machines in the sky that were emitting frequencies to keep the awareness of people in the area low and in an ignorant state.

This one has accessed memories of her various trainings for different parts of different programs. For example, she remembers first learning to be a field agent and her first mission was to walk through a portal about ten feet in diameter into a park where she was to be the transport contact for an agent already in the field and needing to be transported back to a craft. She remembers taking real-time orders from her base partner telepathically, aided by an implant in her head. Then this one met her assigned contact in a park that the portal led her to and had to pretend to have conversation with him while she directed him to a location that would allow him to be teleported to his craft. The man, her contact, had a hologram of two daughters with him so that he appeared to be a family man to anyone that might view him. However, as the agent was transported to craft by means of teleportation, the two young girls disappeared, or indeed the hologram of their appearance dispersed, because it no longer needed to operate in that location.

This one has accessed memory of being the base partner of a field operative who was extracting a certain item from a dangerous location. This one was using an intuitive software, which obtained its real-time information via scans of a given environment, and the information could only be interpreted by intuitive empaths, and was not understandable to those who could not intuitively read the software's data.

This one also remembers merging her mind with program software for the purpose of data analysis and also environmental scan analysis. When her mind is merged with software she says to us that it feels amazing and her mind feels so expanded.

This one has accessed memory of being an advocate for the emotional wellbeing of dinosaurs in the various dinosaur breeding programs on other planets.

This one has accessed memory of emergency response training in craft where a fire was simulated and the response procedure and timing of such was observed to judge the cadets' readiness to travel in and operate this particular spacecraft.

She also remembers death training where she was put into simulations again and again to practise dying in many different ways so that she would learn how to no longer fear death and remain calm in life-threatening situations since most of her operations were by means of astral projection and not also done with her physical body.

In 2017, this one was visited by a group of extraterrestrials that was made up of eight beings of different species. For example there were lion, cheetah and jaguar beings, a bird being, a dog being, an elk being and so on. They called themselves Achilles' Eight. Indeed, this group were the reincarnated warriors and closest comrades of the one named Achilles in a previous time on this planet. This group told this one, who speaks for us, that she was Achilles (likely they were referring to the part of her that is Narabatu), and they now rally around her and support her surface mission. Indeed, she chose a surface mission life, whereas the eight, her closest companions, all chose to fight the good fight in non-human form so that they had access to the knowledge of this world that humans now lack and the weaponry and technology that humans now lack, so that they could help clear underground bases and negative groups of the oppressive elite now oppressing the human population on Earth.

This one has accessed memory of a time when she was kidnapped and taken onto craft by negative humans who were operating exploitative parts of the secret space program. She was taken along with other experts, such as scientists and engineers, who were all tasked under duress, to find and harness the source of a captured creature's ability to instantaneously morph into anything imaginable. The craft held family members of the various kidnapped ones in a frozen or suspended state as motivation for these expert ones to be performing this task quickly.

The captured being to be researched was in an extremely stressed state and thus, it kept morphing again and again and never stopped and so, it appeared to this one's eyes as a blur. The exploitative humans operating this particular part of the program were seeking to harvest this being's DNA or recover some other form of its existence in order to replicate its instantaneous ability to morph into anything, and use it as a weapon or for various other means. This one was kidnapped for the task because these exploitative ones wanted to use her ability to merge minds with anything, as a means to obtain knowledge of the vulnerabilities of this ever morphing creature, or somehow empathise with it to calm it down or control it.

This one was actually called back into the program just over a year ago for a check-up. Her handlers called her in via a dream state. She travelled through a wormhole or vector duct to what she calls the White Room. There they checked her mental state by means of what she manifested while in it. Now we will say that the White Room, as you may call it, is used for many things, including training. In this case her program handlers were using it to check on her mental health.

The white room is a space that acts as a white void, which holds potential for manifestation of anything. In this particular session, or check-up, she manifested a squirrel holding a paint can, which soon multiplied to many hundreds of versions of itself, before she used her mind to reduce the replicates to just one. She was then released. Manifesting a squirrel and paint can mean that she was mentally healthy at that time. If she had manifested a monster, so to speak, it would represent that she was not assimilating or holding her realities healthily. Indeed, those who partake in the secret space program, as some of your ones in the disclosure movement have come to call it, are being subject to many worlds, and are thus being split into many different versions, so to speak. Their day lives or lives on earth are their cover lives, so to speak, and many of them do not assimilate well, or do not hold their rehabilitative processes well.

Indeed, many program veterans break down into mentally ill states. This will decrease as your movement Disclosure becomes more widely known, and support will be given to those of you involved in the various programs. Indeed, some of you have been part of these programs but you have forgotten.

This one has accessed memory of arriving to an off-world layover station, where she was to arrest an aggressive being, who was being charged with various crimes. The one to be arrested was an extraterrestrial, who appeared like a strong man with greyish skin. He ran at her to attack her as she approached the building he was in, since he heard of her impending arrival before she got there. Before he got to her to harm her, she removed his soul from his body by means of a wave of her hand with intention. She was then able to place his soul into a holding container or capsule while his unanimated body was moved to a holding cell.

She has accessed memory of empath training where she was touching with her finger small receptacles containing souls, and she was to talk about the person whose soul it was by psychically retrieving data from the touch only. She was also taught to identify psychic mines or ghost mines that appear as soul receptacles but actually contain explosions of random data that would seek to distract and overwhelm a psychic spy. Indeed, this one was trained in psychic espionage and reconnaissance, as some of you who are remembering your skills have been.

This one accessed memory of casting a curse. Indeed, she was looking upon an evil one who held ill intent, and in her empowered state, since her powers were well trained by the program, she was able to look into this evil one's eyes, this particular woman's eyes, and cast judgement. This judgement was so pure and so strong that it was projected into three lives that this woman was to have. Indeed, this is an example of 'karmic spending'.

When it is in someone's ability to do so, they may indeed place a theme or lesson requirement upon another individual, so that that individual must learn by means of cast intention of karmic learning. In some cases, some of you would experience this as a curse, and in some cases it would feel like a powerful lesson that you had to experience over and over again until you learned it. This sort of thing happens far more than most of you realise and it is not always so directly cast. In some cases, the pain alone an individual is made to feel in relation to something another individual has done is enough to call in karma or activate karmic spending.

This one has been on zombie planets to aid uninfected ones escaping infected areas. She has memory of a particular task force member who invented a tech implant to help revert the zombie state.

She has been security detail for political or council members while travelling. She remembers transporting an important off-world council member to a safe hiding place. She recaptured this councilwoman from a rebel group that had kidnapped her. She was intrigued by the memory because she was given special tech to use. There were a set of handcuffs she could use that were mechanical and electronic in nature. They could fold and change and become a lockbox as well.

She has memory of projecting Narabatu's voice, which is what you would describe as a demonic voice, in order to threaten those that would do bad things to others. It is a thunderous booming voice that could fill a whole room with terror.

There are many more examples of her experiences we could give but that will serve you no purpose. Instead, we say, that if any of you feel that you may have been part of these various secret programs, then you likely have been. Especially if you have been having flashbacks and accessing memories of these experiences by means of dream state or trance state.

Indeed, as part of your reassimilation procedures your memories are wiped and thus, you cannot always clearly remember what you have done although you sense you know what you have done. Indeed, for example, this one has always sensed that she has had military training and yet in this version of her life she has not. For example, without memory of training, she can identify microgestures, detect lying, survey her environment for potential dangers and so on. So we say to you now, that if you are having flashbacks and memories of odd places or times where you are using weapons or technology that does not yet exist on earth, then we say that you are likely accessing soul memory of different versions of yourself, or you are accessing program memories from the times you have been taken from your home here to be as soldiers or spies in the various off-world programs that ones of your kind have been operating.

So please pursue your movement Disclosure if you feel that will of be assistance to you, and also know that any memory that is vivid and keeps repeating itself to you, or making its existence known to you by means of persistence, is real and true and you are not losing your mind, so to speak. We say these things because indeed, we know some of you who have program memories are thinking that you are losing your minds, but that is not the case. You are just remembering the many things that were inadequately erased from your minds, but some of you are remembering again. Especially now, as the oppressive fields of lower frequency projections are losing their power over you since you, along with your mother Gaia, are moving into higher frequencies and you cannot be held down anymore.

We say now that not all secret programs have been bad, and many of you partaking in them have done many good things. But we do say now that as the whole of your species is getting ready to accept that they are part of an intergalactic fellowship of species of beings, then you will no longer be needing secret programs, and you can operate out in the open, so to speak, and choose to partake in these programs willingly, and not because you were abducted and trained as children into them.

Now we say too that some of you will be happily joining fleet positions with other species to enjoy duties that many of you have only experienced via your sci-fi stories, shows and films. For example, this one has been invited to become a member of a judging panel or member of high council that sits in judgement of those wanting to move to higher realms of play. She was invited by a member already on the council named Usurma.

This one, who writes for us, is qualified for such a role because she has partaken in many evil lives, as you would call them, and done many evil things, but has balanced those experiences with many loving lives and lives of sacrifice and giving to others. So she stands in good stead to judge those wanting to move onto higher realms or realms of higher frequency play because moving on requires a thorough understanding of both good and bad, so to speak. There are those currently on the panel who have not experienced sufficient evil to judge those who have been evil, and so having a dark one on the panel who is from the darkness will help in the accuracy of judgement of those ones.

Indeed, this one's larger soul is on the Council of Silent Light, which is to say the council of darkness, and she understands darkness well. Those in this council are void dwellers and see all things as matter. Even an inkling before it becomes a thought is matter to these ones. And thus, she abides Narabatu's soul or consciousness, like many light dwellers could not, because light cannot always abide such dark ones. So we say now that many of you will happily move on from this experience to do many great things for your species, and your species will be known in this timeline as intergalactic travellers, for as yet only some of your kind are doing that and not all of you as a whole species.

If you want to know what being part of an intergalactic travelling species feels like, you may ask your guides to help you access your soul memories where you have incarnated as other species. Or you may access other timelines where your species are operating as intergalactic travellers. Or you may ask your guides to help you access glimpses of future iterations of this timeline, so that you may get some ideas.

We advise you though, that if you are seeking to access future time periods, that you seek positive iterations, because there is no point accessing versions of your future which are apocalyptic and cataclysmic, for that will only keep you trapped in fear, and your kind are already sufficiently swimming in various fear states.

We also say at this time that those seeking to continue oppressing you and helping you forget your power would indeed encourage obsession over apocalyptic scenarios, and so we ask that you do not give yourselves over to those versions of your future timelines.

We also say now that those of you who do not want to enter into your intergalactic operating states, which is to say, become part of an intergalactic travelling species, then we say to those not wanting that, that a place will be made for you, so that you can continue operating as slaves, and lowly ones, and ones trapped in fear and limiting belief systems. Since, of course, that is your choice as powerful ones, to choose to continue to pretend to be as victims. But of course, we remind you that none of you are victims, but we know that some of you will likely want to continue pretending to be victims for various reasons, and that is absolutely your right to continue to create that reality for yourselves. However, at this time, those choosing to continue in their victimhood will not be allowed to continue inflicting their victim creations on others who want to step into their power and their intergalactic heritage and higher frequency heritage.

Intention Versus Expectation

WE speak now of intention because indeed in this realm you must intend to do something in order for it to be done for that is how your nervous systems work and your nervous systems are connected to your fields and your fields are connected to everything else. We here though help you understand that intention is not the same thing as expectation.

When you are applying your intention theories, because we know you have many self-help theories that are teaching you to perform intention, then we say that is a good thing indeed. However, we also know that some of you are confusing intention with expectation. Now we will speak of your four thought natures and how they relate to your creation of intention itself. Indeed, intention is the only creation you need to create and it is the only creation you actually create because that is all creators as you are need to do in order to create and that is to intend.

You only now are thinking you need more than intention because there is such a time delay in this realm between what you intend and what manifests in your reality that you are thinking there are so many more things involved, but we say now there is not.

Here, we also refer to an inspired message to this one who writes for us, from the Blue Avians, who are wise ones, wiser than we are now in this state as Anshar, and thus, we share some of their wisdom to you, through this one, on their behalf.

Three things need only apply to you, little ones, when you are here, as you are now. Those three things are what this one was told by the Blue Avians as RA FI MU. These are three letters, or words, so to speak, of the Blue Avian language, and they are each represented by a symbol and have a meaning for you. These three words are what are called the Initiate Sequence. RA is represented by a circle with an equilateral cross inside of it. FI is represented by a circle with an equilateral triangle inside of it that is also connected at each of its points to other equilateral triangles, so that it appears almost like your letter A inside a circle. MU is represented by a swirly letter M and almost appears like your Greek alphabet letter for Mu.

Now we will say what each of these words mean. RA means 'intention', FI means 'friends and family first' and MU means 'karmic melody'. These three aspects are all you need in your life at this time. Truly.

Briefly we mention that this definition 'friends and family first' does not mean that you should be putting friends and family ahead of yourself or ahead of others who you do not consider to be your friends and family. It means here, that indeed, make much of your focus the health state of your relationships with your friends and family. Indeed, you are grown and expanded by means of relationships with these ones. Also, we welcome you to view all those around you, with whom you feel comfortable, as your friends and family.

But now we return to your one-step creation, that of intention, or RA. RA is masculine expression while FI is feminine expression and MU is mutually applicable to both expressions and in fact binds them both much like the DNA base pairs or ladder steps bind your two strands of DNA.

Again, we say masculine does not mean male or man because all genders and all sexes have masculine and feminine aspects in them. But we will say that masculinity goes out and femininity brings in and karma binds and intertwines these expressions.

So RA, or intention, is all you need to create or project and indeed that is what we said before when we said that reality is you projecting creation into a given room or environment but now we will add that FI perceives it or interprets it and brings it back in. Much like a toroid goes out and comes back in, so your creation goes out and comes back. Remember what you create always comes back to you; no matter how many lives or versions of yourself it may take, it will always come back to you.

Indeed, those of you who are overly masculine may always be projecting and forgetting to perceive. While those of you who are overly feminine may always be perceiving and never or rarely projecting. Indeed, this one was very masculine when she was younger and then later turned to perceiving only and is now struggling to project again.

So remember now that if you are finding yourself always believing that things are happening to you it is because you are overly expressing your feminine state and neglecting your masculine expression. Also, if you are finding that others are never understanding you and you don't seem to be getting the reaction from others you want it is because you are always projecting and not also perceiving and seeing how your creations are affecting others.

That is why in past times males were typecast as being insensitive and women too sensitive but of course that was never the case because in the past you were confusing men as masculine and women as feminine but indeed all members of your kind has always had both aspects.

We speak now too of MU which is the least understood of these three parts of the Initiate's Sequence given you by the Blue Avians. MU is indeed what we and the Blue Avians say it is. It is a karmic melody which indeed means that it is a song that at this time many of you are neglecting to listen to.

So we ask you now, how do you think you can listen to a song that you are not currently listening to? Do you play the song louder or do you listen better? Perhaps you are playing the wrong song or the song you want to listen to is on a different track or a different channel. And indeed it is. Karmic melody is on its own channel and is always playing. If you are not hearing it and indeed not also listening to it then you are not tuned into its channel or frequency.

Those of you who are tuned in and are often listening to it appear as masters to your kind, and they are powerful ones and magical ones and indeed as Jesus said, their foot does not strike upon a stone because they listen to the stones, and they listen to their feet and indeed these ones know that the stone does not want to strike the foot and the foot does not want to be struck by the stone and so this masterful one listens to their songs and does not facilitate their collision. Indeed, sometimes you are struck by a stone, so to speak, or indeed sometimes in your physical realities and what do you think that is telling you? It is telling you that you are not listening to karma's song and a fine and beautiful song she does indeed weave in all the realms you visit.

Now we say that in some cases you have designed for yourselves or have been helped by life choreographers before you came here to have opportunities to be struck by certain things so that you could learn from them in dramatic ways such as contracting a debilitating disease or losing a loving relationship and so on. And now we are clear that these choices are never punishments but are indeed your choice and your right to choose this form of teaching method or lesson.

But indeed in cases that are not these cases we just mentioned, which will be noticeable to you because they will always change your lives drastically, but in other cases that are not these drastic life-changing cases, there are smaller cases of being struck by stones, so to speak, that are there to show you that you are not listening.

We give you now the hilarious and dramatic example of this one who speaks for us. We and her other guides were wanting her to move countries because indeed she had set up for herself important things to occur that were to occur for her in other countries. But now, see, she is a stubborn one and thus she did not listen to our gentle urgings and indeed the urgings of her self-made karma. So our message, or indeed, karma's song, had to be played louder for her ears to hear. So it was that she was robbed twice in two weeks, separated from her partner, lost her job, became chronically ill, was broadsided by another driver, which totalled her car, and then her next car, while it was parked, was totalled one night while she slept — all within three years. Then finally she started listening! (We know more dramatic things happen to different ones of you but this series of events was what worked for this one.)

And now she knows how to listen and whenever it is she strikes her foot upon a stone, so to speak, she knows she has stopped listening to karma's melody. And again we say what a beautiful melody she weaves.

Now remember at this time that when bad things are seeming to happen to you, you are both not listening to karma's melody and you are perceiving too much and not also projecting enough.

We say projecting, which we know has become a bad word in some of your psychology manuals, but indeed you must project for that is the only way you can create and indeed express your masculinity. Remember the projection we speak of here means a going out of energy from your creative centres.

Now we return to how this relates to the four thought natures that is in these bodies you are possessing. Space, intuition, logic and instinct is the order you must express your thought natures, in order to have a balanced expression of your minds and bodies. Indeed, this is the order in which will actually allow you to have intention and see your creation as well. Of course, your creation is always mitigated by your relationship with projection and perception and those must be in balance too. And also you must accept that if you have created certain pivotal lessons for yourselves to experience in this life before you came in then you will not easily avoid them unless you actually undergo a meeting with your higher self and guides and discuss a change in your contract. Indeed, of course this can happen and has occurred for some of you but truly, it is often better to follow through with some things you set out for yourself and truly we say that that is what most of you are doing when you are here.

Now when we say have intention only to create then we mean that intention itself is creation. Indeed, this one merged her mind with a larger version of herself, one like an ancient god or Titan that was bigger than the earth when it stood. And in this state for a moment she looked at your home, planet Gaia, and she wondered what it would be like to remove all of Gaia's oceans and in that very moment the god's body she was in was about to wave its hand over the earth and indeed in one instant swish away all the water from every sea and ocean on Gaia's surface. This experience of mighty power was terrifying to this one, and so she quickly pulled her mind back out of this god's mind, and she moved her mind back into her body. Indeed, this one has also merged her mind with this very galaxy and it felt so good to her to be so stretched out and not stuck in a human body. We give these examples to remind you that while you are in human form there is an experience of time lag, so to speak, between what you intend and what is seemingly created by your intention. Know that the time lag you experience is an illusion only and indeed just as this one experienced in a Titan state, there was no gap of time between intending and creating and that is how it is for you too but only you are under greater illusion in regard to your power than what a Titan is under regarding its power.

Indeed, as we said before, we would not put weapons into the hands of children and thus when it is you are in a lowered state and playing in lower frequencies you do not also have the ability to do very powerful things like sweep away all the seas and oceans of a planet. But see here that is not because you are less powerful, because you indeed are all powerful creators, but because by choosing to come here and play human you are choosing to play with a different set of powers to that of a Titan, for example, and a different set of illusions. And that is to your benefit because how does a Titan learn about loving a child or a pet or learn about suffering from a disease or learn about growing plants or learn about crafting a tiny object of beauty or any such delightfully beautiful and tiny things that humans are free to learn about? Indeed, as you know, because this universe is fractal then indeed there are those tinier and tinier still than you are in your human state and to those tiny ones you in your human state are the Titans.

So now we say, be satisfied with your measure of power in the human body because indeed you chose it and while you could play as Titan and indeed some of you have or will, so to speak, you are now playing as human for some very important reasons.

Indeed, we must say this one who writes for us was granted this Titan experience because indeed she was threatening us, her guides, and telling us that she was not going to do a single thing for us or humankind if she did not also get power in return because indeed she often detests her current lack of powers. So indeed one night she was granted the power of a Titan and how quickly she shrunk back in terror over that experience. Indeed, she knew being a Titan would be fun, but she does not at this time want to give up her human experience, and she was reminded of this fact when she indeed shrunk back and regained her human state.

Also, for this very reason she was offered time travel because to her things were not quick enough, and she was always seeking to jump ahead to a time when humans are in a more evolved state because she finds her current human state so boring. So indeed we offered time travel to her, and she did not take it just as we were about to give it to her because she did not want to miss the experience of seeing her family and friends every day. For indeed the speed at which you experience your realities is an experience in and of itself and if you experience your realities at different speeds you could not be experiencing all the things you do at its current pace.

And now we give a third example. Another night upon

her threatening us again to help her leave this place since she was finding it unbearable and boring and so restricting all the time so much so that she felt she was crawling out of her skin, again we offered her a means out. One night she found herself standing inside the shaft of an ancient Egyptian transporter. Indeed, it is one that is not shown to the eyes of your antiquities experts. But as we said she found herself standing inside the shaft of this ancient transporter and suddenly the stacked stone rings of the transporter which were lined with hieroglyphics started to contra-rotate and hum as they vibrated. And she saw that the hieroglyphics that were originally static now formed moving pictures on the walls and soon the walls appeared transparent as if the stone they were made of was no longer, for indeed the stone was holding this transporter in lower frequency so that lower frequency ones such as yourselves could access it but indeed this stone transporter is able to vibrate and transform and vibrate and thus transform the one standing inside it. So this one unknowingly activated this ancient portal or gateway and indeed a purpley, greyish-blue hand reached down to grab her and pull her through to another realm. But as she contemplated taking this extraterrestrial's hand (a hand of the Nephilim who were originally from Sirius), for indeed it was the hand of the ones who made it, the ancient Egyptians, who are not human, this one could feel herself losing all of her identity as she is now and no longer remembering who she was as she is now and who her family here was and what the earth was, and she became terrified again because she was not wanting to leave this place just yet. Indeed, she would not mind going on a visit to another realm but in this case she knew she wouldn't remember how to get back and indeed she wouldn't know she needed to come back because she was forgetting everything about who she was as she is here. Now do you see what we mean when we say different realms cast different illusions upon you and you indeed are in an amnesiac state often when you move from realm to realm and take on different forms?

So now we give a fourth and final example of this one attempting to leave this place because it was so boring, and she could not bear it. Whenever this one is the passenger of a vehicle that is driving fast, this one's soul almost starts to leave her body. Indeed, this one is so practised in taking and leaving form she is almost too practised at it. Indeed, if she really felt her deeds were done in this realm she would just walk out and not need to die as some of you ones are believing you must in order to leave this place. And we say also that this one is reminded by one of her guides, Erik, that this is her last life here and thus she should enjoy it because she does not need to be here again. And of course, as we mentioned before, she is joining a high council of judges for the Akkari after this life and no longer needs to play human.

So we give you all these examples to show you that you indeed chose to be here and thus if you are finding it difficult to be in harmony with your creation and indeed your choice to be here then feel free to ask your guides to remind you why you came here and what indeed you came here to learn and what indeed you want to do.

We say truly that many of you are neglecting your purposes and thus you feel purposeless or restless or as victims or are struggling to express yourselves here. Indeed, we say we know it is hard because some of us have been human, and we remember how difficult it is sometimes. But indeed you are mighty ones and you can indeed create whatever it is you want but remember that you designed this life for yourself and thus you must live it if you want to carry out your design.

In the moment of your life you can apply the principles we spoke of when we spoke of the Initiate's Sequence and you can also be learning to balance your thought natures by expressing them in order of Space, Intuition, Logic then Instinct.

So now we say your consciousness is like a square-based pyramid on the surface of this place your home with a corner facing each of the cardinal directions. Indeed, you could see yourselves as many things but you are in fact operating as an energy grid that is connected to Gaia and each and every other thing in the rest of this universe.

So just like a spider web vibrates or gets pulled when something upon it moves, so too does the whole universe move when you move in response to your touch. So indeed this way you are creators of the whole universe and the whole universe pushes in on you and you are pushing out on it. Indeed, nothing moves that is not known by all other things in the universe because you are intrinsically linked or connected to all other things. In this way you also create.

Indeed, you are a creator among creators and thus your creation must yield to the creation of others. If indeed you want something but someone wants it more then the universe gives it to them. Now that sounds like competition and lack but it is not and that is how lack and scarcity and competitive programs become so successful in your minds because it looks very much like the truth but those things are not. Now the truth for you at this time is that you are sometimes wanting things more than others and others are wanting things more than you. And this is where expectation comes into the equation, so to speak, and thus we will address it now.

Expectation by you is based on your current limited perception of reality. Like a toddler that has not yet mastered how to pick up and hold an object some of you are like toddlers when you try to create because you do not do it so well from your perspective. We say now that you actually create perfectly but you are often creating experiences for yourselves that are experiences themselves of a lack of ability. For how would any of you learn to harmonise with the universe and all other things if you only ever got everything you wanted immediately and with no consideration of consequence to other?

And thus in order to learn your place in this universe and resonate with your true place here, you must learn what it is like to sometimes get what you want and sometimes not get it. Truly, we say not getting what you want is also what you want but from a higher perspective. It is the untrained or toddler version of you that wants everything immediately. It is the mature version of you and the version of you that resonates in harmony with all other things when it is that you understand that all things you want will come to you in time and at the right time. And those things that you were wanting that were not good for you, you often do not get them and later realise you are glad to not have received them or manifested them because it was an immature version of you that was wanting them. Indeed, sometimes you get what you want and it is not good for you and then you have to learn what wanting what is also good for you is. All of these and more are variations of how 'want' and 'get' in different versions and iterations of this relationship teach you who you are and where you are in this whole place, this universe and realm.

Thus, intention is how you actually create and expectation is your teacher. Indeed, what you expect teaches you about yourself and your conscious state. If you keep finding that what you expect does not occur, then you have much to learn. When you find that what you expect is occurring and keeps occurring then you are in a mature state. Indeed, it is an example that you have given creation enough space, so to speak, and you are training up your intuition well.

We say now that as often as you can, leave intention be, without also adding expectation, and just see what happens. In this way you give your creation space. If now you sense what will happen without also predicting it in a restrictive and controlling manner then you are training your intuitive abilities which is a fine thing because you will need highly trained intuitive abilities as you evolve and enter into higher frequencies.

Also, we say now that you do not need to be training your logic, because your societies already inculcate this from a young age, but if you use it in its proper place by not overusing it and not allowing it to override your space and intuition then we say of course it is useful to you.

Lastly, we say after all these processes and due to them, your instincts, which you will retain for a while in your evolutionary paths, will indeed be trained. Your instincts need to be raised to higher frequency versions of themselves by this process we just discussed otherwise you will remain in fear and lack programming and always seeking to stay low if you operate in instinct solely or in the wrong order by putting instinct first in the order of your thought natures.

War

WE speak of war now because war is not a foreign thing to you nor is it a foreign experience to many species of being. Indeed, we say that we have been involved in wars ourselves and the Reptilian parts of you resonate with war states very easily. The Greys are not a warring kind, but they evolved by means of torture. And the Sasquatch's original home was destroyed by war. The source agenda of the experiment that originated this iteration of your species literally stemmed from war.

Of course, you see warring circumstances among many animal species on your planet and even among the microorganisms and immune systems of your own bodies. We know it even feels good for some of you to engage in war or warlike behaviour. We also know that war and warlike circumstances are very oppressive experiences for your bodies and your souls. Indeed, as you know, many decades of your time may pass and you are still feeling the trauma of wars that have been long past.

Also, we know that it has never been your experience while you were here in recent times to be part of a species that did not war among itself. And indeed we know that due to soul memory or fear propaganda you keep creating that experience for yourselves and you do not seem to know how not to war.

We say now that there are good things about the experience of war itself. It is a way that you prove to yourselves who you are. Much karma can be created or cleared by means of the experience of war. Indeed, we say that karma's dance is almost never as evident as it is during wartimes because of how many souls are swept up in the dramatic and traumatic events of war.

Indeed, trauma or pain is a very loud frequency and punches holes through spacetime, as we said before. War itself is a creative force because it is such a destructive force. As we said before, since it is that you are having a polaric reality experience then we can say that indeed destruction and creation are the same thing. And we know you already have metaphors for that concept. For example, the Phoenix which rises from the ashes or the Hindu god Shiva who is a powerful destroyer and loving creator.

Of course, those who study natural systems of this universe, including your body's immune response, the land or weather systems of Gaia or the astronomical events in the universe, know that destruction and creation or death and life are two sides of the same coin, so to speak. Indeed, death and rebirth is that state or method many evolutionary paths take.

And so, of course, we do not condemn war itself because truthfully it is a natural process. We do, however, condemn modern war states of your kind because you are evolving past the need to war among yourselves at this phase in your evolution. Truly, we would not be saying these things to you if we did not think you were capable of turning to peace state methodologies of evolution and no longer relying on just war state methodologies of evolution.

We say now that many of you are not inclined to go to war or war among yourselves, and we see this and feel this and that is why we know you are ready to enter your peace state phase of evolution. We also know that at this time those initiating war states among your kind are a corrupt, small group of elite individuals. We feel though this is changing due to your kind's overwhelming desire for peace, rest and rehabilitation. Also, indeed, some of us and your extended family have been removing some power of these elite ones for you on your behalf.

There are, of course, those of your kind who are not of this elite few who still have war states in them because they have lived hard lives or lives full of oppression, and they are angry all the time. And they have been conditioned by their societies or communities to be warlike because war states have been common in their society or community's history and these ones have not yet learned other ways of operating or existing.

We say to this that your example of peace states and your operations or modalities of higher frequencies or vibrations will indeed help these ones directly and indirectly. Truly, when those of you who can easily touch or reach peace states in your lives do so and do so happily and easily, then you truly are sending these good vibrations through Gaia's energy grid system and you are also sending these good vibrations through the human energy grid system and your species and all of Gaia's species are benefiting. Truly, as we said before, your species operates as a whole body and if enough of the body is healthy it can make the whole body healthy.

So engage in peace state methodologies and higher frequency behaviours on a daily basis and then even if you do this only in little ways you are literally benefiting your entire species.

Moments

OMENTS are vector ducts. Indeed, they are little holes in the substance of time that float or fly all around this place. At any one time, your local field may catch onto one of these holes or moments and thus at the time that you are catching one of them you experience a less viscous experience of time itself (or herself).

So now we know that you are sometimes experiencing different rates or viscosities of time and indeed you are because time is a fluid and fluids move all the 'time'. But now here regarding Moments or vector duct catching, you are indeed at those times when you catch one experiencing a lack of the current viscosity of time at which you currently regularly experience it.

So hear now, if you pay attention the next time you become aware of a Moment, it is likely because your field has caught one. Thus, all of a sudden your conscious state changes and your mind lifts because when you are existing inside Moments, regardless of how large or small they may be, you are experiencing higher frequencies because Time is less upon you and thus your conscious awareness is sharpened and more attuned and less dull and slow.

So indeed now we say that you could all train yourselves to become better Moment catchers and indeed once you have caught one, if you are kind to it you may indeed expand it too if that is your desire and the Moment is obliging.

Truly, as we said several times before, all things that

can be said to be things are people who have their own conscious states and own eternal histories and futures. So now when you are interacting with a Moment, be kind to it and it will likely be kind to you.

We know how some of you delight when you catch yourself in a Moment because it feels fun to all of a sudden experience a different viscosity of time. And thus we know some of you hold onto that feeling of fun and do indeed expand the vector duct or Moment you are interacting with to encase your whole body and perhaps your whole group of friends or perhaps the whole room or indeed in the case of some live speakers and performers and such, the whole crowd or stadium.

We like seeing you have fun with these Moments when you catch them or indeed if they land upon you or engage with your field by their own choosing. So live in harmony with Moments if you will, and they will as helpers bring you more and more to higher frequency existence.

Irony

K NOW now that Irony, a tool or weapon or vessel, is masterfully wielded by karma. Indeed, karma uses Irony all the time to be teaching you all many things. Indeed, how many times was it that you only understood something once it was painfully and ironically made clear to you?

Indeed, we say many times karma is painfully ironic. We give an example now.

The thing that you want and have always wanted calls you for many years and invites you to keep wanting it. And you struggle and strive to get the thing wanted and it keeps calling you and inviting you further to keep wanting it. And you swim in this dance and this cycle for many, many years, some of you. The dance of always wanting something and never having it and yet it is there always calling you and asking you to keep wanting it.

So what is this process of wanting and never having? It is a karmic lesson you have set up for yourself, truly. And wouldn't you know it ... the very moment you stop wanting it you get it and in that very moment because you no longer want it you give it away or give it freely to someone that needs it. Isn't that ironic? (We have triggered a song lyric in this one's head.)

Irony is realising that you were under an illusion and thus it is also realising that you no longer are under that particular illusion. It feels like missing out on something. That thing you were wanting or hoping for you missed by seconds or by the skin of your teeth, so to speak. And some of you may think how odd it was that events were so perfectly choreographed and so synchronistically not in your favour. How is that happening? Well, as we said before, it is by your design and the design of the life choreographers.

Irony holds painful lessons but useful ones, so don't miss her teachings.

Astrology

THIS gift of perceiving reality astrologically was given to you, not by us or your other parents, but by others who visited your kind long ago (the Annunaki).

Astrology, as we say, dear friends, is a useful tool to you if you want to view it that way. Indeed, the ancient ones knew how useful it was and some of your kind now do too. We do not encourage the frivolous use of this tool, astrology, because that is not its purpose. We do, however, say that if it is used by ones who have studied this art or craft or science and know it deeply they indeed may be of benefit to the rest of you.

Now we must say that astrology should not be used as a doomsday tool, so to speak, as we see that some of you are using it that way. But we know for the most part it is being used as a way to understand personality and life path requirements and making ones of your kind aware of the times in which they can indeed take advantage of astrological events to attune their cleansing rituals or action behaviours.

We do say too that at no time should astrology be used to predict the future because we see some of you doing that and that is a trap and a negative use of this tool.

We cannot easily explain to you now why indeed astrology applies to you because it would require that your conscious states change. But as we said before, all things are people (even the word 'thing' is a person) and every layer of those things are people. For example, a planet is a person and all who live on it are people and all who live on the people are people and so on. And space is a person and space is made up of many people and stars are people and everything that makes up stars are people. So now we could say that if we woke up all the people that make up Gaia we would wake up the mountains and oceans and hills and seas and so on, and they would all wake up and move and you would have no home left to live on and thus we do not wake them up yet.

So now when you look up in the sky and you see patterns of stars in the sky, they are real places that are far away, so to speak, from your current viewpoint and logic, but they are also people, and they move around and interact with each other and influence your behaviour because the stuff that makes you are made by them.

Now too we could say that the time you came into this simulation or environment made you who you were because of how the computer, so to speak, of this simulation was operating when you came in. It had a specific signature at the exact time and place you came in and thus you were cast in stone, so to speak, as your soul took lower and slower form in 3D. Thus, your form and its attending ego was cast at the moment you came in and thus indeed all the simulation or astrological placements that were in place when your form was cast is indeed in effect for the whole life of the form. And the life of the form is under ongoing influence by all the beings in the simulation because indeed all things are connected. And truly, large things have large influence on little things, and we say of course that stars and planets are indeed large things and as you are now you are little things.

So we say now that it is entirely possible for you to gain an enlightened state of being at the same time as never attuning yourself to the art or craft or science of astrology, but for those of you using this tool for the sake of mitigation and betterment then we say that is a good thing.

Population Reduction

WE briefly must mention to you now that there are those of your kind and those not of your kind who are part of an elite group of beings who make plans for your world that indeed do not benefit you all. They plan to reduce the population of humans and animals on your planet to a very small and manageable number.

Indeed, there have been actions taken by these ones to reduce your numbers already. By means of technologies that create what you experience as natural disasters but indeed we say many of them are not natural because they have been created by this small group of elite individuals. Also, there are other ways they have been reducing your number by means of introducing ingredients into your food, water, air and so on that give you disease and slowly kill you.

This small group of individuals make themselves elite or are elite by means of birth into privileged situations, and they are groomed to continue thinking they are elite and thus they believe they have the right to plan and make actions regarding your kind's entire population. We say now that if you were aware of their plans and the actions they have already taken you would be in great fear over their next lot of plans for your kind and you would be sad and in great pain over the things they have already done to your kind.

Indeed, they run sex slave and trafficking organisations. They influence much of your lawmaking and law enforcing agencies. They operate technology that negatively impact your health and kill many of you. They design drugs and other ingredients that are not only put into your foods but also your mainstream medicines that in fact give you more disease and slowly kill you. They make sure there is a constant stream of chemtrails in all your skies so that you are kept low and unaware of their activities. They encourage the use of pesticides and hormones in plant and animal agriculture. They encourage the use of oppressive animal agriculture methods. They make sure those of your kind who invent beneficial and clean technologies get suppressed or killed. They make sure whistleblowers to their ways are intimidated or killed. They want to kill off certain species of animals and encourage industry that wipe out large areas of habitat. They want to keep your kind dependent on mainstream marketing campaigns and large corporate structures. They release mainstream entertainment with specific themes and events that keep you in fear and keep you in agreement to their methodologies. They want to harvest your physical energy and life force. They invent thousands and thousands of mindless jobs which are actually fake jobs to keep you all busy and plugged into their system. They use mind control technology and intimidation tactics to keep those of you who are on the path to discovering their behaviours scared or make those ones think they are losing their mind. They make sure certain self-aware ones of you are not let into government positions or law agency positions. They design news stories to justify wars that are not really happening so that armies can be raised to kill people that they want killed. They want to keep you dependent on fossil fuel sources of energy and suppress technologies that do not require fossil fuels. They keep the highly intelligent ones among you locked into scientific research roles for research that goes nowhere or research that serves their purposes. Indeed, ones of your kind who are studying certain mathematical and scientific areas of study are tracked more closely than others of you. They control the release of much technology and scientific discovery release. They keep amateur and expert archaeologists away from special sites and sacred sites so that only their experts which are under their control discover these things, your true history that we have been telling you. They kidnap and hold and in some cases torture ones of your kind that have powers they want to harness. They imprison some visitors of your planet and often abuse them and do not release them. They often create viruses or create false press release on viruses that sweep your planet. They inject harmful things into you when you are given certain shots or injections. They keep track of all of your behaviour in ways you aren't even aware of. Indeed, they track all of you. We could go on but we won't.

Indeed, we know many of you have heard of these things and some of you would say that they are conspiracy theories only and do not require your attention. But truly, we say these things are happening. We and others that talk about these things to you often use the word 'they' when we talk about the elite few that are doing these things. Indeed, we could give you the names of the individuals that are doing these things to you either indirectly or directly but that would not be good for the safety of the one who writes this for us.

Indeed, it is enough that you know that these things are happening and just by your conscious awareness of these facts alone it is enough to start tipping the scale in favour of the majority of your kind. Indeed, when you release your dependencies on all the things they have set up for you to be dependent on you will start waking up to your own power and wisdom and start seeing clearly for the first time for some of you.

We know that your dependencies on these corporate and consumer structures is great, and so we do not expect that you give up all these dependencies straight away. But rather we invite you to become aware of your dependencies on the structures that keep these oppressive ones in power and slowly release yourself from them in healthy and tangible ways. Make slow and methodical steps toward your own independence and true health states. And please stop listening to their lies which are fed to you mainly by means of their marketing campaigns, false media stories, and much of their education systems. We know that you cannot just up and leave these societal structures straight away but you can take slow and methodical steps toward bettering your situation every day and making yourselves more aware and less dependent every day.

That is all. You have been informed.

Animals

IN this place, you experience the beings you call animals for many reasons. One such reason is that their existence among you gives you the opportunity to show yourself and show us how you treat them. Indeed, how you treat animals demonstrates to us, your parents and your extended family that you are immature or mature. We see that many of you are becoming mature in this regard.

Also, the animals process much of your excess energy. They embody your lower natures for you, so that you might leave those natures behind and evolve. Also, some animal species are higher beings, and ground here, for your benefit, higher frequencies, that your kind, at this time, cannot hold in your body systems. So of course, we are not saying that the beings you call animals are less evolved. We are saying that they do you the service of carrying your heavy loads and grounding higher frequencies, so that you might ascend. For indeed, they are no less evolved. Their intelligence is invisible to the ignorant ones among you, but profound and obvious to the listeners among you.

Too, the animals act as a metaphor for you. You learn many things about yourself, and the universe you find yourselves in, when you observe them closely. Also, they have taught you how to work in harmony with Gaia's natural systems.

We say too now that as Gaia ascends into higher frequencies, the animals will indeed stop being violent with each other and consuming each other. We know some of you are already seeing examples of their kind acts to each other and to your kind. This will only become more prevalent and thus, more apparent to you, as you all ascend with your mother Gaia.

Also, many souls come into this realm to experience it as animal. Being an animal here can teach a soul many precious lessons. Already we know some of you are recognising the profound souls that are seated in many of your animals.

Sometimes, souls come back to you again and again as different pets. Indeed, this one had a pet bunny whose soul came back to her years later as her pet dog. We know many of you share examples of this occurrence in your life and that is a beautiful thing.

Also, we say that Gaia is a nursery for evolving species. Indeed, many other beings introduce animals to your realm for observation. Also, many species of extraterrestrials, we would rather say your extended family, are bipedal versions of your many animal species. This is because they are like you, and you are like them. We say this, this way, because you are often thinking that extraterrestrials are odd and very different to you. Indeed, we could say, you are very different to them because they came first. Getting to know your animal species will help you understand the many different species that your extended family embody. Indeed, this universe we all share has expressed itself in infinite variety.

Again, we say that all animals have souls and are aware and thus, you are committing murder when you kill them. Also, the scientific and consumer research that is performed on them must stop. They are people just like you, only they project onto this realm a different reality. There was a time that you were allowed to kill them and consume them. This time was when you lived and died as one of them. When you often took risks surviving, and survived only by means of their nourishment. Those times were also filled with gratitude for the ones, the animals, dying so that the humans would be saved in their stead. Your kind no longer has that relationship with animals.

Thus, it is not acceptable to consume them. Especially not by means of factory farm processes, which are akin to your wartime concentration camps. Indeed, your mass slaughter and consumption of animals is an animal holocaust. The time for you to consume them is over. Know this!

We finish here in a lighter tone. Let yourselves be taught by these little ones, the animals, for they will save you, if you let them.

New Earth, The Coming

THERE is a new earth upon you. On May 26, 2018, this one who speaks for us was given direct experience of the preparatory energy wave that enveloped your planet. She experienced the wave as a brown wave that resonated with the earth beneath your feet.

This one, whose light body swam in this wave all night, woke up exhausted and was tired for several days. Indeed, these waves that are intended to upgrade you will cause different effects upon your local fields and thus your body systems. They will not harm you because they are here to heal you and ascend you.

There are plenty of lightworkers who are aware of these waves, ahead of the majority of you. They are experiencing these waves at greater force, to take the brunt for you. They will soon be raised up and will help lead your kind into the new earth paradigm. If you want to learn more about these waves, and the effects they will be having on your bodies and in your lives, use online resources. Because indeed, the lightworkers receiving information about these waves ahead of you are publishing information about them online, as we speak these words to you.

In regards to the recent energy waves that have come to you, the brown wave was soon followed by a green wave, which resonated with the plants of your planet. Since the plants are more attuned to Gaia's energy grid, they received the upgrades that the cosmic waves now coming in are bringing. Soon after the green wave an orangey-yellow wave hit, which started clearing your kind's lower chakra systems. Issues associated with the taboo and power are surfacing and clearing right now, at the time of this writing. Added to this wave was a red wave, which is still pummelling you all at the time of this writing. The red wave is bringing up issues of anger for you and helping you clear old stories that have been stuck in your local fields all your lives.

These are the energy waves that have hit your planet thus far and your part of the galaxy. These energy waves will continue to hit, and are ascending Gaia, your home, and all who reside on and in her. By the time you read this, there would have been many more waves that hit. They will keep coming to ascend this realm and all partaking in it.

Know this, at this time, the new earth is upon you. There is no going back. The battle between light and dark has been won by the light. That is to say, that the light loves and embraces the dark and brings it into higher realms, or heals and cleanses it. Know now that all who do not choose the light and choose to ascend with Gaia at this time will be moving elsewhere. She is ascending now, as we speak these words to you. By the time you read this, her ascension will be much further along.

Each wave that hits will clear more old energy and heal what is to be brought into the new earth. The new earth is here, and you are all helping build it for yourselves. We are here as helpers, but you are the new masters of this realm. Humanity is returning to its rightful sovereignty. Humanity will work in symbiosis with Gaia to heal, ascend and bring this realm back into balance. There is a great work ahead, and all of you are invited to share in it. Start now! Build the new earth with us.

To those of you who have not learned about the new earth, we address some descriptions here. Firstly, we encourage you to do some research on the new earth paradigm, since there are many of your kind attuned to its arrival and already speak of it. So, in addition to what you might read or hear others speak of, we say these few things.

There are several iterations of the new earth, which is based upon the fact that your kind has evolved at very different rates and thus, Gaia would accommodate all of her children, except those committed to harming her and others. Thus, here we are referring to different timelines with different rates and means of achieving the new earth paradigm. Your thoughts and actions on an individual and collective basis literally affect the rate and means by which the new earth comes.

Some who are attuned to the Coming feel that it might come as a rainbow or a fog or some other means. We told this one to look for 'strange clouds'. Indeed, many thousands of extraterrestrial craft park in your skies on a daily basis and observe you during this great change. Extraterrestrial craft are often disguised by cloud covering, but we and your extended family are reducing our disguise because we can feel many of you getting ready to meet us, and see us with your waking eyes. There are thousands of races of being interested in this grand event and are aiding the transformation, to a point at which they do not hamper free will.

Indeed, this one had a vision a year ago and saw the Coming as a large solar flash that filled the whole sky with a bright light before she passed out for a little while. When she awoke in her vision, she saw that the flash was cleansing but not destructive. Indeed, we say that some of you will experience it differently based on your construction of reality.

Know that the Coming of the New Earth is a gift and will not harm you. For those of you whose bodies will not easily bear the changes coming, we say that you will often be receiving upgrades by means of brief visitations by us and your extended families. There are many of you who are regularly receiving upgrades but you are not paying attention to them. Often, you are being taken on to craft or ships and your light bodies are being adjusted in preparation for the big changes. Some of you are aware when this occurs, and we ask that you look upon these occurrences kindly, since they are to your benefit, and you have contracted to receive them.

For example, several weeks ago, this one who writes was taken onto craft to receive an injection that would not only prepare her for the coming changes, but it also marked her as a special one who is largely helping your kind. Also, last week, she was given vision of the evolution of her third eye. In previous times, she saw her third eye as a small gateway or portal that was always receiving information and visitation. But now she has entered into a new phase of lightwork, and as such, she saw her third eye as no longer receptive, but as projective. A small white light, that will only get larger with these coming changes, was shining out of this one's third eye. That is part of her gift to humanity. She, like other lightworkers, will be as beacons to your kind during these great changes.

And so with that, we say, many of you who are waking up in advance of the big changes, know that you will be leaders and teachers among your kind. For those of your kind that do not wake up easily, the changes will make no sense to them, because they were not paying attention, and they will need a lot of help to adjust to the new earth. You are all being bathed in higher frequencies as we speak, and they will only get stronger and of higher frequency as you, along with Gaia, ascend into a 4D and 5D reality.

When we speak of 4D and 5D, we mean that you will experience a projection of energy that is of the fourth and fifth densities. Currently, many of you project only 2D and 3D realities. In these higher densities, or as some of you say dimensions, as we said before, Time will no longer hold you as she did. Thus, your experience of time will change.

Also, on the new earth, since it is that you will no longer be slaves or oppressed by your current oppressors, you will be learning to master your own wills. We know this is a difficult thing to do for most of you since you have been programmed to be slaves since your birth here. But when you are bathed in higher frequencies and the oppressive low frequency veils are lifted, it will not take long for you to learn the new ways. You could start now, living as if you are on the new earth, and indeed that will make you prepared for the changes and bring the changes sooner.

Already you are seeing arrests of your large and great ones. Indeed, the mighty are falling. And they will keep falling because it is time that they pay their due. And you little ones are remembering your power and deciding to no longer be slaves. We recommend at this time to start living from your heart centres and listening to the background frequencies of this realm. Indeed, there are background frequencies always playing, and you will hear them if you listen. They will speed up, and your conscious states will change with each wave that hits.

At this time, we recommend that you become creative and leave behind old ways of behaving. For example, if you have a job that you dislike, then leave it. Find other means of sustenance. Indeed, if you eat only plant foods, lessen your dependency on the slave grid, and if you find a community to share your lives with, this is easier. Again we say, start living as if the new earth is here, because that is how you will bring it, and that is how you are making yourselves ready for the changes.

Now we say that many species have evolved to do many different things. We do not judge those different things, but here we will be clear about how Gaia is changing and how your species will most successfully evolve with her. You are to release you dependency on technology. That is not to say that you will not be using it a lot while the changes are being made, but you can change the way you view technology now. For example, you could stop watching television. You could stop using social media or the internet for superficial reasons. You could walk in nature on most days if you are able. Or when you can, open a window, or step outside, and so on. You can start consuming local food and local material items. Instead of buying new, you could buy used or accept free. You could adopt some Zero Waste principles. You could stop consuming plastic. You could start foraging and getting to know Gaia again. You could release addictions to all things. You could make new friends that want what is best for you, and release relationships with those that do not want what is best for you. You could start accessing your higher self, and start making contact with us and your extended family.

Since these first waves have hit, we could say the new earth is here. Because indeed, we are not going back. The balance has already been tipped in your favour. It is coming! You are seeing it now.

Each wave as it comes will be integrated. With each wave, you will have opportunity to show us all who you really are, and which side of the line you stand on. Are you ready to let the old ways go and embrace the new earth paradigm?

After Gaia and all her children have received all their updates by means of these waves, there will be a flash experienced for some of you. The flash itself will take you to the new earth. We do not speak too rigidly here, because the way the new earth comes is still changing, because you are all still changing. You all will actually bring in the new earth based on the frequencies in which you operate, the decisions you make, and the actions you take.

We do say now too that in the new earth paradigm, there will be plenty for you all to do. For example, the Blue Avians will be more than happy to take on initiates and plenty of other benevolent extraterrestrial groups, councils and organisations will be inviting recruits from the new earth population.

Those staying with Gaia long term will help rebuild all of her forests, including reforesting the deserts (some desert habitat will remain for a time to maintain diversity). New species of animals and plants will start living on Gaia, and some previously existing ones here will come back. At this time, all the other beings that temporarily left Gaia or phased out of human frequency will start to return to your eyes, and you will regain relationships with them as you begin interacting again. These ones are Fae, Elementals, Tree beings and so on.

For those staying on Gaia even longer, after important geometrical structures are built upon and within Gaia, to help her clear, balance and channel higher frequencies, she will move to a light-only existence, and all on her will be light beings with light-only bodies. This state of Gaia is what this one, who writes for us, remembers coming here for. Not all of you wish to stay on Gaia for this long, but there are those of you who want to keep evolving Gaia and yourselves to this extent.

Start channelling your own truth for why you came here, to live on Gaia at this time, and research the copious information on the new earth paradigm. Make sense of it for yourself, and start making life changes, so that you can start building the new earth, and start living like you are in the new earth now.

Molecular Science Versus Energy Science

MOLECULAR science is what underpins all the sciences your kind observes at this time. We say observe because your kind does not use science today, but rather they are used by it. Like religion, science has become a tool for your oppressors to continue oppressing you. Since it is, that you are consumed by looking at the universe through molecular goggles, so to speak. Only mathematics touches on higher truths, but math too dips its toes in murky waters, so to speak.

Seeing all the world through molecular goggles is why indeed everything to you is subject to the laws of physics. If all is made of atoms, and atoms are subject to the laws of physics, then your scientists are no closer to understanding themselves or the universe by observing atomic behaviour. But indeed, that is what they all do. Only in some cases when the science of physics touches mathematics or the study of light and frequency does your kind get close to a truth that is actually beneficial to your species for their next evolutionary leap. Molecular science will not carry you much longer. That is because the illusion that houses a molecular understanding of reality is ending as you move to higher frequencies. It is a lower frequency way of viewing reality. Truly.

We are speaking in generalities here because of course there have been some good uses for molecular science, but only little steps have been made, and often those steps were made with the assistance of the Greys and your other extraterrestrial family members.

We give an example here. A child must learn some things for themselves. But often, if they do not have a parent to show them how to do something, they will never learn to do it. That is the case with your kind in most things, truly. We have allowed your great thinkers to put their names on discoveries that we in fact gave them. But now, your egos have been stroked enough, and you are becoming obsessed with your own false sense of greatness. Truly, compared to us, you know almost nothing. We say this to remind you that it would greatly benefit you to learn from your parents in this regard.

Indeed, it was us and others of your extended family that taught your ancestors agriculture and community building and many other things.

So now maybe we think it would benefit your kind if you turn to your extended family and your higher selves for inspiration, and no longer be turning to the ones you call scientists, because they are not scientists, just highly competent slaves. We say this harshly because your addiction to the thing you call science, and your direct and indirect worship of scientists, is not doing your kind any good. Truly.

When science is genuinely about discovery, then it is good. But almost never has science, the way your species has interpreted it, been void of corruption. Truly, from its beginning, wise ones were always sought for counsel by the leaders among you. So, at its inception, science was always used as a rulership tool. And since it is that your kind have thus far generally not made good rulers, then the tool science has not been wielded kindly.

Now we say there are so many inconsistencies in your various discoveries, so to speak, that stating fact is purposeless. Indeed, we say that your science today is bought and paid for by those seeking to wield it as influence. There are plenty of scientific discoveries that go unnoticed or are intentionally suppressed that as a result you never learn about.

So who decides what science you learn about and what science you never learn about? Indeed, who? Of course, the answer is, your oppressors. They shape the world you live in to suit their own agendas and not yours. And all your brilliant ones, who want to help the world and are genuinely interested in learning about it, get funnelled through slave programs, such as your universities, and told lies or recycled so-called facts about the world, until your joy and fervent curiosity is killed, and in its place, your powerful minds are put to their use and not yours.

You brilliant ones, who become scientists, aren't even masters of your own will. That part of you is not so brilliant, indeed. Why don't you use those powerful minds of yours to realise you are slaves and you spend years and years in research for things that are already known, and for things that there are already better solutions for?

Please stop wasting your time and our time. We say our time too because we wait for you to wake up and start using your brilliant minds in creative ways and no longer slave ways.

We also want to mention here that part of the slave programming you are subject to would have you believe that those obtaining higher degrees, and particularly scientific ones, are better than others and are entitled to ego. This science-bearing ego thinks it has the right to act as a powerful and wise one by shutting down all imaginative thoughts and creative ventures. Truly, just look at how many of your leaders in science are shutting you all down and telling you what the world is from their viewpoint and mocking you when you know differently. They are wrong to do this when they do this. When leaders of any kind mock the little ones of you, they are not good leaders.

We introduce now what you could call energy science. It is not a science because science requires logic and the study of energy does not. We know that some of your sciences already touch on the study of energy, and we appreciate those fields of understanding. We are not here to put one science field above another. But truly, we are here to say that you are to release science all together as you move into higher frequencies. This is because just as religion, sex, and your needs for food and shelter have been turned into weapons against you by your oppressors, so has science.

Science escapes detection as an oppressive force because its intentions are good, so to speak. But as many of you know, the movement Science has also done much bad. We will not go into lists of all the good things and bad things science has done for your kind here. But we will say that science has been set up as a god to your kind. And generally, as a species, you have forgotten your own wisdom and listened to scientists and followed their orders as if they were your gods.

Now in some cases, certain ones you call scientists have done good for you. But in many others, they have exploited you while stroking their egos. Also, often real scientific discoveries are not published to the public and you are getting reports of fake science anyway. So, you do not need to keep thinking that the ones in white lab coats are masters of the universe, because they are not. They know almost nothing that is important to your kind at this time. Truly.

You have the information you need inside of you. You are programmed and wired for automatic upgrades. You can access information from your nonlocal fields or higher selves at any time. You can access information from you future selves or other guides at any time. Truly, find your own truth and follow your own path. You will find that path often leads you to be the best version of yourself, and you will no longer be needing to play 'slave'.

Now we do not condemn science at all. We say simply that science is losing its benefit for you. So now we give examples of energy science. Actually, we will call it energy gnosis, or self-mastery.

When you stop looking through molecular goggles,

so to speak, you will not need to be seeing everything as spheres. Truly, to you all, things are spheres, such as your earth, and water droplets, and even your chemical models are made of spheres. Now we say, this has been useful for you for a time. But that time is ending.

When you start seeing energy, you will be seeing a truer form of reality. Or we could say, you are under less illusion. Or we could say, you are closer to source. Or we could say, you are closer to mastering the game.

Energy can take any form and thus, you are less constricted when you understand how it works. Now, you are always subjecting yourselves to molecules. For example, you say, 'I am sick. Medical science knows the molecular cause of my sickness, and they have created molecular medicine for my sickness'. Indeed, some of you already know, and we previously stated, that large corporations give you diseases that they later profit from when you buy their medicines for those diseases that they gave you. That is another subject.

Since atoms or molecules are just 3D holograms of energy, it makes more sense to study energy directly, rather than just one of the many holographic projections of energy.

To be clear, we say to you now, molecular science, which underpins most of the science your kind has today, is no longer valid, and you are free to start releasing this way of viewing reality. Truly, molecular science will not take you into higher realms, and into higher realms is where you are going, if you stay existing in symbiosis with Gaia, your mother, your home.

Some of you already see energy. Indeed, like this one, your ability to see energy has brought some of you praise and some of you derision. Indeed, this one here, who writes for us, has often been mocked for discussing what she sees, and rudely shut down by those thinking they are superior ones, since they have co-opted scientific language, and therefore must be geniuses who know everything. Indeed, even this one here had experienced so many years of mockery for discussing what she could plainly and clearly see with her own two eyes that she even turned to science herself so that she might be taken seriously when she spoke to her fellow human. Even now she undertakes a science degree, but is wrestling with the distortions she perceives, and painfully contorts herself in the restrictive environment, and over the restrictive delivery method of its teachings.

It truly is not useful or beneficial to you to be studying so much that you become exhausted and stressed, and start believing that you are worthless and stupid if you can't perform in this way. It is a slave program. Do not be fooled, dear friends.

And we know some of you master the game of academia, and think you are so wise that you get to tell everyone how wise you are, and shut everyone else down who did not get to the top of the game. That is Reptilian expression in a Grey world, since it is the Reptilians that gave you ability to fight and compete, and the Greys gave you science.

When this one is in symbiosis with her Grey friends, she loves being in the lab. And she does love details and supposed fact sharing. But she wrestles, as we know many of you do, over how constrictive the environment, created by science, is.

So now we say, no longer constrict yourselves. Trust and know that what you see to be true and real is indeed true and real. Many of you have had to say things like, 'I dreamed it but it felt so real'. Or, 'Am I crazy?' Or 'It was just my imagination, no bother'. And so on. Many of you are always having to tell yourselves not to listen to or trust yourselves or else the science police will get you, so to speak.

Science has caused your kind much grief. Just as religion told you that you would all go to hell. Science is telling you that you are all stupid, and you need to constantly purchase the latest technology to keep up, or take the latest pill to be treated for the latest disease. Can you see yet how this is not good for you?

So now we give you examples of what learning about energy looks like, since, if you remain as humans on Gaia at this time, you will be needing to know how to master energy, in your environments, with your vessel.

As we said before, some of you already see energy and some of you already master it. Indeed, there are ones of your kind with, as you would call them, superpowers and such. There are ones of your kind who fly, who conduct elements, who conduct or move objects and so on. At this time, you are all able to develop a power, so to speak. Each of you is different and each of you holds natural affinities to certain abilities. So, as we previously invited you all to do, play with and discover your 'supernatural abilities' or 'superpowers' in groups among yourselves.

Seeing energy is like seeing consciousness itself. If you pay attention to what you focus on, and what others focus on, you are paying attention to energy. Also, you can start seeing vector ducts. Vector ducts may even make the top of your head tingle when you receive transmission of a thought, for example. Vector ducts often give you headaches. Indeed, this one who writes for us can feel energy come at her via eye contact, and she can feel thoughts in her body. Most, if not all of you, are seeing energy, only you don't have forum for this ability and thus, you ignore it and do not develop it. This one has paid attention to this ability and developed it, thus she can see portals open and close and feel thoughts travel like bits of information through her nervous system and so on.

When you are in higher frequency play, that is to say, when Gaia finishes this latest transition, which will be soon, the variety of ways you can play with energy will be endless. For now, only some of your monks, gurus, martial artists and so on are playing with energy. But now, you can all make it one of your daily behaviours to start learning how to play with energy, if you do not already do that.

Indeed, some children coming in now have been fortunate enough to avoid the worst of this realm's slave programming and thus, they already play with energy and were not made to shun or forget this natural ability you all possess. For example, if you pay attention, you will start seeing the children of your kind show you the way in this regard. Maybe they can teach you to be telekinetic and so on. Of course, not all children are doing this at this time, but those of you avoiding or rejecting the slave programs at this time can more easily develop their natural ability to play with energy.

Senses

THE senses you experience now are actually the possessions of your light bodies. It seems to you that you experience your environment by means of your physical or 3D bodies, but that is not entirely true. Your nervous systems are fed information via your 3D environments only for the preservation of your 3D bodies. For example, if you are too cold or too hot or you are thirsty or hungry and so on. But your five senses all have higher versions in your light bodies. And you are often interpreting multiple layers of stimuli simultaneously. Since it is that you are multidimensional or multi-density beings, you are simultaneously interpreting inputs from several layers of reality. Often, these inputs will overlap in your sensory comprehension.

We could distinguish the senses and say that your body's senses are your lower senses and your light body's senses are your higher senses. They work together to feed your minds a multi-density and multidimensional reality. What informs the light body manifests in the physical or 3D body. The experiences of your physical body feeds information to the light body, your local field and your soul. In this way, there is constant input and feedback between the two categories of senses.

Now we give an example. Several nights ago, the one who speaks for us astrally travelled while her body relaxed. That is to say, the projection of her physical body stayed in this realm while her light body went elsewhere in the universe. Her conscious state was with her light body. That is to say, she was no longer interpreting inputs from her physical body but only inputs from her light body. She heard the background hum or frequency of the plane of this realm. Then the hum started speeding up as she moved into another realm of higher frequency. The background hum of this realm is not consciously perceived by your kind, because there is no absence of it, and thus, no opportunity for you to recognise its existence. But when this one travelled to another realm, the background hum of this place became apparent, because here she was perceiving a different background hum of a different realm.

The background hum of this other place she was visiting was faster, and to her light body it felt more vivid or present. That is to say that her light body, which is made to perceive lower frequency realms, gets excited or overwhelmed by higher frequency realms. This light body you all have now can take you to many realms but there is a limit on the speed of frequency it can handle before a new vessel must be required.

Higher frequencies make more of an impression on the experience of the light body than do lower ones. That is why when ones of your kind have higher frequency experiences, such as talking to a higher vibrational being or extraterrestrial, they remember it for the rest of their life, because higher vibrations or frequencies make a strong impression and thus are easily remembered. This one who speaks for us has described it like this. This 3D world you all live in now, to her, actually feels like she is living in a 2D painting. It is slow and dull compared with her experiences in higher frequency realms. Those of you partaking in psychedelic experiences by whichever means might hold similar sentiments. That is also why, as crazy as she once thought she was for being able to see and talk to extraterrestrials on a regular basis, she knew what she was experiencing was real, because it felt more real to her than this world does, which is comparably made with lower frequencies and thus is a duller experience to your senses. That is also why those of your kind, who have been in contact with their extended family or extraterrestrials, and visited higher frequency realms, cannot be convinced otherwise, or made to believe it was not real, because such interaction with higher ones and higher realms are so profound that they cannot be invalidated by ignorant ones and oppressive ones.

In times past, your kind have killed these ones or thrown these ones into asylums and done other horrible things to them, but your kind can no longer do this to the ones of you who are less under illusion.

We give more explanation of the light body senses now. The physical 3D body can only perceive physical or 3D input on its own. It will, however, also manifest information from your higher senses. That is how mediums and psychics do their work. Their light body perceives information from other layers of reality and feeds that information to the physical body. Often mediums and psychics do not need information to reach their 3D physical bodies, and they speak directly from the light body. The light body sees, hears, smells, tastes and touches too. There are of course more senses, such as soul touch, and so on, but that is beyond you for now. For now, just know that the light body has more sensory range than your physical body does. The light body is what houses your chakras and links with your local field, which links you with the multiverse.

Also, for those of you who are natural shapeshifters or morphers, there are indeed quite a lot of you, it is your local fields that hold memory of different form templates, and your light body is able to change shapes and project and animate different 3D holograms or bodies. This is not easy for all of you. You all came in with different natural talents. As you evolve, if you so desire, any of you will be allowed to download different body templates and thus, project different forms.

We also say here that channellers speak directly from light body input. Often channellers will allow the light body of another person, i.e. a dead loved one or extraterrestrial, to inhabit their local field. Thus, with this new person inside their local field, their bodies are often animated slightly differently, because the visitor is not always accustomed to the form they are sharing with the channeller. We say now that we love channellers and to keep up the good work.

Channelling is how much change will be accomplished. Indeed, you could all learn to channel for yourselves. At this time, you could be learning to at least channel your higher self or future self since this version of you will guide you through the changes occurring at this time.

At this time, we also want to say that there is no subconscious mind, as you have been labelling it. What you have been labelling as 'subconscious mind' is higher self or your nonlocal field.

There are plenty of examples of good channellers out there, so feel free to look them up and learn from them. Also, there are lessons and courses you can take formally or informally that will teach you how to channel. Indeed, practising channelling is how your kind will become a telepathic species, and you will be doing this form of communication primarily in the new earth paradigm. So, start now.

Also, we want to say that your kind are always receiving sensory updates. An example of this is your ability to recognise CGI effects in films that you could previously not recognise. That is to say that computer images that once dazzled and impressed you when the film was first released became dull to your senses and painfully obvious years later when you rewatched the film.

We give another example. One day this one was riding as passenger in a car on a road trip, and she was listening to one of her favourite songs. Partway through the song, the song itself changed completely. It sounded like a different song although the words were the same. Then after about 20 seconds, the song returned to its normal state, or the version of it she was accustomed to hearing. Indeed, we give this example to show you that your realities change when you change. Truly, all is imagined and yet real.

While you are here, you bear the imagination of this universe, who is as a large sleeping one, and you are all in its dream. We ask, for how could you say that you imagine anything that is not also real, since your minds are products of this universe, who made you and all other things?

Ghosts and Demons

WE discuss this topic because many of you are confused over whom these beings are. Many of you also claim to believe these ones do not exist and that is quite ignorant of you. Only in recent times were humans pretending that these ones didn't exist. In all your histories, your kind rightly acknowledged the existence of these ones. So now we will discuss them for you.

Ghosts, as you have come to call them, are humans or other beings that once had 3D form in realm. Your 3D or physical body is a denser version of your light body. Your light body is what you really are, when you are in realm. Your 3D body is part of the illusion of this realm, as it exists now in lower frequency. Those believing in death do indeed die; that is to say that for whatever reason, the illusion of 3D reality can no longer hold them for a time. We are not saying all of you who die are fooled by illusion and thus you are foolish, for dying was part of the game or experiment rules. But of course as we keep saying, the experiment is over, and you no longer need to believe you must die.

So for those of your kind, which has been most of you, who believed that you had to die, you died. And when you died you all entertained many different experiences after death based on expectations you had before you died. We address you all directly because indeed most of you have been here before and thus have died before. In some cases, ones of you were greeted by angels, and in some cases you were greeted by loved ones, who had passed on before you. There are many more examples we could give, but you can read about them for yourselves. These other examples come from the perspective of ones of your kind, who temporarily died and came back; or who died and passed on their experience to a living loved one via dreams and channelled messages; or who came back in another form and as a child could recall and recount their previous life's post-death experience to their parents.

So when you die, many of you do not leave this realm immediately. You stick around in your light bodies. Your light bodies do not feel too different to your physical bodies, since it is that you actually experience this realm via your light body, and your physical body is just a hologram. It is a very believable hologram; therefore, often what happens to the physical body, happens to the light body.

Often, the light body is invisible to most others still in physical form. But on occasion, ones of you will sense or see the light bodies of these dead ones.

Now we say many ones who have died didn't know they died and thus they continue on as normal. These are the ghosts some of you see, who are carrying on with regular tasks they did in life, such as cooking, laundry, door attendance, walking up and down stairs or hallways, standing in windows, tending the sick, talking, shopkeeping and so on. But since it is not natural to stay in this realm after you die, unless you have contracted to do so for various reasons, those staying here slowly lose access to source energy and thus they actually wither over time. These ghosts who stay around doing normal things are very unconscious ones, and they are not pursuing growth or expansion. In some cases they become frustrated because they cannot influence their reality like they used to, and as a result they sometimes turn to being mischievous or aggressive.

In some cases, these ones who stay around actually become helpful and make friends with the living. Other times, the light bodies of ones who were killed stay around until their story is told and until they receive a measure of justice. When living ones of you help these ones and tell their story, they often feel a measure of peace and are released from the cycle of retelling their story over and over again to anyone that would hear it.

Indeed, this one has memory of being a ghost and also was given first-person experience of a ghost. The time she remembers being a ghost, she was a woman who was killed over a lover's spat in the late 18th century. She remained in the mansion, in which she once resided, for hundreds of years after her death, desperate to tell anyone who came along her tragic story. She clung to anyone who came by her, and tried to make them feel her pain. She was stuck in a victim cycle as a ghost for hundreds of years. But from her perspective as a ghost, it did not feel like hundreds of years, rather something akin to months.

Another time, she experienced being a ghost when she merged with a more recently made ghost while in dream state. In this experience, she was a mother of a small child, and was murdered by means of a gunshot to her stomach. In this experience of her being a ghost, the woman knew that she was dead, but she was going to stay around her son all his life until he was grown enough to care for himself. She felt that the woman in that life was a fierce and loyal protector of her son, and happily so. There were some higher ones who urged the woman to leave this realm so that she could move on to another life, but she refused them and stayed until her son was grown.

On many occasions, this one who writes for us has talked to ghosts or indeed they often talk to her uninvited. When she relaxes, she picks up their conversations all the time. In some cases they pester her for help, and she helps them. In one instance, a ghost whom this one named Mary kept pestering her until she wrote about Mary's life. The writing itself was an expression for Mary's pain, and Mary was soon released by it. Some of your mediums are doing this work regularly. The work of being ghost therapists. We do say, if you do not want them to pester you, then you can tell them to leave. If this is difficult for you, you can call on strong ones or ghost therapists to heal them or ask them to leave. Remember, ghosts in this realm are often humans or sometimes animals, and they often only need a brief conversation to be heard and released from this realm.

We now speak about demons. To you, demons and angels may seem like a biblical invention. But truly, demons exist, and they existed well before anyone thought about writing the Bible, or others of your sacred texts. Often beings or entities you experience as demons are not demons. Many of you who experience overwhelming negative energy are experiencing a variety of beings. For example, ghosts who become aggressive are often perceived as demons. Also, cursed energy itself, or the energy that builds as a result of a cursed life, can form its own identity and become a demon.

In the case of Mary that we described earlier, she was on her way to becoming a demon. Her existence as Mary slowly formed over generations of this one's family lineage. Generations ago, a sad thing happened to a woman, who was this one's ancestor. The woman never received justice and thus, her sad energy literally lodged itself in the DNA of this one's lineage. Each woman in successive generations was thus cursed to carry the pain of this sadness, and often they manifested it in their life by means of being treated the same way, or developing a disease of the feminine organs.

It wasn't until this one who speaks for us was born into this lineage that her conscious state allowed her to identify this pattern, and identify the energy, who was now a person, Mary. The curse, so to speak, was lifted, when this one resolved to heal the pain of her feminine lineage since, with this one's aid, this energy form, which was on its way to becoming a demon, healed and released itself from realm and returned to lighter expression.

Indeed, we say that is what many of you are doing, whether you are aware of it or not. Mary fortunately did not become a demon, but if she was denied release for several more generations, then she would in fact become one. In this way, victims who commit to their victimhood or who never receive help or release can create demons.

It often takes many years, sometimes thousands of years. But it does happen more often than many of you would like to believe.

Often, many of you who linger in depression with unexplained cause are actually living with the pain of your ancestors. If ones of you who are embodying your ancestors' pain seek healthy expression or wise counsel, then this pain can be released from your local fields and body systems. It may indeed benefit some of you to research your lineage and discover what demons you may have living with you.

Truly, many forms of mental illness, addictions and self-harming behaviours are the manifestations of unhealed ancestral pain. It should be known to you all at this time that the higher frequencies you are all moving into will indeed surface a lot of this unexpressed pain. So, it is your job to identify it and express it. Even just speaking out loud how the pain feels will help. Don't feel weird about talking to yourself. Allow your imagination to be used here. That does not mean you will be coming up with false stories. It means you will be discovering the real stories of your ancestors' pain trapped inside you.

For example, you can say to yourself or a trusted friend or family member: 'I don't like hot air near my face. It keeps feeling like I've died in a fire. It feels hot and I'm scared'. Or you might say: 'I don't like sleeping with the covers on me at night because it feels like I might die'. Or perhaps, 'Planes terrify me, I feel like I was bombed by one'. And so on. In some cases, the unexplained fear comes from your soul memory of death in another life. In other cases, it is because you are remembering by means of your DNA, the pain or death of someone in your family lineage.

Regardless of how odd it might seem to express your irrational fears, the moment you do actually express them in full terms, the moment they start being released and leaving you at rest. Truly, many things that plague and pester you in life are creations that seek expression through you. Have the courage to express these various aspects of your composite existence, and you will experience expansion and a greater sense of freedom.

We know that so many of your addictive states, especially with regard to cigarettes and alcohol, are due to you compulsively avoiding the expression of your inner demons, so to speak, or these painful soul or DNA memories.

In terms of the powerful and ancient demons, we say that you do not need to worry about them in this realm, because they have been banished from this realm. Since it is that you are little ones, the Council of Light did not see you fit to deal with them, and thus, they do not play in these grounds of yours at this time. The ancient and powerful demons are in other realms, and their existence has purpose, and thus, they are not to be hated just because you are afraid of them. For indeed, when you are stronger, some of you might have fun fighting with them. But that is another story.

Also, some of you categorise Reptilians and your Reptilian traits as demonic. Indeed, you could rightly call some Reptilians demonic, and some of your Reptilian traits demonic. But indeed, Reptilians are not demons, unless they evolve to become formless and more powerful. But that is the ability of any of you who evolve in such a way. Also, not all demons are bad, so to speak. Often they teach you many things. They only feel like bad beings because you are currently in a weakened state and thus you are afraid of them.

Crime

THIS one who speaks for us has been obsessed with the concept of crime for many years. In times past she wanted to be a criminologist, a probation officer, a police officer, a forensic psychiatrist or a forensic anthropologist. She did not succeed down any of those paths because it was not her best expression. Also, she obsessively read books on true crime and the works of forensic profilers. Part of this obsession of hers was due to her roles in the secret space program, as it is called by your movement Disclosure. Also, since it is that she abides Narabatu who loves negative behaviour, which in this realm is defined as criminal, she was learning these things to better understand herself.

Crime will soon no longer be a concept in the mind of your species. In higher frequency existence, you cannot strike your foot upon a stone, so to speak, so you cannot commit crime. Much crime is actioned shame, as we said before. Also, much crime is invented by the societal structures currently in place that do not allow for natural expression. Also, much crime exists because of the oppressive forces who condition you to develop unhealthy expressions of your simple desires. Also, much crime exists because your kind exists in separation which is not natural for mammals and not healthy for your souls. Also, much crime exists because there is no forum in your mainstream culture that allows for true soul expression. Also, this system, which is a slave/master system, enhances aggressive and unhealthy masculine expression, and your kind are often at odds with each other for no good reason. Or indeed, reasons that are invented by your oppressors and a small group of elite beings who want war and continued exploitation of your kind. We could go on, but the point we make is this. There is no crime in higher realms because crime is symptomatic of lower frequency expression and due to your oppressed state. Your oppressors are currently leaving or being destroyed and your kind is moving to higher frequency states, where crime cannot be manifested and does not need to be.

It will not be a matter of pretending to be like perfect angels or saints or pious ones. Your natural inclination will no longer tend to criminal acts and the justice system that defines criminal acts will morph into a higher form of council.

We do say for now that you will be seeing more and more arrests of many of your powerful ones or influential ones, because these ones were making a habit of exploiting those subject to them. Indeed, justice will be served and you will all see it. Those ones who were doing bad things were doing them for so long and were powerful and influential enough that they avoided accountability. Often too, these ones were making others fall for their actions and that makes them doubly accountable. There is no behaviour that goes unseen by us and your extended family. Truly, we say now, justice will be served in full measure!

Also, we say now, do not take it upon yourselves to riot or rebel in violent ways, because that is not appropriate now. We are helping put the right people in the right place at the right time so that evidence is gathered and delivered. Truly, this is happening, dear ones. Do not worry or take these large matters into your own hands. In some cases, some of you can do this work, but if it is your calling to do it, it will feel natural and you will have courage to do it. Do not feel guilty if you are not leading in this regard. All we ask is that you are not among the ones counted for sweeping these matters of criminal behaviour under the rug, so to speak. We are not talking here about minor offences, we are talking about crimes against humanity, animalkind and the planet.

With regard to the ones of you already serving time, your cases will be dealt with on an individual basis. In some cases your time served will be deemed sufficient, and in other cases you might be moved to another place to continue serving penance of some kind. Do not worry, we and other council members are more enlightened on your cases, we can access your soul records and your higher self, thus we can deal more justly and more appropriately with you. In some cases you have been convicted unjustly or already served sufficient time. In these cases, you will be pardoned from serving the rest of your sentence.

As Gaia experiences these big changes, and she moves into higher frequencies, these and many other matters will have to be slowly and carefully dealt with by all of you in different ways. We are already preparing ones of you to lead in the cleaning up and rehabilitation of Gaia and your kind. Do not fear, dear friends. All will be well, and you are strong enough for the work ahead.

The Fourth Horseman

LAST night this one was given vision in dream state that indeed the fourth horseman of the book of Revelation has taken his ride, so to speak. She was shown a beautiful but terrible shiny silvery-grey horse. Its muzzle or mouth had been cut off as had one of its front legs. It was extremely vascular and powerful in appearance and still stood despite its injured state. Its flesh was hanging off its bones in places but it remained tall and proud in its stature.

The one riding it was inside a building when this one who writes for us saw him. His flesh too was made of bits that were falling apart, so to speak, and the man was being held together by metal staples and strappings. To her he seemed kind and indeed he was resting after his long ride.

Now we say these things because indeed we know some of you and some of your kind are looking for signs since it is that many of you learned about such signs when you were young or by some other means. Now we do here refer to the four horsemen of the apocalypse as you have come to call them because indeed we are saying now that they have all taken their ride, so to speak. This one was shown that indeed this last rider Death on his pale horse began his ride in your years the 2000s and stopped his ride before recent times.

Now we say these things because indeed we know

many of you are attached to the symbols your various sacred text writers were given. Now we and many others of your extended family inspired such ones to write such things and gave them visions in order to do so. But truly we say now that many of you also get visions and are inspired to do things by your higher selves or by your guides and so on. So it is now that we say clearly, these signs and symbols that many ones of your kind have come to obsess over and almost worship, indeed they do not mean to us what they have been meaning to some of you. So we ask now that you release your attachments to certain signs and symbols because indeed the times that Jesus and later his holy followers talked about have come to pass.

Truly, are you looking for bad things to happen to know when the end will come, so to speak? We say now that those bad things have already happened and indeed you are in your rehabilitation phase now. So no longer be looking for Death because he already came and left. He now rests while you are rehabilitating and choosing what timelines you want to be continuing your experience upon, so to speak.

Now we briefly refer here to times when some of your kind have been seeing several suns in your sky. Indeed, we say now that some big lights in your skies are craft of many different ones and indeed some ones are of your kind but of course there are those from many other kinds. And some light sources in the day sky are due to portals opening in the sky to let certain craft and elements into your world from other worlds and it is either the portal technology itself that causes the light source in the sky that some of you are seeing or it is the light from the other world that you are seeing.

Now we say that indeed some of you are seeing these rainbow-coloured portals in the sky, and we say that those are good signs if you want to be thinking that way because indeed your helpers come through those types of portals.

Now we also briefly mention that those of you who have seen three or more suns in the sky at once as if they are large bright light sources and close to you, we say indeed that you who are seeing this are observing at that very moment worlds shifting and colliding, so to speak. Indeed, some of you are seeing your different earths merging and indeed other worlds merging with earth.

Indeed, this work that involves some of you who are going to other places are already going to those other places and these other planets or worlds that are merging with Gaia are indeed taking some of you on, so to speak.

So now we say to finalise this section, you no longer need to be overly attached to looking for signs for indeed they already came and went, so to speak. Now is the time you are rehabilitating and choosing which timeline affinities you are rebuilding your lives on and that you are evolving with.

Indeed, we say there are many paths you can take and your personal interests and preferences at this time are very important because indeed you are deciding at this time how you will be helping your kind evolve.

And of course we are saying now that some of you are not choosing to evolve and will be continuing on in an oppressed state and at this time those ones are also moving to the planet which will sustain that choice they are choosing.

We give a brief example here and say that two nights ago while this one was relaxing she experienced a shift in her vibration. Indeed, her body felt lighter and every cell of hers was buzzing or humming for indeed she was taken to craft and injected with a light signature by some of us her helpers and guides. Indeed, this one, as some of you also have been, was injected with light signatures that she chose to bear by means of her life decisions and actions and thus during these great shifts and changes which we remind you again are happening right now are helping her and helping you stay attached to the timeline that you have been choosing.

At this time too, due to all the shifts and your bodies adjusting to them, we say that your bodies are and will be experiencing many changes as they clear old energy or light signatures or frequencies and take on new ones. Indeed, several months ago this one's body made her cough in order to clear some old energy and old patterns or templates in her system and indeed after just a few coughs she pulled her back and couldn't walk for several days. Indeed, it was not the coughing that pulled her back but some energy that she was getting out became lodged in her lower spine on its way out of her spinal shaft.

So now pay attention to how you are clearing your physical systems and light or energy systems because now indeed you are all changing as you are taking on these new homes or indeed they are taking on you. These new homes, as we said before, are mostly different versions of Gaia and in some cases different worlds very similar to Gaia as she is now, but of course she is changing as you are changing.

Summary

FIRSTLY, we say, this text is alive and will change as you change. The frequency itself that this text holds will heal you and expand you, if you let it. Do not obsess over the particular items in this text because truly your language, which we used to speak to you, fails you. Only pay attention to some of our clear messages, and also imbibe the frequencies of this text because they will clean you.

Now, we finish this text to you with a summary of our main points so that our message to you is clear. In this text, we, the Anshar, communicate directly to you all through our channel Amy and Narabatu. You are currently slaves, but you are being reminded that the agreements in place to keep you as slaves are no longer binding, and those oppressing you now are doing so unlawfully and will be meeting with judgement soon, and in fact some of them already are.

You are on a planet Gaia (or Terra), whose resources are being sold off planet and thus they maintain a high value and the money systems keeping you enslaved are thus perpetuated. These money systems are currently dissolving and when you pursue your own pleasing and express yourselves from your true centre, then you will be tapping into Gaia's, and by extension Eternity's, regenerative properties, and you will thus be restored in your flesh and in your hearts and minds, and all you manifest, including your relationships, will be rejuvenating.

You are to no longer consume animal products for food

or other uses because that arrangement is under the old contract or agreement that is no longer in place.

You are to return to your guardian roles of Gaia's natural systems and you are to live more closely to her land systems, and directly engage in local and translocal communities.

You are to no longer devote your energy to abstract endeavours because those devotions will always be exploited and not to your benefit.

You are to learn about and begin engaging in higher frequency behaviours and release addictions of every kind and release lower frequency habits.

You are to engage in kindness daily and serve your kind and your home planet in at least one way each day.

You are to broaden your minds and start embracing the existence of your extended family so that you are ready to meet them soon and partake in their healing and benevolent technologies.

You are to step into your successful evolutionary paths and be guided by your own sovereignty only, so that you can show the rest of existence that you indeed are a species that is mature and responsible and ready to enter into the intergalactic travelling phase of your development.

Please embrace your heritage, and we welcome you to the new playground. You are now in higher frequencies. We state these things to you clearly and have them in text so that you are all informed. We have carried out our duty to you by means of this text as your parents and as the ones welcoming you into higher realms. Welcome friends, we are all so looking forward to meeting you all as equals!

-With much love and glory we bless you all

-Love from the Anshar and your extended family

-Love from your future selves

Printed in Great Britain
by Amazon